THE
LYLE
OFFICIAL REVIEW
PAINTINGS
PRICE GUIDE
1993

While every care has been taken in the compiling of information contained in this volume, the publisher cannot accept liability for loss, financial or otherwise, incurred by reliance placed on the information herein.

All prices quoted in this book are obtained from a variety of auctions in various countries during the twelve months prior to publication and are converted to dollars at the rate of exchange prevalent at the time of sale.

The publishers wish to express their sincere thanks to the following for their involvement and assistance in the production of this volume:

NICKY FAIRBURN (Art Director)
EELIN McIVOR (Sub Editor)
ANNETTE CURTIS (Editorial)
CATRIONA DAY (Art Production)
DONNA CRUICKSHANK (Art Production)
FRANK BURRELL (Graphics)
DONNA RUTHERFORD
JACQUELINE LEDDY
JAMES BROWN
EILEEN BURRELL
ANGIE DEMARCO

Cover illustrations

Front: The artist's son Tita, by A. Valette (Christie's)
        A red haired nude, by Gustave Max Stevens (Sotheby's)
        A still life of fruit, by Johannes Cornelis de Bruyn (Sotheby's)
        'King Monmouth', by William H Hopkins (Boardman)
        The pilot's wife, by Hector Caffieri (Christie's)
Spine: A friend in need, by Emile August Hublin (Christie's)
Back: An African pitta, by David Morrison Reid Henry (Christie's)
        'We stood along the edge' 54° 92' South, by Robin Brooks (Christie's)
        A portrait of King Oskar of Sweden as Crown Prince, by Joseph Stieler (Sotheby's)
        Flirtation, by Federico Andreotti (Christie's)

A CIP catalogue record for this book is available from the British Library

ISBN 86248 - 143 - 0
Copyright © Lyle Publications MCMXCII
Glenmayne, Galashiels, Scotland.

Typeset by Word Power, Berwickshire.
Printed and bound in Great Britain by
Butler & Tanner Ltd., Frome and London.

THE

LYLE

OFFICIAL REVIEW

PAINTINGS
PRICE GUIDE
1993

COMPILED & EDITED BY
TONY CURTIS

Introduction

Published annually and containing details of thousands of oil paintings, watercolours and prints. The Lyle Paintings Price Guide is the most comprehensively illustrated reference work on the subject available at this time.

Each entry is listed alphabetically under the Artist's name for easy reference and includes a description of the picture, its size, medium, auctioneer and the price fetched at auction during the twelve months prior to publication.

As regards authenticity of the works listed, this is often a delicate matter and throughout this book the conventional system has been observed.

The full Christian name(s) and surname of the artist denote that, in the opinion of the auctioneer listed, the work is by that artist.

The initials of the Christian name(s) and the surname denote that, in the opinion of the auctioneer listed, the work is of the period of the artist and may be wholly or partly his work.

The surname only of the artist denotes that, in the opinion of the auctioneer listed, the work is of the school or by one of the followers of the artist or painted in his style.

The word 'after' associated with the surname of the artist denotes that, in the opinion of the auctioneer listed, the picture is a copy of the work of the artist.

The word 'signed' associated with the name of the artist denotes that, in the opinion of the auctioneer listed, the work bears a signature which is the signature of the artist.

The words 'bears signature' or 'traces of signature' denote that, in the opinion of the auctioneer listed, the work bears a signature or traces of a signature which may be that of the artist.

The word 'dated' denotes that the work is dated and, in the opinion of the auctioneer listed, was executed at that date.

The words 'bears date' or 'inscribed' (with date) denotes that, in the opinion of the auctioneer listed, the work is so dated and may have been executed at about that date.

All pictures are oil on canvas unless otherwise specified. In the dimensions (sight size) given, the height precedes the breadth.

Although the greatest possible care has been taken to ensure that any statement as to authorship, attribution, origin, date, age, provenance and condition is reliable, all such statements can only be statement of opinion and are not to be taken as statements or representations of fact.

The Lyle Paintings Price Guide offers a unique opportunity for identification and valuation of paintings by an extremely broad cross section of artists of all periods and schools.

We firmly believe that dealers, collectors and investors alike will treasure this and subsequent annual editions of the Lyle Paintings Price Guide (published in September each year) as changing trends in the fluctuating world of art values are revealed.

Tony Curtis

Auction Acknowledgements

AB Stockholms Auktionsverk, Box 16256, 103 25 Stockholm, Sweden
Allen & Harris, St Johns Place, Whiteladies Road, Clifton, Bristol BS8 2ST
Jean Claude Anaf, Lyon Brotteaux, 13 bis place Jules Ferry, 69456 Lyon, France
Anderson & Garland, Marlborough House, Marlborough Crescent, Newcastle upon Tyne NE1 4EE
The Auction Galleries, Mount Road, Tweedmouth, Berwick upon Tweed TD15 2BA
Auktionshause Arnold, Bleichstr. 42, 6000 Frankfurt a/M, Germany
Australian Art Auctions, Suite 333, Park Regis, 27 Park Street, Sydney 2000, Australia
Bearnes, Rainbow, Avenue Road, Torquay TQ2 5TG
Biddle & Webb, Ladywood Middleway, Birmingham B16 0PP
Bigwood, The Old School, Tiddington, Stratford upon Avon
Bonhams, Montpelier Street, Knightsbridge, London SW7 1HH
Bonhams Chelsea, 65–69 Lots Road, London SW10 0RN
Michael Bowman, 6 Haccombe House, Near Netherton, Newton Abbot, Devon TQ12 4SJ
Butterfield & Butterfield, 220 San Bruno Avenue, San Francisco CA 94103, USA
Butterfield & Butterfield, 7601 Sunset Boulevard, Los Angeles CA 90046, USA
Christie's International SA, 8 place de la Taconnerie, 1204 Genève, Switzerland
Christie's, 8 King Street, London SW1Y 6QT
Christie's, 502 Park Avenue, New York, NY 10022, USA
Christie's East, 219 East 67th Street, New York, NY 10021, USA
Christie's, Cornelis Schuytstraat 57, 1071 JG Amsterdam, Netherlands
Christie's (Monaco), S.A.M, Park Palace 98000 Monte Carlo, Monaco
Christie's SA Roma, 114 Piazza Navona, 00186 Rome, Italy
Christie's Scotland, 164–166 Bath Street Glasgow G2 4TG
Christie's South Kensington Ltd., 85 Old Brompton Road, London SW7 3LD
Bruce D Collins Fine Art Gallery, Box 113, Denmark, Maine, USA
David Dockree Fine Art, 224 Moss Lane, Bramhall, Stockport SK7 1BD
Du Mouchelles Art Galleries Co., 409 E. Jefferson Avenue, Detroit, Michigan 48226, USA
Duran Sala de Artes y Subastas, Serrano 12, 28001 Madrid, Spain
Eldred's, Box 796, E. Dennis, MA 02641, USA
Finarte, 20121 Milano, Piazzetta Bossi 4, Italy
Fraser-Pinney's, 5627 Ferrier, Montreal, Quebec, Canada H4P 2M4
Galerie Koller, Rämistr. 8, CH 8024 Zürich, Switzerland
Galerie Moderne, 3 rue du Parnasse, 1040 Bruxelles, Belgium
Germann Auktionshaus, CH 8032 Zürich, Zeltweg 67/Ecke Markurstr., Switzerland
Glerum Auctioneers, Westeinde 12, 2512 HD's Gravenhage, Netherlands
Graves Son & Pilcher, 71 Church Road, Hove, East Sussex, BN3 2GL
Greenslade Hunt, 13 Hammet Street, Taunton, Somerset, TA1 1RN
Halifax Property Services, 53 High Street, Tenterden, Kent
Hauswedell & Nolte, D-2000 Hamburg 13, Pöseldorfer Weg 1, Germany
Hotel de Ventes Horta, 390 Chaussée de Waterloo (Ma Campagne), 1060 Bruxelles, Belgium
P Herholdt Jensens Auktioner, Rundforbivej 188, 2850 Nerum, Denmark
Hobbs & Chambers, 'At the Sign of the Bell', Market Place, Cirencester, Glos.
G A Key, Aylsham Saleroom, Palmers Lane, Aylsham, Norfolk, NR11 6EH
Kunsthaus am Museum, Drususgasse 1–5, 5000 Köln 1, Germany
Kunsthaus Lempertz, Neumarkt 3, 5000 Köln 1, Germany
W.H. Lane & Son, 64 Morrab Road, Penzance, Cornwall, TR18 2QT
Lawrence Fine Art, South Street, Crewkerne, Somerset TA18 8AB
David Lay, The Penzance Auction House, Alverton, Penzance, Cornwall TA18 4KE
John Maxwell, 133a Woodford Road, Woodford, Cheshire SK7 1QD
Phillips, Blenstock House, 7 Blenheim Street, New Bond Street, London W1Y 0AS
Phillips, 65 George Street, Edinburgh EH2 2JL
Phillips Marylebone, Hayes Place, Lisson Grove, London NW1 6UA
Riddetts, Richmond Hill, Bournemouth
Ritchie's, 429 Richmond Street East, Toronto, Canada M5A 1R1
Selkirk's, 4166 Olive Street, St Louis, Missouri 63108, USA
Skinner Inc., Bolton Gallery, Route 117, Bolton MA, USA
Sotheby's, 34–35 New Bond Street, London W1A 2AA
Sotheby's, 1334 York Avenue (at 72nd Street), New York, NY 10021, USA
Sotheby's Monaco, Le Sporting d'Hiver, Place du Casino, 98001 Monte Carlo, Monaco
Henry Spencer, 40 The Square, Retford, Notts. DN22 6DJ
Tennants, 27 Market Place, Leyburn, Yorkshire
Woolley & Wallis, The Castle Auction Mart, Salisbury, Wilts SP1 3SU

PAINTINGS PRICE GUIDE 1993

There is no shortage of calamitous figures to apply to the art market in 1991, where it is said that picture sale turnover during that period fell by a whopping 70% worldwide. The 50% collapse in the Impressionist and Modern picture market must bear most of the responsibility for this, coupled to the deepening recession on both sides of the Atlantic.

Those who made most out of the boom years of Impressionism obviously stood to lose most by the market's collapse, and both Christie's and Sotheby's have seen their profits tumble – Christie's offering £6.4 million pre-tax profit on sales of £583 million and Sotheby's £12 million on sales of £639 million. At least both stayed in the black, but a fall in profits of over 90% comes as a shock to the system, and drastic cost cutting, with numerous redundancies followed.

The pattern of where art is being bought and sold also changed. The Art Sales Index quotes up to July 91 that New York claimed 38.6% of the market, London 24% and Paris 13% by value of pictures sold. New York the previous year had looked set to sail through the 50% barrier with 49.6% in 1989–90, so in fact fell back 11%. In contrast with this, and with the French decline of 3.6%, a fall of just over 1% for London looks downright positive, though it continues the steady decline of the past few years.

In London, however, the picture, if the pun may be used, has been complicated by various factors, such as the threats of Labour victories, of the end of the tax free import of Art from outside the EEC and of a ban on the export of works of art in private hands, without compensation, which are deemed to be of national importance.

The first of these has, of course been put back in the closet for the next five years or so. The second, however, rumbles on in the deliberations of the EEC. If it is adopted, the prices of paintings sent for sale in London from, say Switzerland, will obviously fall to reflect the 17.5% VAT which would be payable. Vendors can then hardly be blamed for taking their goods to sell in New York (the 50% barrier may, after all, not be completely out of sight), where, without tax, they will undoubtedly do better. Similarly, the tax would also fall on those trying to repatriate art which may have earlier fetched up in the US during one of the frequent haemorrhages we have suffered to that country. Most other EC countries do tax imports of art (which may explain their secondary importance as art sales centres) and, as usual, are lined up against the UK on this issue. However, there are indications that France, where taxing anything foreign is almost a way of life, may have realised the threat posed to Paris by this decree and see that their interest too lies in a free trade policy.

The third threat was a Conservative proposal to list important paintings and heritage objects to stop them being imported. This was finally disposed of early in June, when the Secretary of State for National Heritage, David Mellor, announced that the scheme had been abandoned. The disadvantages, he said, would far outweigh the benefits, and he listed the former as the diminution of owners' rights to dispose of their property, and the distortion of art market values. Nevertheless, the mere threat of such a ban could quite possibly have been a moving factor in the sale of three pictures which have caused arguably the greatest excitement over the last twelve months.

These were all to be auctioned at one sale on 15 April at Christie's London. The first was Holbein's Portrait of a Lady with a Squirrel, offered by the Marquess of Cholmondeley to help pay for maintenance and improvements on his estates. More than £15 million was hoped for. The second was Rembrandt's Daniel and

Cyrus before the Idol of Bel (est. at £8 million), and the third was Canaletto's view of the Old Horse Guards (£5–7 million).

In fact, they were all to meet with very different fates. The Holbein never even made it to the sale, as a deal was struck with the National Gallery whereby they were able to buy it for £10 million payable over a period. The Rembrandt was bought in at £6.2 million and it was left to the Canaletto to provide the triumph of the day, when it was sold to the composer Andrew Lloyd Webber for £9.2 million plus premium.

Thus two out of three at least were saved for the nation. However, while the megastars of the entertainment world are, it seems, increasingly heavily into painting (Mick Jagger, Eric Clapton and Madonna to name but three) we can hardly rely upon philanthropic and patriotic private buyers stepping in in future to save the day. The National, having even with help exhausted itself in this one purchase, will not be in a position to buy anything else of importance for at least three years, unless there is a radical change of policy by the government whereby they finally increase the museums' purchasing clout (now frozen since 1985, for heaven's sake!). Doubtless this is one of the reasons why the export ban had its attractions as an easy and cheaper option than actually shelling out some cash. Its effects on distorting the art market would, however, be incalculable.

HANS HOLBEIN II (1497/8–1543) – Portrait of a Lady with a Pet Squirrel – oil on panel – 56 x 38.5cm. Bought by the National Gallery

REMBRANDT HARMENSZ VAN RIJN (1606–1669) – Daniel and Cyrus before the Idol of Bel – signed and dated *1633* – oil on panel – 23.4 x 30.1cm.

GIOVANNI ANTONIO CANAL, il Canaletto (1697–1768) – The Old Horse Guards, London, from St. James's Park – oil on canvas – 117 x 236cm.
(Christie's)   £10,120,000 $17,600,000

9

REMBRANDT HARMENSZ VAN RIJN (1606–1669) – Portrait of Johannes Uyttenbogaert – bears signature and date – oil on canvas – 132 x 102cm.
(Christie's) £4,180,000 $8,067,400

Attributed to JACQUES DUMONT called le Romain (Paris 1701–1781) – A biblical scene – oil on canvas – 71.5 x 96cm. *(Christie's)* £7,700 $14,861

It was sad, and even strange, that it was the Rembrandt that failed, since this has certainly been the Master's year. He has been the subject of two major exhibitions in London, The Master and his Workshop at the National, and his drawings at the British Museum. In the background – as often, indeed, in the foreground – too, there have been the Dutch scholars of the Rembrandt Research Project, busily beavering away to disattribute Rembrandts left, right and centre and to reassign them to his assistants or pupils.

The problem was, as has recently become clear, that Rembrandt, in common with many other 16th and 17th century painters, ran what amounted to a small art factory. He, however, seems to have been happy to go a step further and to give tasks to his assistants to carry out in Rembrandt style, then have the result signed with his name. It thus often becomes impossible to sort out exactly who did what, but certainly a swathe has been cut through what were previously thought to be bona fide examples of Rembrandt's work. For example, of twelve 'Rembrandts' owned by the Wallace Collection a hundred years ago only one genuine article

now remains. Some of these disattributions are incontrovertible, while others are more debatable. However, until the Project have taken it under their microscope and duly pronounced, no owners of a putative Rembrandt can sleep easy in their beds.

So why did the Rembrandt fail? One theory puts it down to the nature of the painting itself. In contrast to the Canaletto, it was a dark and sombre piece, both in colour and in content, and it may just be that the dark and the difficult are thoroughly out of fashion in these times. Lightness and accessibility certainly characterise the Impressionists, and by pursuing this theory we may yet find a reason for their meteoric rise.

That said, however, Sotheby's successfully sold Rembrandt's Portrait of Johannes Uyttenbogaert (duly authenticated by the RRP) in London on July 8th. This was consigned by another aristocrat in need of funds for his estate, the Earl of Rosebery. The painting was modestly estimated at £3–4 million and in fact sold for £4.18 million, a fact which reportedly caused great satisfaction at New Bond Street, as the rivalry between the two giants sharpens in a very much leaner market.

Attributed to FRANCESCO ZUCCARELLI – Italianate River Landscapes with Anglers and other figures on river banks – oil on canvas – 57 x 42cm. – a pair
(Christie's) **£33,000 $55,925**

It is, however, Old Masters at all levels which have been providing much of what joy there has been in the art market over the past year, and the Italians are to these, in some measure, what the Japanese were to the Impressionists at the height of their popularity. Where all the money is coming from, given the perpetually wacky state of the Italian economy, is anyone's guess. Every auctioneer I questioned on the subject simply replied darkly, 'We don't enquire!' What is undeniable, however, is that buying they are as if there was no tomorrow. The most popular of all are Venetian and Neapolitan views which tended to be painted for the English as mementos of their Grand Tour, so much so that few or none were left in their cities of origin. Now the Italians are buying them back with a vengeance. At Phillips in March, for example, a Neapolitan view by Gaspar van Wittel, known as Vanvitelli, bought a top price of £140,000 where only £30–50,000 had been looked for. The Italians, however, do deign to purchase English Old Masters as well, though, again, academic subjects tend to present a few more problems than the lighter scenes.

Even down at the more modest end of the market, the story is the same. Christie's South Ken. report a series of excellent sales with success rates running at over 80%. At their sale of 2 April 1992, two Zuccarelli attributions (pleasant, light pieces both) made £33,000 against estimates of £6–8,000. Even 19th century copies are finding ready buyers with, at the same sale, copies of Boucher's Rape of Europa and Venus and Vulcan going for over £6,000, having been estimated at £1–1,500. Bonhams too report that pictures estimated at only a few hundreds pounds regularly double their estimates.

BENJAMIN WILLIAM LEADER – Summertime, Llandulas, North Wales – signed and dated 1878 – oil on board – 15³/₄ x 24in.
(Lawrence Fine Arts) **£9,680 $17,230**

JAN BREUGHEL the Younger and DAVID TENIERS the Younger – Christ and the Woman of Cana of Galilee in a landscape with a view of the Pont Neuf, Paris – bears the monogram of Teniers – oil on copper laid down on panel – 63.5 x 89cm.
(Jean Claude Anaf) **£58,789 $101,117**

13

Dutch and Flemish Old Masters remain steady, again appealing principally to their countrymen. At Christie's sale of 15 April, even with a rather high bought in rate, a van den Eeckhout sold for £374,000, a record for the painter. Here as ever, provenance was a major factor, for the painting came from an old collection with impeccable credentials.

A late Old Master surge was looked for from Spain, which is enjoying something of an annus mirabilis, what with Expo and the Olympics. Christie's celebrated this in May 1992 with a stunning Spanish sale, containing major works by Zurbarán and Murillo, not to mention El Greco and Goya. Spain is cash rich and the economy is booming, and Spanish buyers are more and more visible internationally, again snapping up their own painters. Christie's described the sale as 'incredibly successful'. In reality, however, it was the Old Masters who again saved the day, and there were major failures even here. El Greco's The Disrobing of Christ comfortably broke a record for the master when it sold for £1,870,000 against a previous high of £1.5 million. The altarpiece of the The Last Supper by the Perea Master, (£308,000) and works by Coello (£264,000) and Antonio Vazquez (£46,200) also set records, but fell well within estimate, (the El Greco was pitched at £1.5–£2.5 million), as did the Murillos. Sadly, the lovely and reflective (but dark!) Zurbarán of Christ and the Virgin in the House at Nazareth failed completely on an estimate of £1.2–£1.6m, bought in at £900,000. The Goya portrait of Dõna Maria Teresa de Vallabriga y Rozas, again highly estimated and also over-cleaned, met a similar fate.

BARTOLOME ESTEBAN MURILLO (1617–1682) – The Immaculate Conception – 167 x 111.5cm.
(Christie's)   £242,000 $438,020

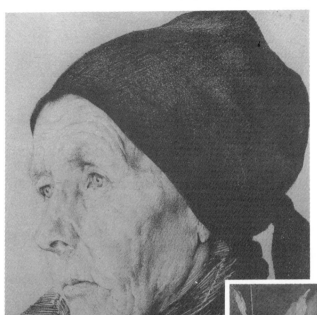

WILHELM MARIA HUBERTUS
(1844–1900) – An old woman – pencil
on paper – 21 x 15.6cm.
(Christie's) **£14,850 $27,470**

DOMENIKOS THEOTOKOPOULOS, El
Greco (1541–1614) – The Disrobing of Christ –
signed – oil on panel – 56.6 x 32cm.
(Christie's) **£1,870,000 $3,384,700**

The main cause of all the doom and gloom, i.e. post 1870 art, was trotted out again by both major auction houses at what has come to be the expected times in November and May in New York. November saw the fine Hall Tremaine collection being offered by Christie's, in which all pictures had been off the market for some twenty years. Several works were considered by the experts to stand in the same relation to their painters as did Dr Gachet to van Gogh or Au Moulin de la Galette to Renoir. One of these was Fernand Leger's Le Petit Dejeuner. Estimated at $8–10 million, it sold to a European collector for $7m, which constituted about half the record price of £8.5 million paid for Leger's Contraste de Formes in the heady days of 1989. Another important work on offer was Robert Delauney's Premier Disque. This had been in the Tremaine collection since 1953, and was valued at $2–3 million. In the event it went for $4.7 million. Juan Gris' Cubist still life Poires et Raisins came in exactly at low estimate. It seems that in the present climate prospective buyers are not to be tempted by ambitious estimates into parting with their funds. If the work appears to be valued too high, they simply won't bother to bid.

The recession has also had its effect on the most secure reputations among living contemporary artists. The most notable of these are de Kooning and Johns. It will be remembered that in 1989 de Kooning's Interchange sold to the Japanese for $20.9 million and John's False Start in 1988 for $17.05 million. Now in November 1991 a de Kooning Long Island landscape failed at $2.09 million, a fifth off low estimate, Johns' Device Circle from his same 1959 series made only $4.4 million at Christie's in New York, while Sotheby's the following evening managed to do only a little better with Jubilee at $4.95 million. Now in a realistic world these are still leading, and thoroughly respectable, prices for works by living artists. It's the difference that shocks (especially if you happened to buy at the top).

JASPER JOHNS (b. 1930) – Device Circle – signed and dated '59 – oil, encaustic, newspaper, collage, wooden arm and metal screw on canvas – 101.7 x 101.7cm. *(Christie's)* £2,430,939 $4,400,000

ROBERT DELAUNEY (1885–1941)
– Premier Disque – oil on canvas –
134.6cm. diameter
(Christie's)   **£2,596,685 $4,700,000**

FERNAND LEGER (1881–1955) – Le Petit Dejeuner – signed and dated *21* – oil on canvas – 96.5 x 129.5cm.
(Christie's)   **£3,846,154 $7,000,000**

ANNE WALKER (circa 1888–1965) – Children Playing – signed – oil on canvas – 24 x 29in.
(David Lay)

£1,000 $1,700

EMILE BAES – Nude, back view – signed – oil on canvas – 80 x 120cm.
(Galerie Moderne)

£890 $1,522

WALT KUHN (1880–1949) – Kansas (Portrait of the Artist as a Clown) – signed and dated 1932 – oil on canvas – 81.3 x 35.9cm.
(Sotheby's) £159,777 $286,000

The other names to suffer from the withdrawal of Japanese interest (in Sotheby's in November their Impressionists expert reported just one Japanese face among the audience 'and he went to sleep') are their favourites, such as Utrillo, Vlaminck and Buffet. Sotheby's had the enterprising thought of taking the market to the erstwhile purchasers, and held a prints sale in Tokyo. The material on offer was all very carefully directed towards the Japanese taste, with Renoir, Laurencin and Warhol featuring largely. Nevertheless, they still recorded a 37% rate unsold, and of those that did sell many went under low estimate.

It is however the May sales in New York where all the records have traditionally been broken, and these can still be looked upon as a litmus paper for the state of the market. There was, indeed, much to encourage. More pictures had come forward for sale this year, and the total sold by both houses came to $85.2 million, well up on the dreadful $41 million of a year ago (all things, of course being relative!).

LLOYD LOZES GOFF (1917–83) – The Sensational Lady Godiva – signed – oil on canvas – 76.8 x 61cm.
(Sotheby's) £3,750 $6,600

By and large, post 1904 works did much better than the Impressionists, with twenty pictures and sculptures topping $1 million in contrast to just seven last May. The two single owner sales of Contemporary Art offered by Christie's from the collections of Fredrik Roos and William McCarty Cooper (both AIDS victims) were near sell-outs, and Sotheby's sales in the succeeding days, though perhaps less high-profile, met with a similarly wide and enthusiastic response. Top lot was Braque's Studio VIII, which made $7.7 million at Christie's. Christie's too saw a bid of $2.86 million for Chagall's Bouquet de Fleurs, while Sotheby's managed $2.1 million plus premium for Renoir's. Portrait de Jean. Again, it was the pictures that were fresh to the market which found favour, and those being reoffered by vendors hoping for a quick resale were ignored. A major casualty among such was Renoir's La Loge, bought in this time at Christie's at $5.2m. Interestingly, the Americans were back with money in their pockets, but they were spending it very selectively indeed.

MARC CHAGALL (1887–1985) – Bouquet de Fleurs – signed and dated – oil on canvas – 99 x 71cm.
(Christie's)
£1,554,348 $2,860,000

PIERRE-AUGUSTE RENOIR
– Portrait de Jean – signed – oil
on canvas.
(Sotheby's)
　　　　　£1,166,666　$2,100,000

GEORGES BRAQUE (1882–1963) – Atelier VIII – signed – oil on canvas – 132.1 x 196.9cm.
(Christie's)　　　　　　　　　　　　　　　　　　　**£4,191,617　$7,700,000**

Turning to less dramatic parts of the market, we find 19th century Continental paintings aping to some degree Old Master trends. Here again the Italians are very active. At Sotheby's March sale, for example, Al Sole, by Vincenzo Cabianca, sold at a very respectable £115,000 (£126,000 including premium) against an estimate of £60–80,000. However, there still does not seem to be that much quality material about; sales are rather slimline, and bidders are buying very much along nationalistic lines. In addition to the Italians, the Greeks snap up Greek offerings and so on. Even the Maltese were around at Bonhams' watercolour sale, bidding for views of Valetta. Sotheby's, however, have reported a resurgence of new buyers, and the reappearance of some collectors who had abandoned the salerooms when prices soared. Perhaps this is a sign of better things to come, and more vendors will be encouraged to consign their goods again.

ALEKSEI ALEKSEEVITCH HARLAMOV (1840–1922?) – Portrait of a young girl – signed – oil on canvas – 44.5 x 30.5cm.
(Christie's) £26,400 $49,104

VINCENZO CABIANCA – Al Sole – signed and dated *1866* – oil on canvas – 71 x 89cm.
(Sotheby's) £126,500 $218,845

XAVERIO DELLA GATTA – The 1799 Revolution against French rule in Naples – watercolour – 22 x 30in.
(Bonhams) £74,800 $126,412

SIR ARTHUR ELSLEY – Goodnight – signed
(Christie's) £100,570 $176,000

British Victorian pictures also benefited at home and abroad from an upsurge of interest. This is a market where private buyers have always been of great importance. They often go for decorative, sentimental subjects, and these are proving to be the backbone of this particular sector. Typical of this was the record achieved for a Halle; his Paolo and Francesca made £110,000 at Christie's sale of 13 March. The criterion here, as elsewhere, is that pictures should be fresh to the market. This was certainly so in the case of Lord Leighton's portrait of Lady Sybil Primrose, which had been discovered high on the wall of a house belonging to a member of the sitter's family. It sold to a Far Eastern collector at Christie's for £231,000.

CHARLES SPENCELAYH – The Unexpected – signed – oil on canvas – 51 x 38cm.
(Sotheby's) **£24,000 $41,760**

CHARLES EDWARD HALLE – Paolo and Francesca – bears inscription – oil on canvas – 186.7 x 123.8cm.
(Christie's) **£110,000 $185,900**

EUGENE FAURE (1822–1879) – A Woodland
Idyll – signed – oil on canvas – 86 x 48in.
(Christie's)   **£11,000 $20,460**

FREDERIC, LORD LEIGHTON – Lady Sybil Primrose – oil on canvas –
121.9 x 87cm.
(Christie's)   **£231,000 $390,390**

RICHARD DADD (1817–1886) – Contradiction: Oberon and Titania – signed and dated *1854–1858* – oil on canvas – 61 x 75.5cm.
(Christie's)

£1,600,000 $2,896,000

Christie's put the cherry on the cake in their sale of 12 June when Contradiction: Oberon and Titania, by the deranged painter Richard Dadd, fetched £1.6 million, a record for a Victorian painting. This picture has a notable performance history in the saleroom, for it broke records too when it was sold to an American in 1983 for £550,000, having originally sold in 1964 for £7,000. Altogether it has proved quite a sound investment over the years!

British pictures are even doing well in the States, where John Elsley's sentimental 'Goodnight' sold for $176,000 at Christie's, and Lavery's Golf Links, North Berwick, went for £121,000. (Golfing pictures are proving as popular as ever – another Lavery, this time of The First Green, North Berwick, sold the following month at Phillips for £77,000.)

JONATHAN EASTMAN JOHNSON (1824–1906) – The confab – signed – oil on board – 55.9 x 31cm.
(Christie's)

£36,300 $66,000

SIMONY JENSEN – Monk eating oysters – signed – 38 x 45cm.
(Herholdt Jensen) **£393 $684**

JOHN LAVERY – Golf Links, North Berwick – signed and dated *1919* – oil on canvas – 63.5 x 76.2cm.
(Christie's) **£121,000 $211,750**

JOHN SINGER SARGENT – The green parasol – pencil, watercolour and bodycolour – 47.5 x 35cm.
(Christie's)   £286,000 $517,660

ROBERT BEVAN (1865–1925) – Horse Dealers at the Barbican – signed – oil on canvas – 55 x 64.5cm.
(Christie's)
                              £104,500 $189,145

WILLIAM RUSSELL FLINT – Jasmin – signed and inscribed – watercolour and tempera – 33 x 61.6cm.
(Bonhams) £16,000 $27,200

FRANCIS CRISS (1901-1973) – Alma Sewing – signed – oil on canvas – 83.8 x 114.3cm.
(Sotheby's) £12,905 $23,100

29

The Spaniards suffered mixed fortunes, however, in the New York Continental sales in February. Christie's failed to sell two likely pictures in the $50–100,000 bracket by Ruiz y Ortega and Gallegos y Arnosa, while Sotheby's made records the following day, selling Sorolla y Bastida's Barcas for $500,000 and Gallegos y Arnosa's La Botica for $180,000. (And just to prove they have not abandoned ship completely, the Japanese trade splashed out on a small Corot landscape for all of $170,000!)

The boot was on the other foot, however, when it came to the Latin Americans. It will be remembered that the two giants differed sharply on their reading of this market, with Sotheby's closing down their Latin American department in New York, and Christie's on the other hand predicting great things for this sector. The closure caused considerable indignation among insulted Latins, and the department was finally recreated. They were rewarded with an early success when José Maria Velasco's Valle de Mexico set a new record for a Latin American painting of £1.4 million, but then had to put the champagne promptly back on ice when Christie's went one better and sold Diego Rivera's the Flower Seller for a record £1.659m ($2.97m) the following evening.

With regard to watercolours, Bonhams report that those from the late Victorian period, which had been enjoying a boom over the last few years, show signs of levelling off. Those by earlier painters on the other hand have done very well. At their sale of 27 November, however, it was again the Italians who were most in evidence, when they paid £68,000 for a Neapolitan gouache which had been estimated at a mere £10–15,000.

Other favourites still assured of a welcome are Seago and Flint. Bonhams gave the latter another exclusive airing on February 19, when the top price was the £16,000 paid for Jasmin, and they have every intention of continuing with these sales. Their doggy and marine theme sales also did well, as did Christie's bird sale in February, where private buyers from Britain and US and the Continent heavily outnumbered the trade.

DIEGO RIVERA (1886–1957) – The Flower Seller (Vendedora de Flores) – signed and dated *1942* – oil on masonite – 122 x 122cm.
(Christie's) £1,659,000 $2,970,000

ARCHIBALD THORBURN (1860–1935) – Clearing after Rain; Red Grouse among Heather – signed and dated *1920* – pencil, watercolour and bodycolour – 533 x 756mm.
(Christie's)   **£44,000 $76,560**

WILLIAM HENRY HAMILTON TROOD (1848–1899) – Uncorking the Bottle and a Surprising Result – signed and dated *1887* – oil on board – 16 x 22in. – **a pair**
(Bonhams)   **£10,000 $17,000**

LIAO CHI-CH'UN – Kuei-shan Island – signed – oil on canvas – 72.5 x 91cm.
(Sotheby's)   NT 7,040,000

Modern paintings have met with mixed fortunes as buyers in a recession understandably chase the safer options. The heyday of the Scottish colourists seems to be over for the present, replaced perhaps to some extent by Irish pictures from the same period, which have proved winners at several sales during the year.

So what can be deduced from all this? The first criterion of a successful sale seems to be that the works should be clean and fresh to the market, which is very sensitive at picking up something which has been touted around for a while. It is perhaps a sign of uncertain times that the top dealers have so many fine pictures to sell at present. They can hold pictures in a difficult market pending the discovery of a buyer at the right price, instead of the instant but very public result of the auction room, where a picture which fails can be 'burnt' for the foreseeable future.

The second important factor is that buyers will no longer be cajoled upwards by high estimates. If the auction houses get it wrong, the buyers will simply refuse to play. This must make estimating a perfectly horrendous business at present – as it is, they seldom get it right more than 50% of the time, which may be why Christie's are reportedly toying with the idea of only handing out estimates for big sales on the previous day.

Finally, it pays to be inventive and innovative and, driven by necessity, all the auction houses have been casting around for new ideas to attract the punters. Sotheby's picked a winner when they trotted off to Taiwan for their first sale ever devoted to modern Chinese paintings and sculpture. Two records were set when a painting by Liao Chi Chien of Turtle Mountain Island off the Taiwanese coast sold for NT 7,040,000, and a landscape by Yu Cheng-yao made NT 6,820,000. I haven't seen one sale report (not even Sotheby's own) which translates these prices into a more Christian currency, but they must be good, as Sotheby's are now planning regular sales out there, the first scheduled for October 1992.

By and large the prognosis then is good, and realism prevails. Profits may be down but, at the end of the day, it does seem to the onlooker an altogether saner way of running a railway!

EELIN McIVOR

PAINTINGS PRICE GUIDE 1993

WILLIAM ACHEFF (b. 1947) – Santo Domingo dipper –
signed and dated *1982* – oil on canvas – 30.5 x 45.7cm.
(Sotheby's)   **£5,806 $10,450**

Attributed to HANS VON AACHEN (1551/2–1615) –
Portrait of Duke Wilhelm V of Bavaria (1548–1626) and
his son Albrecht – oil on canvas – 229 x 140.5cm.
(Sotheby's)   **£22,000 $39,600**

JULIUS ADAM (1852–1913) – Best friends – signed – oil
on panel – 14.4 x 20cm.
(Christie's)   **£3,300 $5,412**

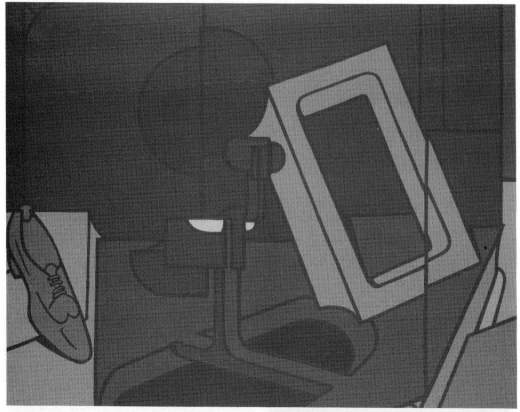

VALERIO ADAMI (b. 1938) – The shop window – signed
and inscribed – oil on canvas – 80.5 x 99.5cm.
(Christie's)   **£14,300 $23,166**

JOHN CLAYTON ADAMS (1840–1906) – On the Tweed
– signed – oil on canvas – 106.7 x 152.4cm.
(Christie's)   **£9,020 $15,965**

VALERIO ADAMI (b. 1935) – On the riverbank – signed
and inscribed – acrylic on canvas – 116.2 x 88.2cm.
(Christie's)   **£12,100 $20,086**

**EDMUND WORNDLE VON ADELSFRIED (1827–
1906)** – Christ the carpenter – signed and dated *1860* – oil
on canvas – unframed – 48.2 x 73.6cm.
(Christie's)   **£7,700 $12,551**

Studio of PIETER COECKE VAN AELST (1502–1550)
– Joseph of Arimathaea – oil on panel – 91.5 x 31.8cm.
(Sotheby's) £12,100 $21,780

Studio of PIETER COECKE VAN AELST (1502–1550)
– Mary Magdalen – oil on panel – 86 x 31.8cm.
(Sotheby's) £13,200 $23,760

WILLEM VAN AELST (1627–circa 1683) – A still life of hunting paraphernalia with a partridge and a cockerel – bears traces of a signature – oil on canvas – 98 x 77.5cm.
(Sotheby's)   **£13,200 $23,760**

EILEEN AGAR (b. 1899) – Abstract composition – signed – oil on canvas – 59.5 x 49cm.
(Christie's)   **£1,870 $3,104**

FRANZ THEODOR AERNI (German, 1853–1918) – Market street – signed and dated '86 – oil on canvas – 110.5 x 74cm.
(Sotheby's)   **£22,000 $38,940**

Follower of PIETER AERTSEN – The prodigal son feasting – oil on canvas – 101.5 x 110cm.
(Sotheby's)   **£27,500 $49,500**

AUGUSTO ALBERICI (b. 1846) – Stallholders outside The Temple of Minerva, Rome – signed – oil on canvas – 75.5 x 62.2cm.
(Christie's)   **£7,150 $12,512**

JOSEF ALBERS (1888–1976) – Towards Fall I – signed with monogram and dated *58* – oil on masonite – 61 x 61cm.
(Christie's) £23,100 $37,422

JOSEF ALBERS (1888–1976) – Study for Hommage to the Square: 'Wait' – signed with monogram and dated *63* – oil on masonite – 76 x 76cm.
(Christie's) £24,200 $42,834

PIERRE ALECHINSKY (b. 1927) – Composition – signed and dated *1978* – watercolour on paper – 75 x 59cm.
(Christie's) £8,939 $15,821

FRANCESCO ALBOTTO (Italian, 1722–1757) – Venice, the Rialto Bridge from the south – oil on canvas – 55.7 x 84.6cm.
(Sotheby's) £110,000 $198,000

PIERRE ALECHINSKY (b. 1927) – Légèrement parlant
– signed and dated *1985* – acrylic and black ink on paper
laid down on canvas – 273.5 x 249cm.
(Christie's)　　　　　　　　　**£44,000　$77,880**

FRANCESCO ALEGIANI (late 19th century) – A
trompe l'oeil with portraits by Raphael pinned to a wooden
panel – signed and inscribed – oil on canvas –
50.8 x 34.6cm.
(Christie's)　　　　　　　　**£6,820　$11,867**

ROBERT L. ALEXANDER, R.S.A. (1840–1923) – The
evening meal – signed and dated *1884* – oil on canvas –
104 x 137cm.
(Christie's)　　　　　　　　　**£8,800　$14,432**

ROBERT WEIR ALLAN (1851–1942) – Fishing boats in
a harbour – signed – pencil and watercolour with scratching
out – 280 x 534mm.
(Christie's)　　　　　　　　　**£2,200　$3,564**

ROBERT WEIR ALLAN (1851–1942) - Cairo, looking
towards the Citadel – signed and inscribed – pencil and
watercolour – 508 x 750mm.
(Christie's)　　　　　　　　　**£825　$1,337**

MARION BOYD ALLEN (American, 1862–1941) – A young girl and boy by the fireside – signed and dated *1918* – oil on canvas – unframed – 102.5 x 128cm.
(Sotheby's)   **£1,760 $3,115**

HELEN ALLINGHAM, R.W.S. (1848–1926) – The black kitten – signed – watercolour with scratching out – 325 x 251mm.
(Christie's)   **£26,400 $43,560**

HELEN ALLINGHAM (1848–1926) – A thatched cottage near Peaslake, Surrey – signed – watercolour with scratching out – 230 x 245mm.
(Christie's)   **£7,480 $12,118**

HELEN ALLINGHAM (1848–1926) – The view from Tennyson's window, Farringford, Isle of Wight – signed – pencil and watercolour – 165 x 210mm.
(Christie's)   **£2,420 $4,404**

HELEN ALLINGHAM, R.W.S. (1848–1926) – Near Witley, Surrey – signed – watercolour with scratching out – 480 x 375mm.
(Christie's)   **£46,200 $76,230**

HELEN ALLINGHAM, R.W.S. (1848–1926) – In the primrose wood – signed – watercolour with scratching out – 362 x 285mm.
(Christie's)   **£22,000 $37,180**

ADRIAN ALLINSON (1890–1959) – Portrait of Mr. Watkins – oil on canvas – 56 x 68.5cm.
(Christie's)   **£7,700 $12,782**

SIR LAWRENCE ALMA-TADEMA (1836–1912) – Portrait of the singer George Henschel playing Alma-Tadema's piano, Townshend House – signed and inscribed with opus no. – oil on panel – 48.3 x 34.2cm.
(Christie's)   **£46,200 $78,540**

RUDOLF VON ALT (Austrian, 1812–1905) – In the park of the spa at Teplitz – signed – watercolour over traces of pencil – 28.5 x 27.5cm.
(Sotheby's)   **£5,720 $10,124**

MARIANO ALONSO-PEREZ (Spanish, 19th/20th century) – Retrieving the bonnet – signed – oil on canvas – 72 x 58.5cm.
(Sotheby's)   **£3,300 $5,841**

ALEXANDRE ALTMANN (Russian, b. 1885) – A village – signed – oil on canvas – 59 x 71.5cm.
(Sotheby's)   **£3,300 $5,841**

RUDOLF VON ALT (Austrian, 1812–1905) – The cemetery at Gastein – signed and dated '889 – watercolour – 28 x 27cm.
(Sotheby's)   **£4,400 $7,788**

FEDERICO ANDREOTTI (Italian, 1847–1930) – Flirtation in the wine cellar – signed – oil on canvas – 63 x 46.5cm.
(Sotheby's)   **£8,800 $15,576**

FILIPPO ANGELI, called Filippo Napoletano (circa 1595–1630) – Figures on a rocky coastal landscape –
oil on copper, oval – 15 x 20.5cm.
(Sotheby's)   **£12,100 $21,780**

RICHARD ANSDELL, R.A. (1815–1885) – Going to market, Spain – signed and dated *1858* – 61 x 105.5cm.
(Christie's)   **£6,600 $10,692**

PIETRO ANTONIANI (Italian, circa 1740/50–1805) –
Naples, view of the Largo del Castello during the Cuccagna
Festival held on 5 June 1766 – inscribed on reverse – oil on
canvas – 31 x 41cm.
(Sotheby's) **£31,900 $57,420**

PIETRO ANTONIANI (Italian, circa 1740/50–1805) –
The eruption of Vesuvius on 19 September 1767 –
inscribed on reverse and signed with initials – oil on canvas
– 31 x 41cm.
(Sotheby's) **£17,600 $31,680**

KAREL APPEL (b. 1921) – Figure and birds – signed –
acrylic on paper mounted on canvas – 89 x 148cm.
(Christie's) **£17,190 $30,426**

SHUSAKO ARAKAWA (b. 1936) – Landscape – signed,
inscribed with title and dated *1969* – 122 x 183cm.
(Christie's) **£27,500 $44,550**

Manner of JUAN DE ARELLANO – Carnations, poppies
and other flowers in a basket with fungi – oil on canvas –
66 x 87.7cm.
(Christie's) **£3,080 $4,805**

OUMBERTOS ARGYROS (early 20th century) –
Childhood memories – signed and dated *929* – oil on
canvas – 100.3 x 75.5cm.
(Christie's) **£6,050 $10,587**

43

MAXWELL ASHBY ARMFIELD (1882–1972) – Fungi
– signed with monogram – tempera on gesso-prepared
panel – 23 x 28.5cm.
(Christie's)   **£3,080 $5,298**

JOHN ARMSTRONG (1893–1973) – Entry to the circus
– signed with initials – tempera on board – 48 x 37.5cm.
(Christie's)   **£47,300 $78,518**

ALOIS ARNEGGER – On the Neapolitan coast – signed
– oil on canvas – 101.7 x 101.7cm.
(Christie's)   **£2,200 $3,784**

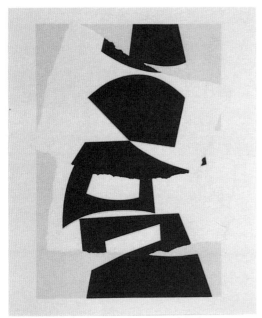

JEAN ARP (1887-1966) – Sketch for a tower – signed on
backboard – 66.5 x 49.5cm.
(Christie's)   £7,150 $11,583

FRANK AUERBACH (b. 1931) – Portrait of E.O.W. III –
oil on board – 36 x 30.5cm.
(Christie's)   £19,800 $32,076

REGINALD ARTHUR (fl. 1881–1896) – Joseph interpreting Pharaoh's dream – signed and dated *1894* – oil
on canvas – 101.6 x 127cm.
(Christie's)   £44,000 $74,800

MILTON AVERY (1893–1965) - Spring time – signed
and dated *1957* - oil on canvasboard – 71.1 x 55.9cm.
(Christie's) **£11,484 $19,800**

MICHAEL AYRTON (1921–1975) – The white boat –
signed and dated *47* – oil on panel – 25 x 35cm.
(Christie's) **£3,520 $6,160**

HENRY BACON (1839–1912) – Christmas prayers –
signed and dated *1872* – oil on panel – 45 x 34.5cm.
(Christie's) **£4,466 $7,700**

FIRMIN BAES (1874–1945) – Still life with lemons –
signed and dated 1932 – pastel on paper – 43 x 53cm.
(Hôtel de Ventes Horta)   **£1,724 $3,000**

ARTHUR BAKER-CLACK (d. 1955) – Boatyard –
signed and dated *1913* – oil on panel – 26.7 x 34.9cm.
(Christie's)   **£3,850 $6,776**

ALICE BAILLY (Swiss, 1872–1938) – Young woman
brushing her hair – oil on board – 84 x 102cm.
(Germann)   **£5,263 $9,368**

CHARLES THOMAS BALE (fl. 1868–1875) – Primroses
in a basket, japonica and a bird's nest; and Grapes, peaches
and plums on a mossy bank – signed – oil on canvas –
35.5 x 45.7cm. – a pair
(Christie's)   **£2,090 $3,804**

ENRICO BAJ (b. 1924) – Untitled – signed – mixed
media on cloth – 146 x 114cm.
(Finarte)   **£31,873 $54,343**

CHARLES THOMAS BALE (fl. 1868–1884) – A mallard
and a woodpigeon with a basket of apples and grapes on a
wooden ledge – signed with monogram and dated *1884* –
oil on canvas – 51 x 61cm.
(Christie's)   **£2,860 $4,633**

PEDER BALKE (1804–1886) – Stockholm by moonlight
– signed – oil on paper laid down on canvas –
17.8 x 22.8cm.
(Christie's)   **£6,050 $10,527**

GIACOMO BALLA (1871–1958) – Bambino – signed –
oil on canvas – 61.5 x 50cm.
(Christie's)   **£46,200 $74,844**

GIACOMO BALLA (1878–1958) – Nude against the light
– signed and dated *1908* – pastel on board – 130 x 61.5cm.
(Finarte)   **£227,092 $387,192**

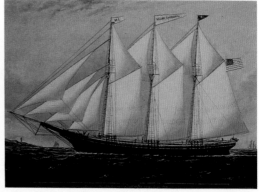

GIACOMO BALLA (1871–1958) – Il Pugile futuristo
(recto) – signed – pencil and watercolour on paper –
Composizione futurista (verso) – pen and ink and crayon on
paper – 10.7 x 17.2cm.
(Christie's)   **£5,500 $9,680**

THADDEUS BANNISTER (b. 1915) – The schooner
William Churchill – signed and inscribed – oil on canvas –
62 x 88.8cm.
(Christie's)   **£2,420 $4,308**

THADDEUS BANNISTER (b. 1915) – The schooners
Fleur de Lys and Phantom in a match race – signed and
inscribed – oil on canvas – 62.8 x 88.3cm.
(Christie's) £2,640 $4,699

EDUARD BARGHEER (1901–1979) – Dreamtown in
fireworks – signed and dated *52–53* – oil on canvas –
71.5 x 99.7cm.
(Christie's) £13,750 $24,337

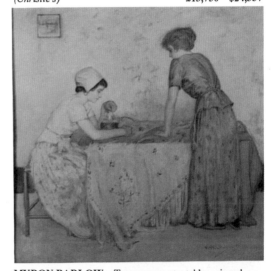

**GIOVANNI FRANCESCO BARBIERI, called Il
Guercino** – Study of a female nude, possibly Susanna –
pen and brown ink, on paper laid down on canvas –
23.8 x 18.7cm.
(Bonhams) £5,200 $8,268

MYRON BARLOW – Two women at a table – signed –
oil on canvas – 29^1/2 x 29^1/4in.
(Du Mouchelles) £3,944 $7,000

MCCLELLAND BARCLAY (1891–1943) – Dinner under the stars – signed – oil on canvas – 71 x 127cm.
(Christie's) £1,914 $3,300

EDWARD HERBERT BARNES (FL. 1855–1909) – A gift of tobacco – signed and dated *1877* – oil on canvas – 71 x 91.5cm.
(Christie's)   **£3,300 $5,841**

MAURICE BARRAUD (Swiss, 1889–1954) – Nude – signed and dated *1945* – oil on canvas – 65 x 81cm.
(Germann)   **£22,177 $35,262**

WILLIAM H. BARTLETT (1858–1932) – The neighbours – signed and dated *1881* – oil on canvas – 99 x 128.2cm.
(Christie's)   **£20,900 $35,530**

PIETRO BARUCCI (1845–1917) – Flock at sunset –
signed and inscribed – oil on canvas – 100.5 x 200.5cm.
(Christie's)   **£17,600 $28,688**

DAVID BATES (1840–1921) – A pool, Malvern – signed
and dated *1881* – oil on canvas – 35.6 x 45.8cm.
(Christie's)   **£1,100 $1,947**

LUIGI BASILETTI (1780–1860) – An Italianate
Capriccio landscape with the Falls at Tivoli – signed with
monogram and dated *1839* – oil on canvas – 109 x 174cm.
(Christie's)   **£14,300 $23,309**

DAVID BATES (1840–1921) – A Warwickshire streamlet
– signed and dated *1896* – oil on canvas – 61 x 91.5cm.
(Christie's)   **£7,150 $11,583**

STEPHEN JOHN BATCHELDER – Wherry passing
Irstead Church – signed – watercolour – 14 x 18in.
(G.A. Key)   **£1,850 $3,275**

DAVID BATES (circa 1841–1921) – In the vale of the
Conway – signed and dated *1905* – pencil and watercolour
– 350 x 514mm.
(Christie's)   **£1,540 $2,495**

GUSTAV BAUERNFEIND (1848–1904) – A back street,
Jaffa (?) – signed and dated *82* – oil on panel –
28.6 x 45cm.
(Christie's)   **£16,500 $26,895**

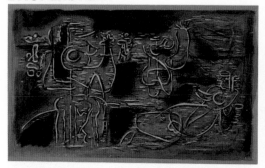

WILLI BAUMEISTER (1889–1955) – From Esther, 1946
– signed and dated *46* – gouache and charcoal – 28 x 48cm.
(Lempertz) **£17,993 $28,699**

PETER BAUMGARTNER (1834–1911) – St. Martin's
goose – signed and dated *1869* – oil on canvas –
76.2 x 93.4cm.
(Christie's) **£11,000 $17,930**

EDWARD BAWDEN (1903–1989) – January, 10 am –
signed – pencil, watercolour and bodycolour – 44.5 x 56cm.
(Christie's) **£6,050 $10,587**

WALTER BAYES (1869–1956) – Sous Bois - signed and
dated *1923* – oil on canvas-board – 45.6 x 46.4cm.
(Christie's) **£3,520 $5,843**

WILLIAM A. BAZIOTES (1912–1963) – Puppet forms –
signed – watercolour and gouache on paper –
27.7 x 35.3cm.
(Christie's) **£6,061 $10,450**

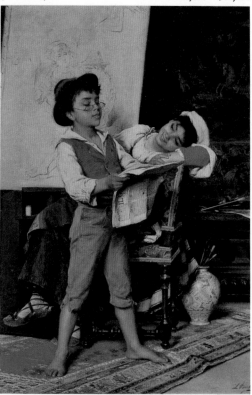

LUIGI BECHI (Italian, 1830–1919) – Reading the news
in the artist's studio – signed – oil on canvas –
143 x 103cm.
(Sotheby's) **£31,900 $56,463**

GIOVANNI BATTISTA BEINASCHI (1636–1688) –
Saint Peter – numbered on reverse – oil on canvas –
133.4 x 96.1cm.
(Christie's) £8,934 $14,830

JOHN BELLANY (b. 1942) – Self portrait – signed – oil
on canvas – unframed – 173 x 76cm.
(Christie's) £5,720 $10,010

VANESSA BELL (1879–1961) – The walled garden at
Charleston – inscribed on the reverse – oil on canvas –
46 x 35.5cm.
(Sotheby's) £4,950 $8,811

BERNARDO BELLOTTO (1721–1780) – The Fortress of
Königstein – oil on canvas – 133 x 235.7cm.
(Sotheby's) £3,410,000 $6,138,000

BERNARDO BELLOTTO (1721–1780) – View of the Piazza Navona, Rome – oil on canvas – 88 x 149cm.
(Christie's)   **£1,295,372 $2,150,317**

GEORGE BELLOWS (1882–1925) – The fisherman – inscribed by the artist's wife – oil on panel –
45.7 x 55.9cm.
(Sotheby's)   **£45,833 $82,500**

JEAN BENNER (1836–1909) – The rose garden – signed
and dated *1861* – oil on canvas – 132.1 x 97.8cm.
(Christie's)   £7,480 $13,015

THOMAS HART BENTON (1889–1975) – T.P and Jake
– signed – egg tempera on canvas mounted on panel –
121.9 x 78.7cm.
(Sotheby's)   £152,778 $275,000

FRANK MOSS BENNETT (1874–1953) – The price of a
song – signed and dated *1903* – oil on canvas –
91.5 x 127cm.
(Christie's)   £2,860 $4,633

WILLIAM RUBERY BENNETT (1893–1987) –
Kangaroo Valley – signed – 38.2 x 45.7cm.
(Christie's)   £4,620 $8,131

Attributed to CLAES PIETERSZ BERCHEM (1620–
1683) – Rocky, Italianate landscape with a woman on a
donkey and a shepherd at a ford – oil on panel –
49.5 x 42.5cm.
(Sotheby's)   £5,500 $9,900

BERCHERE

NARCISSE BERCHERE (1819–1891) – An Arab caravan at the entrance of a town - signed – oil on panel – 37.5 x 61.6cm.
(Christie's) £7,700 $13,398

PETRUS-AUGUSTUS BERETTA (Italian, 1805–66) – Unloading a hay barge, Rotterdam – signed – oil on panel – 37 x 49cm.
(Sotheby's) £3,300 $5,841

BERGAMO SCHOOL (circa 1630–40) – Portrait of a young man, dressed in red – oil on canvas – 170 x 110cm.
(Christie's) £11,167 $18,537

JULIUS HUGO BERGMANN (1861–1940) – Marauding lions – signed and dated *90* – oil on canvas – 137 x 221cm.
(Christie's) £33,000 $53,790

OSCAR EDMUND BERNINGHAUS (1874–1952) – Five miles to Taos – signed – oil on canvas – 50.8 x 61cm.
(Christie's) £12,760 $22,000

OSCAR E. BERNINGHAUS (1874–1952) - Two horses – signed – oil on canvasboard – 22.9 x 33cm.
(Sotheby's) £5,806 $10,450

H. BETZOLD (20th century) – A still life of mixed flowers in a glass bowl, on a draped table – signed – oil on canvas – 80.7 x 66cm.
(Christie's)   **£2,750 $4,785**

Follower of JOACHIM BEUCKELAER – A fish stall with an amorous couple observed by a fishseller – oil on canvas – 106.6 x 156.8cm.
(Sotheby's)   **£8,250 $14,850**

JOSE BEULAS (b. 1921) - Torla – signed – oil on canvas – 130 x 97cm.
(Duran)   **£10,028 $18,000**

PETER BIEGEL (1913–1988) – Tally Ho! – signed – oil on canvas – 49.5 x 39.5cm.
(Christie's) £2,310 $3,835

EUGEN VON BLAAS (1843–1932) – A Mediterranean beauty – signed – oil on canvas – 57.8 x 44.7cm.
(Christie's) £6,600 $11,484

ELIZABETH BLACKADDER (b. 1931) – Interior with self-portrait – signed and dated *1972* – oil on board – 81 x 112cm.
(Christie's) £8,250 $14,437

EUGEN VON BLAAS (1843–1932) – The water carrier – signed and dated *1880* – oil on canvas – 63 x 98cm.
(Christie's) £30,800 $50,204

WILLIAM KAY BLACKLOCK (Exh. 1897–1921) – The shepherdess – oil on canvas – 20 x 30in.
(W.H. Lane & Son) £6,600 $10,659

WILLIAM KAY BLACKLOCK (Exh. 1897–1921) –
The flower seller – signed and dated *1912* – oil on board –
20 x 26.5cm.
(Christie's) £2,200 $3,784

CHARLES BLACKMAN (b. 1928) – Young girl and old
cat – signed – oil on canvas laid down on board –
124.5 x 154.9cm.
(Christie's) £6,600 $11,616

JEAN-CHARLES BLAIS (b. 1956) – Never again – signed three times, inscribed and dated on reverse *X II 83*
– oil on torn posters – 266.7 x 233.7cm.
(Christie's) £26,400 $46,728

JEAN-CHARLES BLAIS (b. 1956) – Head - signed and dated *84* – gouache, pins and paper collage on paper – 45.6 x 50.8cm.
(Christie's)   £7,700 $12,782

JEAN-CHARLES BLAIS (b. 1956) – Untitled – signed and dated *86* – oil on torn posters – 90 x 135cm.
(Christie's)   £14,300 $23,166

THOMAS BLINKS (1860–1912) – Full cry – signed and dated *96* – oil on canvas – 50.8 x 76.2cm.
(Christie's)   £6,380 $11,293

JAN FRANS VAN BLOEMEN, called Orizzonte (Flemish, 1662–1749) – Two Classical landscapes – oil on canvas – 38.5 x 65.5cm. – a pair
(Sotheby's)   £55,000 $99,000

BERNARDUS JOHANNES BLOMMERS (1845–1914) – Return from the beach – signed – oil on canvas – 68 x 56.5cm.
(Christie's)   £19,250 $33,687

BERNARDUS JOHANNES BLOMMERS (Dutch, 1845–1914) – A frugal meal – signed – watercolour – 37 x 51.5cm.
(Sotheby's)   £5,280 $9,346

SANDRA BLOW (b. 1925) – Abstract – signed and dated on reverse *1954* – oil on canvas – 127 x 79cm.
(Christie's)   £1,870 $3,272

ERIC BODOM (1829–1879) – A waterfall in Norway – signed and dated *1853* – oil on canvas – 98 x 83cm.
(Christie's)   £6,380 $10,399

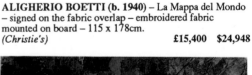

ERNEST LEONARD BLUMENSCHEIN (1874–1960) – Indian in a white robe – signed – oil on canvas – 51.4 x 40.6cm.
(Butterfield & Butterfield)   £37,822 $66,000

ALIGHERIO BOETTI (b. 1940) – La Mappa del Mondo – signed on the fabric overlap – embroidered fabric mounted on board – 115 x 178cm.
(Christie's)   £15,400 $24,948

Attributed to HENRY JOHN BODDINGTON (1811–1865) – A view of Windsor Castle from the Thames – oil on canvas – 71.1 x 91.5cm.
(Christie's)   £3,850 $6,237

BRAM BOGART (b. 1921) – Aux fêtes rouges – signed and dated *60* – pigment and composition on canvas – 161 x 213cm.
(Christie's)   £71,500 $115,830

FRANK BOGGS (1855–1926) – The harbour at Marseilles
– signed – oil on canvas – 55 x 112cm.
(Christie's)   **£17,600 $30,976**

GUY PENE DU BOIS (1884–1958) – Sin twisters –
signed and dated – oil on panel – 51 x 38cm.
(Christie's)   **£66,990 $115,500**

GUY PENE DU BOIS (1884–1958) – Patience – signed
and dated – watercolour and ink on paper – 38.8 x 33.6cm.
(Christie's)   **£2,871 $4,950**

GUY PENE DU BOIS (1884–1958) – Portrait of Patrick
Henry Bruce – signed – oil on canvas – 101.5 x 81.3cm.
(Christie's)   **£4,785 $8,250**

GIOVANNI BOLDINI (1842–1931) – A gentleman,
seated in an armchair, reading a book and smoking a pipe
(recto); and A reclining lady (verso) – signed – pencil and
watercolour on paper (recto); pencil and brown wash
(verso) – 23.5 x 21.9cm.
(Christie's)   **£7,150 $12,512**

ELIAS PIETER VON BOMMEL – A Dutch canal landscape with a hay barge moored by a church – signed and dated *1876* – oil on canvas – 39.3 x 58.4cm.
(Christie's) £1,760 $3,027

MAURICE BOMPARD (French, 1857–1936) – An antiquarian shop in Venice – signed and inscribed *Venise 1894* – oil on canvas – 80 x 64cm.
(Sotheby's) £3,850 $6,814

MAURICE BOMPARD (1857–1936) – View of Venice – signed – oil on panel – 94 x 133cm.
(Hôtel de Ventes Horta) £3,793 $6,600

MAURICE BOMPARD (1857–1936) – Waiting: Odalisques in an interior – signed – oil on panel – 53 x 65cm.
(Christie's) £8,800 $14,344

BONHEUR·

ROSA BONHEUR (1822–1899) – Un vieux baudet (The head of a donkey) – signed and dated *1878* – oil on canvas – 101 x 82cm.
(Christie's) £20,900 $36,575

ROSA BONHEUR (French, 1822–99) – A wounded chamois – signed – oil on canvas – 48 x 64cm.
(Sotheby's) £3,300 $5,841

A. BONIFAZI (late 19th century) – A captivated audience – signed, inscribed and dated *1876* – oil on canvas – 60 x 106cm.
(Christie's) £30,800 $50,204

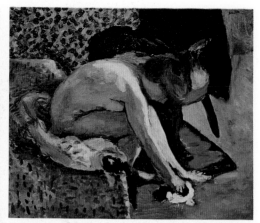

PIERRE BONNARD (1867–1947) – Young woman putting on stockings – with studio stamp – oil on canvas – 53 x 63cm.
(Christie's) £330,000 $541,200

PIERRE BONNARD (1867–1947) – At the embroiderer's (Women at the window) – signed – oil on panel – 34.2 x 40.6cm.
(Christie's) £126,500 $207,460

CARLO BONONI (1569–1632) – Perseus – oil on canvas, framed as an oval – 94.5 x 128cm.
(Sotheby's) £25,300 $45,540

FRANCISCO BORES (1898–1972) – The blue roof –
signed with initial and dated *37* – oil on canvas –
38.1 x 46.4cm.
(Christie's) £6,600 $11,616

FRANCISCO BORES (1898–1972) – The sailor musician
– signed and dated *37* – oil on canvas – 130 x 97cm.
(Christie's) £19,800 $32,076

AMBROSIUS BOSSCHAERT the Elder – A still life of
a rose, a tulip, and other flowers in a Wan Li bottle jar, on a
ledge with butterflies – oil on copper – unframed –
23.8 x 17.9cm.
(Bonhams) £195,000 $310,050

BOTERO

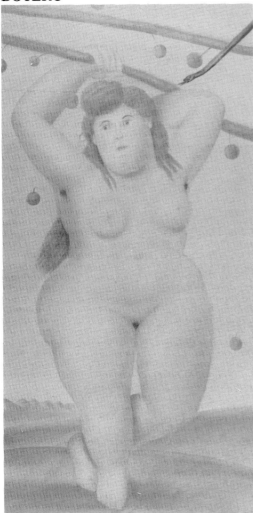

EMIL BOTT (19th century) – The Idlewild – signed and dated *1881* – oil on canvas – 40.6 x 79.4cm.
(Sotheby's) £9,778 $17,600

EUGENE BOUDIN (French, 1824–1898) – Etretat/La falaise d'Amont – signed and dated *90* – oil on panel – 14³/₄ x 18¹/₄in.
(Skinner Inc.) £39,207 $69,300

FERNANDO BOTERO (b. 1932) – Eva, 1982 – watercolour on paper – 180.3 x 95.2cm.
(Finarte) £71,713 $122,271

JESSIE ARMS BOTKE (American, 1883–1971) – The explorers, geese in a garden – signed and dated *1932* – oil on masonite – 32¹/₂ x 40in.
(Skinner Inc.) £11,825 $20,900

EUGENE BOUDIN (1824–1898) – Le Port de Trouville – signed and dated *94* – oil on panel – 40 x 32.3cm.
(Christie's) £30,800 $54,208

EUGENE BOUDIN (1824–1898) – The pasture – signed with initials – oil on canvas – 33 x 40.7cm.
(Christie's) £9,900 $16,038

GEORGE HENRY BOUGHTON (1833–1905) – Portrait of Esmé Robb, bust length – oil on canvas – 45.7 x 45.7cm.
(Christie's) £4,950 $8,415

CYPRIEN-EUGENE BOULET (French, 1877–1927) – A woman resting against a tree – signed – oil on canvas – 80 x 59cm.
(Sotheby's) £4,400 $7,788

CHARLES EDOUARD BOUTIBONNE (Austrian, 1816–97) – Mermaids frolicking in the sea – signed and dated *1883* – oil on canvas – 151 x 230cm.
(Sotheby's) £16,500 $29,205

BOUVARD

ANTOINE BOUVARD (French, d. 1956) – A Venetian scene – signed – oil on canvas – 52 x 79cm.
(Sotheby's)   £4,620 $8,177

ANTOINE BOUVARD (d. 1956) – A Venetian backwater – signed – oil on canvas – 53 x 80.6cm.
(Christie's)   £5,500 $9,570

ANTOINE BOUVARD (d. 1956) – The Giudecca, Venice; and The Molo, Venice – both signed – oil on canvas – 24.2 x 33cm. – a pair
(Christie's)   £6,600 $11,484

ANTOINE BOUVARD (d. 1956) – On the Giudecca, Venice – signed – oil on canvas – 59.8 x 80.6cm.
(Christie's)   £9,350 $16,269

OWEN BOWEN (1873–1967) – Where the World comes not – signed and dated *1898* – oil on canvas – 101.5 x 152.5cm.
(Christie's)   £7,150 $11,583

JANE MARIA BOWKETT (fl. 1860–1885) – Pushing off – signed with monogram – oil on canvas – 61 x 45.5cm.
(Christie's)   £1,320 $2,138

ALAN BOWYER – American whaler in Antarctic waters, Alice Mandell of New Bedford, 1851 – signed – oil on canvas – 24 x 36in.
(Eldred's)   £318 $550

HERCULES BRABAZON BRABAZON (1821–1906) –
The Salute, Venice – signed with initials – watercolour with
touches of white heightening on grey paper –
235 x 307mm.
(Christie's) £6,600 $12,012

ROBERT BRACKMAN (1898–1980) – Self portrait –
signed – oil on canvas – 25.5 x 20.5cm.
(Christie's) £1,531 $2,640

HERCULES BRABAZON BRABAZON (1821–1906) –
The Piazzetta from the Canal – signed with initials – pencil,
watercolour and bodycolour – 254 x 355mm.
(Christie's) £5,720 $9,266

ROBERT BRACKMAN (1898–1980) – Arrangement
No. 9 with figure – signed – oil on canvas – 71 x 91.5cm.
(Christie's) £4,466 $7,700

BASIL BRADLEY (1842–1904) – An English and a
Gordon setter; and An Irish setter and a pointer in a
landscape – signed – pencil and watercolour heightened
with white – 26.7 x 19cm. – a pair
(Christie's) £1,650 $2,706

SIR FRANK BRANGWYN, R.A. (1869–1956) – An eastern port – signed with initials and dated *94* – watercolour and bodycolour – 50.5 x 75.5cm.
(Christie's)   **£1,540 $2,649**

ANTONIETTA BRANDEIS (Austrian, b.1849) – A view of the Piazzetta and S. Maria della Salute; A view of the Doges' Palace and the Piazzetta, Venice – both signed – oil on panel – each 17 x 24cm. – a pair
(Sotheby's)   **£11,000 $19,470**

GEORGES BRAQUE (1882–1963) – The apples – signed – brown crayon on paper – 13.5 x 28.3cm.
(Christie's)   **£11,000 $19,360**

ANTONIETTA BRANDEIS (b. 1849) – The Piazzetta, Venice, with San Giorgio Maggiore beyond; and The Tiber with the Castel Sant'Angelo and St Peter's, Rome – both signed – oil on panel – 16.2 x 22.8cm. – a pair
(Christie's)   **£9,350 $16,269**

GEORGES BRASSEUR (Belgian, 1880–1950) – The fortune teller – signed – oil on canvas – 192 x 134cm.
(Hôtel de Ventes Horta)   **£1,110 $1,898**

MAURICE BRAUN (1877–1941) – San Diego hills – signed – oil on canvas – 41 x 50.5cm.
(Christie's) **£4,147 $7,150**

ALFRED DE BREANSKI (1852–1928) – Highland cattle by a loch, Perthshire – signed – oil on canvas – 61 x 91.5cm.
(Christie's) **£13,200 $22,440**

ALFRED DE BREANSKI (1852–1928) – Dhu Loch, near Balmoral – signed – oil on canvas – 61 x 91.5cm.
(Christie's) **£11,000 $17,820**

ALFRED DE BREANSKI (1852–1928) – The River Tay – signed – oil on canvas – 50.8 x 76.2cm.
(Christie's) **£6,050 $9,801**

ALFRED DE BREANSKI (1852–1928) – Sheep grazing by a lake at sunset – signed – oil on canvas – 76 x 127cm.
(Christie's) **£4,620 $7,484**

JOHN EDWARD BRETT, A.R.A. (1830–1902) – Val
d'Aosta – inscribed on reverse – pencil, watercolour and
gum arabic heightened with white and scratching out –
245 x 194mm.
(Christie's)   £15,950 $25,839

J. PERIS BRELL (Spanish, 19th century) – A matador;A
picador; A toreador – all signed and dated '86, '86 and 1887
– oil on canvas – two 55 x 35cm.; one 68 x 48cm. – three
(Sotheby's)   £5,500 $9,735

**JOHANN GEORG MEYER VON BREMEN (1813–
1886)** – The flood – signed and dated 1846 – oil on canvas
– 128 x 168.2cm.
(Christie's)   £55,000 $89,650

ALFRED THOMPSON BRICHER (1837–1908) –
Autumn boating – signed and dated *1870* – oil on canvas –
22.7 x 45.5cm.
(Christie's) **£14,036 $24,200**

Follower of JAN BREUGHEL II – Virgin and Child with
the infant John the Baptist, surrounded by a garland of
flowers and fruit – oil on copper – 74 x 60cm.
(Christie's) **£23,451 $38,929**

C. BRIAND – Music; and Spring – signed – oil on canvas
and oil on panel – 57.3 x 24.2cm. – two
(Christie's) **£2,200 $3,784**

FREDERICK ARTHUR BRIDGMAN (American,
1847–1928) – Young boy with black ram – signed and
dated *1874* – oil on canvas – 13 x 16in.
(Skinner Inc.) **£4,668 $8,250**

ALFRED THOMPSON BRICHER (1837–1908) – Dusk
on the hill side – signed and dated *1872* – oil on canvas –
61 x 51cm.
(Christie's) **£10,208 $17,600**

FREDERICK ARTHUR BRIDGMAN (1847–1928) –
Odalisque – signed and dated *1878* – oil on canvas –
27.3 x 40.6cm.
(Butterfield & Butterfield) **£3,152 $5,500**

JULES RUINART DE BRINANT (1838–1898) – The concert – signed and dated *89* – oil on panel – 38.4 x 26.3cm.
(Christie's) £2,640 $4,594

BRITISH SCHOOL (early 19th century) – Macacus monkey from Hindustan, India – watercolour on wove paper – 53.3 x 38.7cm.
(Butterfield & Butterfield) £946 $1,650

LOUIS LE BROCQUY, R.H.A. (b. 1916) – Finale – signed – pencil and oil on board – 59.5 x 49cm.
(Christie's) £5,500 $9,625

ALFRED BROGE (Danish, b. 1870) – A lady watering a plant by a window – signed and dated *1915* – oil on canvas – 49 x 63cm.
(Sotheby's) £2,640 $4,673

WILLIAM BROMLEY (fl. 1835–1888) – Watching the nibble – signed – oil on canvas – 35.5 x 45.7cm.
(Christie's) £6,050 $11,011

WILLIAM BROMLEY (fl. 1835–1888) – The Contract – signed – oil on canvas – 23 x 33cm.
(Christie's) £1,650 $2,673

WILLIAM BROMLEY (fl. 1835–1888) – A rest by the
gate – signed and dated *1866* – oil on canvas –
30.4 x 25.4cm.
(Christie's) £2,640 $4,277

ROBIN BROOKS (20th century) – 'We Stood Along the
Edge' 54° 92' South, 14 December 1772' – signed – oil on
canvas – 40.6 x 60.9cm.
(Christie's) £1,980 $3,524

ADRIAEN BROUWER (1605–1638) – Tavern scene –
signed with monogram – oil on panel – 47.3 x 36cm.
(Hôtel de Ventes Horta) £2,560 $4,378

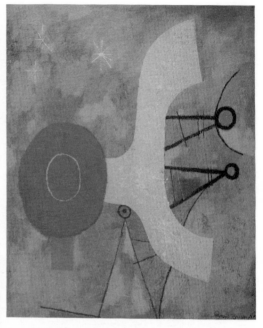

BYRON BROWNE (1907–1961) - Flying disc – signed
and dated *1949* – oil on masonite – 71 x 61cm.
(Christie's)   **£2,424 $4,180**

FORD MADOX BROWN (1821–1893) – King René's
honeymoon – signed with monogram and dated *64* –
watercolour – 26.7 x 17.8cm.
(Christie's)   **£15,400 $26,180**

**ABRAHAM BRUEGHEL (1631–1697) and
FRANCESCO SOLIMENA (1657–1747)** – A girl picking
grapes from a trellis, a still life of flowers in a silver urn
and fruit nearby, in a landscape setting – oil on canvas –
76 x 101.5cm.
(Sotheby's)   **£44,000 $79,200**

**JAN BRUEGHEL the Younger (1601–1678) and Studio
of FRANS FRANCKEN the Younger (1581–1642)** – The
Assumption of the Virgin within a wreath of flowers – oil
on panel – 99 x 73.5cm.
(Sotheby's)   **£27,500 $49,500**

JOHN GEORGE BROWN (1831–1913) – Portrait of
Douglas B. Wesson – signed and dated *1895* – oil on
canvas – 61 x 40.6cm.
(Butterfield & Butterfield)   **£5,043 $8,800**

BRUGES SCHOOL (circa 1510) – Double sided triptych
wing: recto, Kneeling cleric with St Donatien; verso:
Scenes from the life of the Virgin – oil on wood –
61 x 37.5cm.
(Lempertz)   **£23,404 $39,787**

**ALFRED ARTHUR BRUNEL DE NEUVILLE (1852–
1941)** – The paper mouse – signed – oil on canvas –
54.6 x 66cm.
(Christie's) £1,980 $3,247

**ALFRED ARTHUR BRUNEL DE NEUVILLE (1852–
1941)** – Kittens playing with a ball of wool – signed – oil
on canvas – 38.1 x 45.7cm.
(Christie's) £2,200 $3,608

FRANÇOIS BRUNERY (French, 19th century) – A wrong note – signed – oil on canvas – 81 x 100cm.
(Sotheby's) £37,400 $66,198

STEFANO BRUZZI (Italian, 1835–1911) – A
shepherdess and her flock – signed – oil on canvas –
35 x 65cm.
(Sotheby's)   **£18,700 $33,099**

MARCEL BRUNERY (French, 20th century) – A
shared joke – signed – oil on canvas – 61 x 50.2cm.
(Bonhams)   **£7,000 $11,130**

MARCEL BRUNERY (French, 19th/20th century) –
The sonata – signed – oil on canvas – 58 x 72cm.
(Sotheby's)   **£8,800 $15,576**

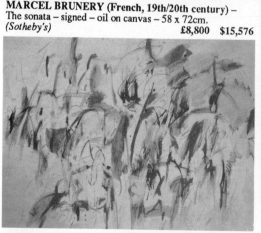

PETER BRUNING (1929–1970) – Untitled–Nr. 133 –
signed and dated *62* – oil and coloured crayon on canvas –
88 x 114cm.
(Christie's)   **£46,200 $74,844**

CHARLES A. BUCHEL (fl. 1895–1935) – Solo – signed
and dated *99* – oil on canvas – 106.7 x 61cm.
(Christie's)   **£5,500 $6,490**

KARL BUCHTA (Austrian, 1861–1928) – Young boys in a horsedrawn carriage – signed and dated *1907* –
oil on canvas – unframed – 71.5 x 111.5cm.
(Sotheby's)   **£3,080 $5,452**

BERNARD BUFFET (b. 1928) – La Mairie – signed and dated *67* – oil on canvas – 90 x 130cm.
(Christie's)   **£44,000 $77,440**

BURCHFIELD

CHARLES BURCHFIELD (1893–1967) – Old house and spring dawn – signed with monogram and dated *1965* – conte crayon and watercolour on paper – 30.5 x 38.1cm.
(Sotheby's) £10,389 $18,700

CHARLES BURCHFIELD (1893–1967) – Old tavern at Gardenville – signed with monogram and dated *1927* – watercolour and pencil on paper – 50.8 x 68.6cm.
(Sotheby's) £15,278 $27,500

JOHN BAGNOLD BURGESS, R.A. (1830–1897) – Anticipation – signed and inscribed on label attached to the reverse – oil on panel – 25.4 x 20.7cm.
(Christie's) £1,430 $2,531

HEINRICH BURKEL (1802–1869) – The inn on the alm – signed – oil on wood – 26 x 38cm.
(Lempertz) £2,908 $4,944

CHARLES EPHRAIM BURCHFIELD (1893–1967) – Back alley – signed – watercolour on paper laid down on board – 61 x 38cm.
(Christie's) £14,036 $24,200

SIR EDWARD COLEY BURNE-JONES (1833–1898) – The Princess Sabra led to the dragon – signed with initials and dated *1866* – oil on canvas – 108 x 96.6cm.
(Christie's) £93,500 $158,950

SIR EDWARD COLEY BURNE-JONES (English, 1833–98) – Study for 'Hope' – oil on canvas – 49.5 x 38cm. *(Sotheby's)* £14,300 $25,311

SIR EDWARD COLEY BURNE-JONES (English, 1833–98) – Study for 'The wine of Circe' – sanguine – 30.5 x 29cm. *(Sotheby's)* £19,800 $35,046

SIR EDWARD COLEY BURNE-JONES (1833–1898) – A study for The Call of Perseus – signed with initials and dated *1883* – coloured chalks on brown paper laid down on linen – 699 x 394mm. *(Christie's)* £4,400 $7,436

SIR EDWARD COLEY BURNE-JONES (1833–1898) – The stoning of St. Stephen: three cartoons for stained glass – coloured chalks and watercolour heightened with white, each on three joined sheets – 225 x 43cm. *(Christie's)* £11,000 $18,700

BURRA

EDWARD BURRA (1905–1976) – The lute players (recto); Two girls in a cafe (verso) – signed – pencil, watercolour and bodycolour (recto), pencil, pen and black ink (verso) – 46 x 37cm.
(Christie's) £12,100 $20,086

THOMAS BUTTERSWORTH (English, 1768–1842) – Euryalus (Capt. Blackwood), Thunderer and Ajax leaving Plymouth on the way to Cadiz and the Battle of Trafalgar (1805), lugger in foreground – signed – oil on canvas – 46.3 x 59.1cm.
(Bonhams) £6,000 $9,900

JAMES E. BUTTERSWORTH (1817–1894) – Ships approaching port – signed – oil on board laid down on masonite – 23.7 x 30.5cm.
(Christie's) £5,104 $8,800

Attributed to THOMAS BUTTERSWORTH (1768–1842) – A naval action during the American War of 1812 – oil on canvas – 50.8 x 60.9cm.
(Christie's) £2,420 $4,308

THOMAS BUTTERSWORTH (fl. 1798–1827) – The Spanish prizes captured after the Battle of Cape St Vincent off Lisbon – signed – oil on canvas – 83.7 x 142.2cm.
(Christie's) £18,700 $33,286

Attributed to VINCENZO CABIANCA (Italian, 1827–1902) – A view of a town on the Roman coast – oil on canvas – 31 x 39cm.
(Sotheby's) £8,800 $15,576

ANTONIO CABRAL Y BEJARANO (Spanish, 1822–91) - A Spanish lady with a fan – signed and dated *1855* on reverse – oil on canvas – 60 x 39cm.
(Sotheby's) £1,870 $3,310

GUGLIELMO CACCIA, called Moncalvo (1568–1625) – The Assumption of the Virgin with angels and two kneeling saints – oil on canvas – 124.5 x 81.5cm.
(Sotheby's) £3,300 $5,940

RICARDO LOPEZ CABRERA (Spanish, 1864–1950) – A sunlit view of the Alcalá River – signed and inscribed – oil on canvas – 59 x 74cm.
(Sotheby's) £1,870 $3,310

FRANCOIS-CHARLES CACHOUD (French, 1866–1943) – Village at evening – signed – oil on canvas laid down on board – 26.7 x 38.7cm.
(Butterfield & Butterfield) £1,008 $1,760

CADMUS

PAUL CADMUS (b. 1904) – Envy #1 – signed – graphite, charcoal, white chalk and watercolour on tissue – 59.7 x 33.7cm.
(Sotheby's) **£1,863 $3,410**

IPPOLITO CAFFI (Italian, 1809–66) – A view of the Forum, Rome – signed and dated *1830* – oil on canvas – 34 x 58cm.
(Sotheby's) **£46,200 $81,774**

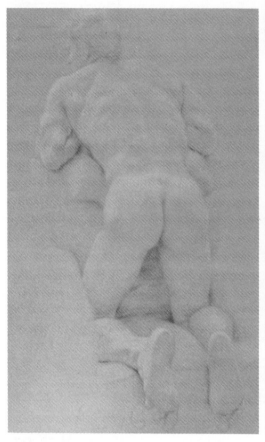

PAUL CADMUS (American, b. 1904) – Male nude kneeling in an armchair – signed – graphite and pastel on tan paper – 22¼ x 14½in.
(Skinner Inc.) **£4,115 $7,150**

HECTOR CAFFIERI – On a donkey – signed – watercolour heightened with bodycolour – 13½ x 9½in.
(Bearne's) **£1,450 $2,516**

CAVALIERE IPPOLITO CAFFI (1809–1866) – The Piazza di San Pietro, Rome – signed and dated *1843* – oil on canvas – 44 x 69.5cm.
(Christie's) **£57,200 $93,236**

HECTOR CAFFIERI (1847–1932) – Fisherfolk unloading the catch in a harbour – signed – watercolour, on Whatman board – 349 x 521mm.
(Christie's) **£2,200 $3,718**

WALTER WALLOR CAFFYN (fl. 1876–1898) –
Carting hay near Brockham, Surrey – signed and dated
1887 – 61 x 91.5cm.
(Christie's)   **£3,300 $5,346**

CHARLES D. CAHOON (American, 1861–1951) –
Two-masted schooner – signed – oil on board – 11 x 11in.
(Eldred's)   **£891 $1,540**

LEON CAILLE (French, 1836–1907) – The reading
lesson – signed and dated *1867* – oil on panel –
32.5 x 24cm.
(Sotheby's)   **£3,850 $6,814**

CALDERON – Altar boys in the garden – signed – oil on
panel – 27 x 35cm.
(Duran)   **£134 $237**

LEON-EMILE CAILLE (French, 1836-1907) – Mother
and child in front of a fireplace – signed – oil on mahogany
panel – 6 x 4in.
(Du Mouchelles)   **£541 $900**

WILLIAM FRANK CALDERON (1865–1943) – How
four Queens found Sir Lancelot sleeping – signed and dated
1908 – oil on canvas – 122 x 182.9cm.
(Christie's)   **£16,500 $28,050**

JOHN CALIFANO (1864–1924) – California coast –
signed – oil on canvas – 30 x 50in.
(Du Mouchelles)   **£1,042 $1,800**

JOHN CALLOW (British, 1822–1878) – Unloading the
catch – signed – oil on canvas – 45 x 81cm.
(Butterfield & Butterfield)   **£756 $1,320**

ISAAC HENRY CALIGA (American, b. 1857) – Profile
of a young woman – monogrammed and dated *1884* – oil
on panel – 5¼ x 3¾in.
(Skinner Inc.)   **£506 $880**

WILLIAM CALLOW (1812–1908) – Heidelberg – signed
and dated *1893* – watercolour – 333 x 473mm.
(Christie's)   **£3,300 $5,808**

J.L. CAMARERA – A Spanish fiesta – signed – oil on canvas – 45.7 x 40.7cm.
(Christie's) £825 **$1,426**

CAMERON – English antique portrait after Sir Henry Raeburn – John Fawse, Esq. of Stobshiel – 36 x 28in.
(Du Mouchelles) £347 **$600**

G. CAMMIDGE (circa 1874) – Fishermen salvaging a wreck on a rocky beach – signed and dated *1874* – oil on canvas – unframed – 71.1 x 102.3cm.
(Christie's) £1,540 **$2,741**

Attributed to LUCA CAMBIASO – The Holy Family with St. John the Baptist – watermark – pen and brown ink with wash – 26.6 x 21.9cm.
(Bonhams) £1,100 **$1,749**

CAMMILLIERI – H.M. Ship Revolutionaire – signed and inscribed – watercolour – 13³/₄ x 20in.
(Bearne's) £1,050 **$1,822**

CAMOIN

STEVEN CAMPBELL – The dream of every ostrich is to
own its own home – oil on canvas – 206.4 x 183cm.
(Bonhams) **£9,000 $15,660**

CHARLES CAMOIN (1879–1965) – The horsewoman –
with atelier stamp on reverse – oil on canvas - 80 x 53cm.
(Christie's) **£22,000 $35,640**

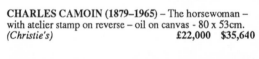

STEVEN CAMPBELL (b. 1953) – Study for man
possessed by a demon of the retina – oil on paper –
203 x 163cm.
(Christie's) **£4,400 $7,700**

GEORGE CAMPBELL (b. 1917) – Malaga, winter –
signed – oil on board – 48 x 58cm.
(Christie's) **£1,870 $3,104**

HEINRICH CAMPENDONK (1889–1957) – Figures
with animals and alarm clock – signed by Edith
Campendonk on reverse – oil on canvas – 70.5 x 81cm.
(Christie's) **£27,500 $44,550**

GEORGE BRYANT CAMPION (1796–1870) – The
press gang – with inscriptions on the mount – pencil and
watercolour heightened with white, on grey paper –
292 x 477mm.
(Christie's) **£880 $1,549**

GEORGE BRYANT CAMPION – Fisherfolk on the
shore at Dover – pencil and watercolour heightened with
white, arched top – 26¹/₂ x 40¹/₂in.
(Christie's) **£770 $1,365**

MASSIMO CAMPIGLI (1895–1971) – Young ladies –
signed – oil on canvas – 45 x 26.5cm.
(Finarte) **£39,841 $67,929**

FEDERICO DEL CAMPO (Italian, 19th century) – The
Santa Barbara Canal, Venice – signed – oil on panel –
17.5 x 28cm.
(Sotheby's) **£9,350 $16,549**

MASSIMO CAMPIGLI (1895–1971) – Ladies in the sun
– signed and dated *40* – oil on canvas – 72 x 91cm.
(Finarte) **£235,060 $400,777**

FEDERICO DEL CAMPO (late 19th century) – The
Zattere, Venice – signed – oil on canvas – 36.2 x 59.7cm.
(Christie's) **£11,000 $19,250**

**Manner of GIOVANNI ANTONIO CANAL, il
Canaletto** – A Caprice of the Grand Canal, Venice with the
Ca' Grande – oil on canvas – 43.8 x 64.8cm.
(Christie's) £1,650 $2,574

VITTORIO CAPOBIANCHI (Italian, fl. 1870–80) – At
the antiquarian – signed and dated *1880* – oil on panel –
48 x 65cm.
(Sotheby's) £8,250 $14,602

JACQUES CARABAIN (1834–1892) – St. Goar on the
Rhine, with St. Goarshausen and Katz Castle beyond –
signed – oil on canvas – 58.2 x 48.5cm.
(Christie's) £11,000 $17,930

CLAUDE CARDON (fl. 1892–1920) – In the pigsty –
signed and dated *1920* – oil on canvas – 43 x 47.5cm.
(Christie's) £1,320 $2,138

CONSALVO CARELLI (1818–1900) – Villagers
gathered by the harbour, Vietri; and a Shepherd and his
dog, with Paestum beyond – signed and inscribed – pencil
and watercolour on paper laid down on card –
36.8 x 50.8cm. – a pair
(Christie's) £6,380 $11,101

CONSALVO CARELLI (1818–1900) – A view of Capri
from Costiera Sorrentina – signed – oil on panel –
27 x 43cm.
(Christie's) £7,150 $12,512

CONSALVO CARELLI (Italian, 1818–1900) –
Fisherfolk in Capri – signed and inscribed – oil on panel –
26 x 40cm.
(Sotheby's) **£7,700 $13,629**

CONSALVO CARELLI (Italian, 1818–1900) – Peasants
and a herd of goats in a landscape – signed and inscribed –
watercolour – 34.5 x 52cm.
(Sotheby's) **£5,280 $9,346**

CONSALVO CARELLI – Peasants resting on a coastal
path above Naples – signed – pencil and watercolour
heightened with varnish – 9$^{1}/_{2}$ x 14in. – and six other
watercolours
(Christie's) **£3,300 $5,676**

CONSALVO CARELLI (1818–1900) – A view of Naples
from Posillipo – signed – oil on panel – 27 x 43cm.
(Christie's) **£13,200 $23,100**

GIUSEPPE CARELLI (1858–1921) – The Bay of Naples
– signed and inscribed – oil on canvas – 62.4 x 105cm.
(Christie's) **£18,700 $30,481**

MAX CARLIER – Nude on a divan – signed and dated 1928 – oil on canvas – 60 x 90cm.
(Hôtel de Ventes Horta)   £2,586 $4,500

GIUSEPPE CARELLI (1858–1921) – Fishing boats on the shore, Sorrento – signed – oil on panel – 48.2 x 27.7cm.
(Christie's)   £4,950 $8,613

Attributed to MODESTE CARLIER (French, 1820–1878) – Still life with game and flowers on a ledge – signed – oil on canvas – 90.2 x 60.3cm.
(Butterfield & Butterfield)   £1,891 $3,300

LUCA CARLEVARIS (Italian, 1663–1730) – Venice, the Piazza di San Marco, looking towards the Piazzetta – oil on canvas, in a carved and gilt wood frame – 70.8 x 118.8cm.
(Sotheby's)   £330,000 $594,000

CARLO INNOCENZO CARLONE (1686–1775) – A hero greeted by the Muse of History – oil on paper laid on canvas – 35.5 x 50cm.
(Sotheby's)   £7,700 $13,860

JOHN FABIAN CARLSON (1875–1945) – February gaiety – signed – oil on canvas - 63.5 x 76.5cm.
(Christie's) **£8,294 $14,300**

DEDO CARMIENCKE (1840–1907) – A goat herder in the Sertigthal Valley, Switzerland – signed and dated *1885* – oil on canvas – 113.6 x 79.3cm.
(Christie's) **£1,650 $2,871**

JOHN WILSON CARMICHAEL (1800–1868) – Benton Park, Newcastle upon Tyne – signed and dated *1837* – pencil and watercolour – unframed – 197 x 312mm.
(Christie's) **£990 $1,594**

JOHN WILSON CARMICHAEL (English, 1800–1868) – Peel Castle, Isle of Man – signed and dated *1868* – oil on canvas – 50.8 x 81.3cm.
(Bonhams) **£2,600 $4,290**

JEAN CAROLUS (Belgian, 19th century) – The music lesson – signed and dated *1858* – oil on panel – 59 x 48cm.
(Sotheby's) **£4,950 $8,761**

PAINTINGS PRICE GUIDE

PAUL ARCHIBALD CARON (1874–1941) – Sainte-Adèle, Québec – signed and dated *40* – watercolour – 36.7 x 46.2cm.
(Fraser–Pinneys)   **£1,754 $3,043**

LYELL CARR (b. 1857) – Calm after the Battle of El Caney – signed and dated *1898* – oil on canvas – 53.3 x 78.8cm.
(Christie's)   **£870 $1,540**

CARLO CARRA (1881–1966) – Coast after sunset – signed and dated *941* – oil on canvas – 70 x 80cm.
(Finarte)   **£117,530 $200,389**

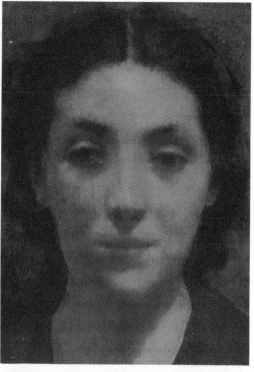

EUGENE CARRIERE (1849–1906) – Portrait of a woman in a red coat – oil on panel – 27 x 19cm.
(Christie's)   **£6,600 $10,758**

After **JACOPO CARRUCCI** called Il Pontormo (Italian, 1494–1557) – Madonna and Child with St. John the Baptist – oil on panel – 29 x 24¹/₂in.
(Skinner Inc.)   **£622 $1,100**

HENRY WILLIAM CARTER (1867–1893) – A Staffordshire bull terrier with a tabby cat – signed and dated *1890* – oil on canvas – 25.3 x 31cm.
(Christie's)   **£4,180 $6,855**

P. CARUSO – Landscape with figure and cows – signed – oil on canvas – 20 x 30in.
(Du Mouchelles)   **£145 $250**

WILLIAM DE LA MONTAGNE CARY (American, 1842–1906) – Buffalo Bill and Geronimo passing the peace pipe – signed with monogram – oil on canvas – 10^1/2 x 16in.
(Skinner Inc.)   **£2,023 $3,575**

ENRIQUE CASANOVAS Y ASTORZA (late 19th century) – An extensive rocky landscape with an ox and cart on a path – signed – oil on canvas – 80 x 130cm.
(Christie's)   **£3,080 $5,359**

JOHN CARTER (1748–1817) – The Erpingham Gate, Norwich, with the cathedral beyond – pencil, pen and grey ink and watercolour – 448 x 254mm.
(Christie's)   **£1,430 $2,517**

CASORATI (late 19th century) – The evening conversation – signed – oil on canvas – 103.5 x 130.1cm.
(Christie's)   **£1,540 $2,679**

CASORATI

FELICE CASORATI (1886–1963) – Seated woman –
signed – oil on board – 48.9 x 35cm.
(Christie's) £46,200 $81,312

ANTON CASTELL – Lago di Como – signed, inscribed
and dated *1841* – oil on canvas – 55.8 x 80cm.
(Christie's) £1,650 $2,851

MANUEL CASTELLANO (1828–1880) – Church door –
signed – oil on board – 13 x 7.5cm.
(Duran) £364 $641

F. CATANO – The cloisters, Italy – signed – pencil and watercolour heightened with white – 13 x 23¹/₂in.
(Christie's) **£286** **$494**

LEONARDO F.G. CATTERMOLE – Middlesex, Peggy, a bay hunter and foal in a landscape – signed and dated 1870 – 23¹/₂ x 35¹/₂in.
(Bearne's) **£740** **$1,284**

FRANZ LUDWIG CATEL – A girl at the entrance of a ruined abbey – oil on canvas – 52.8 x 47cm.
(Christie's) **£1,210** **$2,081**

EUGENE-HENRI CAUCHOIS (1850–1911) – Chrysanthemums in a bowl – signed – oil on canvas – 53.6 x 64.7cm.
(Christie's) **£3,300** **$5,742**

GEORGE CATTERMOLE (1800–1868) – A lady with her maid in an interior – pencil and watercolour heightened with white – 302 x 407mm.
(Christie's) **£660** **$1,063**

PATRICK CAULFIELD (b. 1936) – Upright pines – signed on reverse – oil on board – 122 x 122cm.
(Christie's) **£4,620** **$8,085**

JULES CAYRON (French, 1868–1940) – The boat –
signed – oil on canvas – 72 x 99cm.
(Sotheby's)   £5,720 $10,124

PER WILHELM CEDERGREN (1823–1896) – Boats in
Ladugards Bay – signed – oil on canvas – 25 x 35cm.
(AB Stockholms Auktionsverk)   £478 $819

ETTORE CERCONE – A gipsy girl – signed and
inscribed – oil on board – 11$^{1}/_{2}$ x 6$^{1}/_{4}$in.
(Bearne's)   £750 $1,301

19th CENTURY SCHOOL – Still life of spring and
summer flowers in a French porcelain vase – 24 x 19in.
(Spencer's)   £850 $1,356

Attributed to GIUSEPPE CESARI called Cavalier
d'Arpino (1568–1640) – Nymphs crossing a river – oil on
limewood panel – 57 x 45cm.
(Christie's)   £4,467 $7,415

PAUL CEZANNE (1839–1906) – The house Jas de Bouffan – oil on canvas – 60 x 73cm.
(Christie's)   **£1,760,000 $2,886,400**

ERNEST ALBERT CHADWICK (1876–1955) – Old farmhouse near Rowington – signed – pencil and watercolour with touches of white heightening – 381 x 543mm.
(Christie's)   **£1,980 $3,208**

ERNEST ALBERT CHADWICK (1876–1955) – East Garston, East Berkshire – signed – pencil and watercolour with scratching out – 274 x 387mm.
(Christie's)   **£1,540 $2,495**

PAUL EMILE CHABAS (1869–1937) – Young girls collecting shells – signed – oil on canvas – 152.2 x 103cm.
(Christie's)   **£7,700 $12,550**

HENRY DANIEL CHADWICK (fl. 1879–1896) – Macbeth and the witches – signed – oil on canvas – 98 x 153.5cm.
(Christie's)   **£2,860 $4,633**

CHAGALL

MARC CHAGALL (1887–1985) – The lovers – signed
and dedicated – dated *1952* – gouache, brush and black ink
on paper – 26.9 x 20.5cm.
(Christie's)   **£20,900 $33,858**

MARC CHAGALL (1887–1985) – Violinist in the village
– signed in cyrillic and dated *1913* – watercolour and pencil
on paper – 20 x 12.7cm.
(Christie's)   **£39,600 $69,696**

MARC CHAGALL (1887–1985) – Mother and child with
bouquet – signed – oil on canvas – 35 x 24cm.
(Christie's)   **£88,000 $142,560**

ALICE MAY CHAMBERS (fl. 1880–1893) – Portrait of
a lady, bust length – signed with monogram – red chalk
heightened with touches of white chalk – 382 x 343mm.
(Christie's)   **£3,740 $6,321**

GEORGE CHAMBERS – Entrance to the harbour, Shields – oil on canvas – 61 x 91.5cm.
(Woolley & Wallis) **£2,800 $4,788**

Follower of PHILIPPE DE CHAMPAIGNE – Portrait of a cleric in a black robe and cap with a white lawn collar, holding a book – with signature, inscription and the date *A Haubor fecit, Ats. 64 1658* – oil on canvas – 76 x 63.5cm.
(Christie's) **£880 $1,373**

GEORGE CHAMBERS (1803–1840) – The whaler Phoenix entering Whitby Harbour – signed and dated *1825* – oil on canvas – 63.4 x 91.4cm.
(Christie's) **£7,700 $13,706**

GEORGE CHAMBERS (1803–1840) – Hauling in the nets – signed and dated *1836* – oil on canvas – 48.4 x 71.1cm.
(Christie's) **£2,750 $4,895**

After PHILIPPE DE CHAMPAIGNE – Full length portrait of a child wearing a skull cap, yellow dress and apron, a tethered hawk perched on her left hand – oil on ivory – 10 x 8cm.
(Spencer's) **£420 $670**

PHILIPPE DE CHAMPAIGNE (1602–1674) – Scene from the life of St. Benoit – oil on canvas – 93 x 148cm.
(Christie's) £89,336 $148,298

JAMES WELLS CHAMPNEY (1843-1903) – Portrait of a young woman – pastel on board – 59.4 x 49.5cm.
(Sotheby's) £1,623 $2,970

JEROME-FRANÇOIS CHANTEREAU (1710–1757) – Two young peasant boys standing, wearing hats – red, white and black chalk – 220 x 190mm.
(Christie's) £16,750 $27,805

JOHN WATKINS CHAPMAN (fl. 1853–1903) – The Old Curiosity Shop – signed – oil on canvas – 50.8 x 66cm.
(Christie's) **£9,900 $18,018**

JAMES ORMSBEE CHAPIN (1887–1975) – Studio window – signed and dated *30–44* – oil on canvas – 84.5 x 53.5cm.
(Christie's) **£2,871 $4,950**

FRANTZ CHARLET (Belgian, 1862–1928) – Selim, the street singer of Algiers – signed – oil on canvas – 99.5 x 144.5cm.
(Sotheby's) **£3,850 $6,814**

JOHN LINTON CHAPMAN (19th century) – Appian Way – signed and dated *1870* – oil on canvas – 76.2 x 181.6cm.
(Christie's) **£16,588 $28,600**

WILLIAM MERRITT CHASE (1849–1916) – Portrait of a woman: the white dress – signed – oil on panel – 40.6 x 30.5cm.
(Sotheby's) **£110,000 $198,000**

GEORGE CHARLTON (b. 1899) – The Baltic Exchange and St. Mary Axe – signed – oil on board – 91.5 x 61cm.
(Christie's) **£770 $1,324**

WILLIAM MERRITT CHASE (1849–1916) –
Shinnecock studio interior – signed – pastel on paper – unframed – 40.6 x 50.8cm.
(Sotheby's) **£385,000 $693,000**

WILLIAM MERRITT CHASE (1849–1916) – Ordering lunch by the seaside – signed – an unsigned woodland interior appears on the reverse – oil on canvas – unframed – 43.2 x 38.1cm.
(Sotheby's) **£122,222 $220,000**

PIERRE PUVIS DE CHAVANNES (1824–1898) –
Perseus freeing Andromeda – signed – oil on canvas –
140 x 106cm.
(Lempertz)   **£24,823 $42,199**

JAN VON CHELMINSKI (Polish, 1851–1925) –
Cossacks awaiting a French cavalry charge – signed –
watercolour and gouache on paper – 38.1 x 61cm.
(Butterfield & Butterfield)   **£883 $1,540**

SANDRO CHIA (b. 1946) – The flute player – signed and
dated *83* – oil and mixed media on panel – 150 x 105cm.
(Finarte)   **£25,896 $44,153**

PAINTINGS PRICE GUIDE

SANDRO CHIA (b. 1946) – The crock of gold – signed, inscribed with title and dated on the reverse *1980* – oil on canvas – unframed – 162.5 x 129.5cm.
(Christie's) £30,800 $51,128

EDUARDO CHICHARRO (b. 1905) – Segovian woman – indistinctly signed and dated on reverse – oil on canvas – 37 x 48cm.
(Duran) £784 $1,380

GAETANO CHIERICI (Italian, 1838–1920) – Feeding baby – signed – oil on canvas – 56.5 x 80cm.
(Bonhams) £74,000 $117,660

GEORGE CHINNERY (1774–1852) – The Bay of Macao with the Praya Grande and the old Penha Church on the hill beyond – pencil, pen and brown ink and watercolour – unframed – 256 x 277mm.
(Christie's) £16,500 $29,040

GEORGE CHINNERY (1774–1852) – A mother with two children and a dog – pen and brown ink and watercolour – 150 x 103mm.
(Christie's) £9,350 $15,053

CAVALIERE GIACOMO DI CHIRICO (Italian, 1845–84) – A religious procession in winter – signed – oil on panel – 73 x 58cm.
(Sotheby's) £15,400 $27,258

GIORGIO DE CHIRICO (1888–1978) – Portrait of a lady – signed and dated *1940* – oil on board –
50.5 x 62cm.
(Finarte) £45,817 $78,118

GIORGIO DE CHIRICO (1888–1978) – Still life –
signed – oil on panel – 21.5 x 27cm.
(Finarte) £21,912 $37,360

GIORGIO DE CHIRICO (1888–1978) – Piazza d'Italia –
signed – oil on canvas – 51 x 61cm.
(Christie's) £8,800 $14,256

GIORGIO DE CHIRICO (1888–1978) – Nymphs by a
stream – signed – oil and tempera on board – 32 x 25cm.
(Finarte)   **£16,733 $28,530**

GIORGIO DE CHIRICO (1888–1978) – Trophy – signed
and dated *1926* – pastel on buff paper – 103 x 73cm.
(Christie's)   **£220,000 $360,800**

GIORGIO DE CHIRICO (1888–1978) – Piazza d'Italia (1942) – mosaic – 82 x 157.5cm.
(Finarte)

£39,841 $67,929

GIORGIO DE CHIRICO (1888–1978) – Gladiators and referee – signed – oil on canvas – 84.5 x 65.7cm.
(Finarte)   **£163,347 $278,507**

ALFRED CHOUBRAC (French, 1853–1902) –
Mourning the deceased – signed and dated *1879* – oil on canvas – 129 x 91cm.
(Sotheby's)   **£4,400 $7,788**

M. CHOSSON – The reading lesson – signed – oil on panel – 34.3 x 25.4cm.
(Christie's)   **£1,045 $1,797**

ROBERT CHRISTIE (fl. 1891–1903) – Study of a head –
signed with initials and dated *1892* – oil on panel –
30.5 x 25.4cm.
(Christie's)   **£1,540 $2,803**

CHRISTO

CHRISTO (b. 1935) – The umbrellas (joint project for Japan and USA) - signed, inscribed and dated *1986* – collage with fabric, coloured crayon, gouache, and pencil on card – 77.5 x 66.7cm.
(Christie's)   **£30,800 $51,128**

HOWARD CHANDLER CHRISTY (1873–1952) – A point of contention – signed – oil on masonite – 61.6 x 45.7cm.
(Sotheby's)   **£1,563 $2,860**

FREDERICK STUART CHURCH (1842–1923) – Stonehenge – signed and dated *1907* – oil on canvas – 81.9 x 137.2cm.
(Sotheby's)   **£1,683 $3,080**

CHRISTO (b. 1935) – The Pont Neuf Wrapped (Project for Pont Neuf, Paris) – signed, inscribed with title and dated *1985* – collage with fabric, string, coloured crayon, pencil, gouache and diagram on cardboard – top panel: 28 x 71cm. – bottom panel: 55.2 x 71cm.
(Christie's)   **£20,900 $36,993**

SIR WINSTON SPENCER CHURCHILL, O.M., Hon. R.A. (1874–1965) – Scuola di San Marco, Venice – signed with initials *WSC* – oil on canvas – 51 x 61cm.
(Christie's)   **£36,300 $60,258**

NICOLAS CIKOVSKY (b. 1894) – The tradewinds –
signed – oil on canvas – 40.6 x 50.8cm.
(Sotheby's)   £1,382 $2,530

JOSEPH CLAGHORN (b. 1869) – Meeting on the road –
signed and dated 1900 – watercolour on paper –
45.7 x 71.1cm.
(Butterfield & Butterfield)   £536 $935

GIACOMO FRANCESCO CIPPER, called Il
Todeschini – An old peasant and a maid at a table – oil on
canvas
(Bonhams)   £14,000 $22,260

VINCENT CLARE – Primroses, blossom and a bird's nest
on a mossy bank; and Primroses and polyanthus on a mossy
bank – signed – oil on board – 24.2 x 19cm. – a pair
(Christie's)   £2,750 $4,565

Manner of PIETER CLAESZ – A ham on a pewter
salver, glasses, grapes, a stoneware jug, bread and a lemon
on a draped table – oil on canvas – 40.7 x 63.5cm.
(Christie's)   £1,210 $1,888

JAMES CLARK – The bolting horse – signed – oil on
canvas – 51 x 76.2cm.
(Christie's)   £770 $1,278

111

JAMES CLARK – A bay hunter in a loose box – signed
and inscribed – oil on canvas – 50.8 x 60.9cm.
(Christie's)   **£1,210 $2,009**

MATT CLARK (b. 1903) – Mining camp – signed – oil
on canvas – 61 x 92.1cm.
(Butterfield & Butterfield)   **£630 $1,100**

JOSEPH CLARK (1834–1926) – The very image – signed
and dated *1884* – oil on canvas – 88.2 x 67.5cm.
(Christie's)   **£7,700 $12,474**

SAMUEL JOSEPH CLARK (late 19th century) – A
farmyard scene – signed and dated *1878* – oil on canvas –
90.2 x 151.7cm.
(Christie's)   **£5,500 $10,010**

WILLIAM ALBERT CLARK – Haddon Marphil, a carriage horse before a stable yard entrance – signed and dated *1914* – oil on canvas – 49.5 x 75cm.
(Christie's) £2,860 $5,069

S.J. CLARK – A farmer and his wife with cattle, poultry and a dog; and a Farmgirl nursing a calf – both signed – oil on canvas – 50.2 x 76.2cm. – a pair
(Christie's) £2,750 $4,874

S.J. CLARK (British, 19th century) – Southchurch, Essex – signed – oil on canvas – 20 x 30in.
(Skinner Inc.) £760 $1,320

WILLIAM CLARK of Greenock (fl. 1827–1841) – The ship Malabar and the barque Isabella in the Clyde – signed and dated *1836* – oil on canvas – 58.4 x 87.6cm.
(Christie's) £16,500 $29,370

A.M. CLIFTON – The Thames near Iffley; and Spring blossoms – both signed – pencil and watercolour – 9³/₄ x 13¹/₂in. – two
(Christie's)   £440 $768

BERTHE DES CLAYES (1877–1968) – Maple Sugar House, Rougemont – signed – oil on canvas – 46.3 x 61cm.
(Fraser–Pinneys)   £5,013 $8,697

WINFIELD SCOTT CLIME (American, 1881–1958) – Morning at the dock – signed – oil on board – 12 x 16in.
(Skinner Inc.)   £996 $1,760

ROBERT CLEMINSON – Waiting for master; and Setters on a moor – signed – oil on canvas – 25.4 x 35.6cm. – a pair
(Christie's)   £825 $1,370

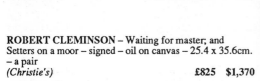

MARTEN VAN CLEVE (1527–1581) – The bride's wedding procession – oil on panel – 42.2 x 76.4cm.
(Sotheby's)   £35,200 $63,360

Manner of FRANÇOIS CLOUET (French, 1522–1572) – Portrait of an elegant lady – oil on panel – 10¹/₄ x 7³/₄in.
(Skinner Inc.)   £685 $1,210

TOM CLOUGH – A village street scene with a horse drawn cart in the middle distance, a girl standing beside a cottage to the right – signed and dated *1912* – 47 x 71cm.
(Spencer's) £1,400 $2,419

LEONARDO COCCORANTE (Italian, 1680–1750) – Capriccio views with classical ruins beside the sea – oil on canvas – 63.5 x 99.6cm. – a pair
(Sotheby's) £26,400 $47,520

JOHN COBURN (b. 1925) – The Red King – signed – oil on masonite – 91.4 x 55.8cm.
(Christie's) £1,100 $1,936

XAVIER DE COCK (Belgian 1818–1896) – The Clearing – signed – oil on panel – 26.5 x 37cm.
(Hôtel de Ventes Horta) £3,692 $6,443

EDWIN COCKBURN (fl. 1837–1868) – Peace and war –
signed and dated *1856* – oil on canvas – 56.5 x 75cm.
(Christie's) £3,850 $6,815

CHARLES ROBERT COCKERELL, R.A. (1788–1863)
– Rome from the Trinità dei Monti – with inscription on
mount – pencil and watercolour heightened with gold –
208 x 270mm.
(Christie's) £4,620 $7,438

CHARLES ROBERT COCKERELL, R.A. (1788–1863)
– The Piazza dei Miracoli, Pisa, with the Battistero, Duomo
and Campanile – with inscription on the mount – pencil and
watercolour – unframed – 85 x 101mm.
(Christie's) £935 $1,505

Circle of VIVIANO CODAZZI – A palace interior with
Belshazzar's feast – oil on canvas – 115 x 95.5cm.
(Sotheby's) £7,150 $12,870

VICTORIANO CODINA Y LANGLIN (1844–1911) –
Diverted attention – signed and indistinctly dated *1880(?)* –
oil on canvas – 26 x 20.9cm.
(Christie's) £6,600 $11,484

J. COGGESHALL-WILSON (British, 19th–20th century) – Pont-Aven – signed – oil on canvas – 89.5 x 89.5cm.
(Butterfield & Butterfield) £1,891 $3,300

FREDERICK E. COHEN (d. 1858) – Coming to the New World – signed and dated *1851* – oil on canvas – 77.5 x 96.5cm.
(Butterfield & Butterfield) £1,261 $2,200

MAX ARTHUR COHN (b. 1903) – Washington Square – signed – oil on canvas – 51 x 61cm.
(Christie's) £2,042 $3,520

COIGNET

JULES-LOUIS-PHILIPPE COIGNET (1797–1860) –
On the Nile – signed – oil on canvas – 40 x 58.4cm.
(Christie's) £3,300 $5,775

**ALPHAEUS PHILEMON COLE (American, 1876–
1900)** – The early bird – signed – oil on canvas – 12 x 16in.
(Skinner Inc.) £218 $385

DAVID COL (Belgian 1822–1900) – Daily reading –
signed and dated on reverse 1885 – oil on panel –
37 x 28cm.
(Hôtel de Ventes Horta) £4,138 $7,200

GEORGE COLE (1810–1883) – Harvesters resting by a
cornfield – oil on canvas – 106.7 x 152.4cm.
(Christie's) £8,800 $15,576

SALVATORE COLACICCO (20th century) – The
America's Cup yacht Susannah off the coast of Canada –
signed; also signed and titled on reverse – oil on board –
65.4 x 80cm.
(Sotheby's) £1,954 $3,575

GEORGE VICAT COLE (1833–1893) – Wargrave,
looking from the wharf up the river – signed with
monogram and dated *1880* – oil on canvas – 40.6 x 61cm.
(Christie's) £4,400 $7,128

The Hon. JOHN COLLIER (1850–1934) – May, Agatha, Veronica and Audrey, the daughters of Colonel Makins M.P. – signed and dated *1884* – oil on canvas – 183 x 213.4cm.
(Christie's)   **£45,100 $76,670**

RAPHAEL COLLIN (French, 1850–1916) – An Arcadian concert – signed – oil on canvas – 45.7 x 38.1cm.
(Butterfield & Butterfield)   **£5,043 $8,800**

GEORGE EDWARD COLLINS – Sleepy chicks; and Thirsty chicks – one signed with initials – pencil and watercolour heightened with white – 5 x 8in. – a pair
(Christie's)   **£385 $682**

ITHELL COLQUHOUN (Exh. 1930–1935) –
Stockhausen Poles – monogrammed and dated 1976 –
mixed media on board – 24 x 23in.
(W.H. Lane & Son) £300 $507

JAMES COLLINSON (1825–1881) – Study of an old
lady – signed – pencil and black and white chalk, on brown
paper, corners cut – 310 x 270mm.
(Christie's) £770 $1,301

Attributed to EBENEZER COLLS (fl. 1852–1854) –
Two-deckers off Longships Lighthouse, Land's End – oil on
canvas – 66 x 87cm.
(Christie's) £5,500 $9,790

EDWARD THEODORE COMPTON – A castle in the
mountains – signed and dated *1873* – pencil and
watercolour – 9¹/₄ x 17¹/₂in.
(Christie's)   **£440 $780**

NICHOLAS CONDY (English, 1793–1857)
– From St. Nicholas Island, Plymouth – gouache –
10.1 x 15.2cm.
(Bonhams)   **£600 $990**

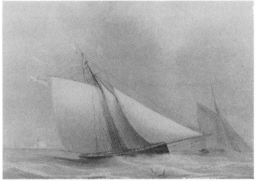

**Attributed to NICHOLAS CONDY (English, 1793–
1857)** – Two gaff-rigged racing yachts flying the flags of
the Royal Yacht Squadron in the Solent – oil on board –
25.4 x 35.6cm.
(Bonhams)   **£2,000 $3,300**

CHARLES CONDER (1868–1907) – Orchard on the
Seine near Vetheuil – signed and dated *1893* – oil on
canvas – 74 x 58.5cm.
(Christie's)   **£18,700 $31,042**

NICHOLAS MATTHEW CONDY (1818–1851) –
Hauling in the nets on Teignmouth Beach, the Ness beyond
– pencil, watercolour and bodycolour – 108 x 162mm.
(Christie's)   **£770 $1,355**

DAVID DE CONINCK (1646–after 1701) – A cat with
pigeons, chickens and rabbits in a landscape – oil on canvas
– 74.6 x 97.6cm.
(Sotheby's)   **£19,800 $35,640**

PHILIP CONNARD, R.A. (1875–1958) – Landscape with rainbow – signed with initials – oil on canvas – 56 x 69cm.
(Christie's) **£1,650 $2,838**

BENJAMIN CONSTANT (1845–1902) – An eastern beauty (The tambourine girl) – signed – oil on canvas – 116.8 x 78.8cm.
(Fraser-Pinneys) **£8,252 $14,523**

CONSTANT (Belgian, 1886–1952) – Sunset in Flanders – signed – oil on canvas – 70 x 88.5cm.
(Hôtel de Ventes Horta) **£7,167 $12,256**

CONSTANT (b. 1920) – Waldo – signed – watercolour, black chalk and coloured crayons on paper – 53 x 73cm.
(Christie's) **£8,939 $15,821**

TITO CONTI (1842–1924) – Off duty – signed – oil on canvas – 108 x 81.3cm.
(Christie's) **£23,100 $40,425**

CONTINENTAL SCHOOL (17th century) – Holy
Family with female Saint – oil on panel – 14½ x 18in.
(Skinner Inc.)   £4,979 $8,800

CONTINENTAL SCHOOL (18th century) – Portrait of a
female Saint surrounded by an ornate floral garland –
indistinctly inscribed on reverse – oil on canvas –
26 x 19in.
(Skinner Inc.)   £1,369 $2,420

CONTINENTAL SCHOOL (late 19th century) – An
Italianate landscape with classical ruins with figures by a
stream – oil on canvas – unframed – 200 x 200cm.
(Christie's)   £3,520 $6,083

CONTINENTAL SCHOOL (19th century) – Moorish
interior – signed, inscribed and dated 87 – oil on canvas –
24 x 15½in.
(Skinner Inc.)   £190 $330

CONTINENTAL SCHOOL (late 19th century) – An artist's palette, decorated with figure studies, landscapes and other subjects – signed by various artists – oil on panel – 67.3 x 101cm.
(Christie's)   **£15,400 $26,950**

CONTINENTAL SCHOOL (19th century) – A town square with a gothic cathedral – signed indistinctly and dated *58* – watercolour on paper – 31.1 x 25.4cm.
(Butterfield & Butterfield)   **£410 $715**

BERYL COOK – Nathans – signed – oil on board – 24 x 18½in.
(W.H. Lane & Son)   **£11,000 $20,460**

WILLIAM COOK OF PLYMOUTH (fl. 1850–1870) –
Salvaging the hulk – signed with monogram and dated *79* –
pencil and watercolour with touches of white heightening –
375 x 680mm.
(Christie's) £990 **$1,604**

B. COOLEY (19th century) – Portrait of Stephen Douglas
– signed and dated *1867* – oil on canvas – 132 x 94cm.
(Christie's) £5,593 **$9,900**

EDWARD WILLIAM COOKE (1811–1880) – Vesuvius
from Capri – signed and dated *1864* – pencil and
watercolour with touches of white heightening and
scratching out – 130 x 203mm.
(Christie's) £935 **$1,646**

EDWARD WILLIAM COOKE, R.A. (1811–1880) –
Zuider Zee fishing craft drying nets and sails in the Harbour
of Spaarendam – with strengthened signature and the date
1847 – 45.7 x 91.4cm.
(Christie's) £28,600 **$50,908**

125

COOMBS

DELBERT DANA COOMBS (American, 1850–1938) –
Shower weather – New Gloucester meadows – signed and
dated *1909* – oil on canvas – 20 x 35in.
(Skinner Inc.) **£996 $1,760**

ABRAHAM COOPER – A chestnut hunter in a
landscape; and a bay hunter in a landscape – oil on canvas –
50.8 x 60.9cm. – **a pair**
(Christie's) **£1,540 $2,730**

COLIN CAMPBELL COOPER (1856–1937) – New
York skyline – initialled *CCC* – gouache on paper –
11.4 x 17.8cm.
(Butterfield & Butterfield) **£630 $1,100**

GERALD COOPER – Hollyhocks and honeysuckle –
signed and dated *1946* – oil on board – 49.5 x 38cm.
(Christie's) **£5,280 $8,765**

THOMAS SIDNEY COOPER (1803–1902) – Cattle
resting in a meadow – signed and dated 1883 – oil on board
– 30.5 x 45.7cm.
(Christie's) **£3,300 $5,841**

COLIN CAMPBELL COOPER (1856–1937) – Middle Eastern market scene - signed and dated *1904* - oil on
canvas laid down – 21.6 x 71.1cm.
(Butterfield & Butterfield) **£2,206 $3,850**

THOMAS SIDNEY COOPER, R.A. (1803–1902) – Cattle and sheep – signed and dated *1859* – watercolour – 14½ x 21in.
(David Lay)   **£650 $1,168**

THOMAS SIDNEY COOPER, R.A. (1803–1902) – A cow and a calf in a barn – signed with initials and dated *1877* – oil on canvas – 61 x 50.8cm.
(Christie's)   **£3,300 $5,841**

THOMAS SIDNEY COOPER, (1803–1902) – A cow and sheep in a water-meadow – signed and dated *1851* – oil on panel – 30.5 x 45.7cm.
(Christie's)   **£2,420 $4,404**

THOMAS SIDNEY COOPER (1803–1902) – Cattle and sheep in the Canterbury meadows – signed and dated *1853* – 122 x 189.2cm.
(Christie's)   **£30,800 $52,360**

COOPER

A. COPPOLA (late 19th century) – Mending the nets by the Bay of Naples – signed – bodycolour – 34 x 62.2cm.
(Christie's) £880 $1,531

THOMAS SIDNEY COOPER, R.A. (1803–1902) – Cattle in a sunlit landscape – signed and dated *1875* – oil on panel – 43 x 53.3cm.
(Bonhams) £3,400 $5,406

THOMAS SIDNEY COOPER, R.A. (1803–1902) – Cattle and sheep in a water meadow – signed and dated *1881* – oil on canvas – 69.8 x 104.1cm.
(Christie's) £5,720 $9,266

G. CORALE – The serenade – signed – oil on canvas – 58.4 x 41.8cm.
(Christie's) £1,870 $3,216

MATTHEW RIDLEY CORBET, A.R.A. (1850–1902) – Laundry women at the Washing Well, San Gimignano, Italy – signed and dated *1898* – pencil and watercolour – 635 x 355mm.
(Christie's) £1,375 $2,228

WILLIAM SIDNEY COOPER – Evening at Herne, Kent – signed and dated *1907* – oil on canvas – 60.5 x 91cm.
(Christie's) £1,100 $1,777

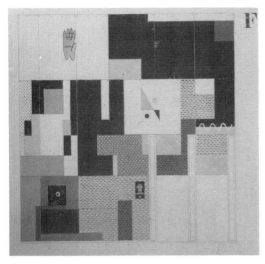

LE CORBUSIER (Charles Edouard Jeanneret) (1887–1965) – Chandigar tapestry – signed with initials – gouache, pencil and collage on paper – 46.5 x 54cm.
(Christie's) £5,500 $8,910

LE CORBUSIER (Charles Edouard Jeanneret) (1887–1965) – Large still life – signed and dated *23–44–49–52–53* – oil on canvas – 113 x 146cm.
(Christie's) £110,000 $193,600

LOVIS CORINTH (1858–1925) – Self portrait, etching: View of the Walchensee – two etchings – 19.8 x 15.9cm. and 19.5 x 24.8cm.
(Lempertz) £1,799 $2,869

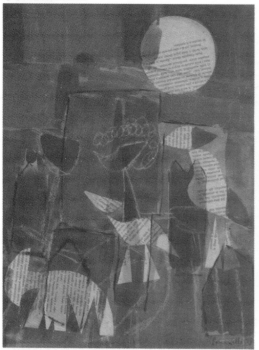

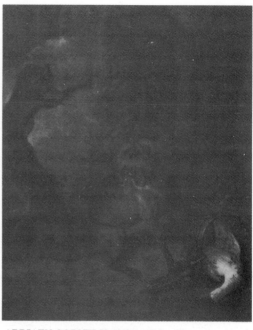

ADRIAEN CORNELIS (1625–1705) – The trap – signed
– oil on panel – 57.5 x 43.5cm.
(Hôtel de Ventes Horta)   **£1,706**   **$2,917**

CORNEILLE (b. 1922) – Dierentuin – signed and dated
48 – watercolour, gouache, coloured crayons and collage on
paper – 46.5 x 35cm.
(Christie's)   **£8,251**   **$14,604**

CORNEILLE (b. 1922) – Nude with rose – signed and
dated *'80* – gouache on paper – 49.5 x 65cm.
(Christie's)   **£3,438**   **$6,085**

DEAN CORNWELL (1892–1960) – Reclining nude –
signed – oil on canvas – 84.5 x 146.1cm.
(Sotheby's) £4,809 $8,800

DEAN CORNWELL (1892–1960) – Capturing the gang –
signed – oil on canvas – 53.3 x 128.3cm.
(Sotheby's) £3,606 $6,600

JEAN BAPTISTE CAMILLE COROT – Fisherman near
the bank hauling in his net – signed – oil on canvas –
33.5 x 40.4cm.
(Sotheby's) £35,200 $62,304

JEAN BAPTISTE CAMILLE COROT (1796–1875) –
Line of trees in the countryside – signed – oil on board –
9.2 x 13.6cm.
(Christie's) £28,600 $46,332

Follower of JEAN-BAPTISTE-CAMILLE COROT – A
wooded landscape with figures resting beneath a tree – oil
on canvas – 116.8 x 91.5cm.
(Christie's) £2,200 $3,784

JEAN-BAPTISTE CAMILLE COROT (1796–1875) –
The Sevres heights, the Troyon road – oil on canvas –
23.5 x 36.8cm.
(Christie's) £121,000 $198,440

HERMANN DAVID SALOMON CORRODI (Italian, 1844–1905) – Bringing in the nets on the Venetian lagoon by moonlight – signed and inscribed – oil on canvas – 165.1 x 86.4cm.
(Butterfield & Butterfield) £14,183 $24,750

HERMAN DAVID SALOMON CORRODI (1844-1905) – On the veranda – signed and inscribed – oil on canvas – 101.6 x 63.5cm.
(Christie's) £9,900 $17,226

HERMANN DAVID SALOMON CORRODI (1844–1905) – Neapolitan fisherfolk, Mergellina, Naples – signed – oil on canvas – 86 x 165cm.
(Christie's) £37,400 $60,962

EDOUARD CORTES (1882–1969) – Porte St. Denis,
Paris – signed – oil on canvas – 33.5 x 46cm.
(Christie's) **£11,550 $20,212**

EDOUARD CORTES (1882–1969) – La Place de la
République, Paris – signed – oil on canvas – 33 x 46cm.
(Christie's) **£10,780 $17,571**

EDOUARD CORTES (1882–1969) – Place de L'Opéra,
Paris – signed – oil on canvas – 45.7 x 76.2cm.
(Christie's) **£20,900 $36,575**

JENNESS CORTEZ (b. 1945) – Horse and terrier in stall
– signed and © *1981* – oil on canvas – 40.6 x 50.8cm.
(Sotheby's) **£1,743 $3,190**

EDOUARD CORTES (1882–1969) – Place de la
Madeleine at dusk, Paris – signed – oil on canvas –
54 x 67.7cm.
(Christie's) **£19,800 $34,452**

RICHARD COSWAY, R.A. (1742-1821) – Portrait of
Lady Heathcote, standing by an urn in a garden – signed –
pencil with touches of watercolour – 279 x 216mm.
(Christie's) **£3,850 $6,198**

JOHN SELL COTMAN (1782–1842) – Portrait of Anne Miles, Cotman's wife, wearing a white bonnet – black and white chalk, on grey paper – 283 x 223mm.
(Christie's)   £825 $1,452

FRANCIS COTES (1725–1770) – Portrait of a lady, half length, in a blue dress wearing a pearl necklace, said to be the Countess of Winchelsea – pastel laid on linen – 598 x 445mm.
(Christie's)   £660 $1,162

FRANCIS COUDRIL (d. 1989) – Restless sun worshipper – signed – oil on board – 19¹/₂ x 24¹/₂in.
(David Lay)   £260 $467

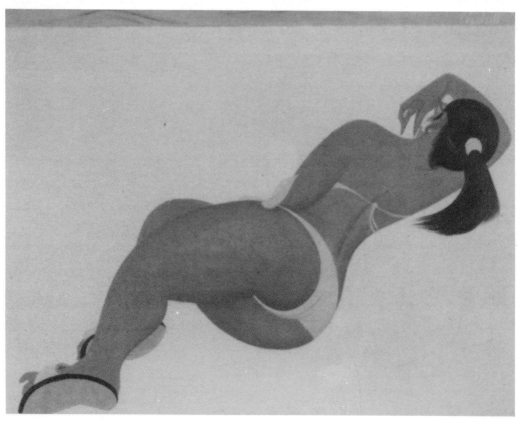

FRANCIS COUDRIL (d. 1989) – Holiday maker – signed
– oil on board – 14 x 12in.
(David Lay) **£160 $288**

GUSTAVE COURBET (1819–1877) – Le Château de
Chillon – signed and dated 77 – oil on canvas –
49.5 x 61cm.
(Christie's) **£71,500 $125,840**

FRANZ COURTENS (Belgian 1854–1943) – Shepherd at
dusk – signed – oil on canvas – 112 x 163cm.
(Hôtel de Ventes Horta) **£7,241 $12,600**

FRANZ COURTENS (Belgian 1854–1943) – Ray of
sunshine –oil on canvas – 110 x 160cm.
(Hôtel de Ventes Horta) **£5,172 $8,999**

EANGER IRVING COUSE (1866–1936) – Sketches
depicting Indian life – one sketch inscribed – pencil on
paper – various sizes: approx. 12.7 x 15.2cm. – seven
(Butterfield & Butterfield) **£1,576 $2,750**

E. IRVING COUSE (1866–1936) – Sacred deer bowl
ritual – signed – 59.7 x 73cm.
(Sotheby's) **£16,500 $29,700**

Attributed to PAUL AMABLE COUTAN (French, 1792–1837) – Castor and Pollux delivering Helen – oil on canvas – 112 x 145cm.
(Sotheby's) **£15,950 $28,231**

SIR NOEL COWARD (1900–1973) – Boy peeling an orange – signed – oil on canvas-board – 33 x 23cm.
(Christie's) **£2,200 $3,652**

GORDON COUTTS (Scottish/American, 1880–1937) – Crossing the plains – signed – oil on canvas – 24 x 28¹/₂in.
(Du Mouchelles) **£1,952 $3,250**

WILLIAM COWEN – Rome from Palatine Hill – signed and dated *April 21, 1826* – pencil and watercolour – 15³/₄ x 22⁵/₈in.
(Christie's) **£1,650 $2,838**

JAN VAN COUVER – On the Waal, Holland – signed – pencil and watercolour heightened with white – 14 x 20¹/₂in.
(Christie's) **£220 $384**

RUSSELL COWLES (American, b. 1887) – The Romantics – signed – oil on canvas – 45 x 48in.
(Skinner Inc.) **£1,556 $2,750**

RUSSELL COWLES (1887–1979) – The watchful
shepherd – oil on canvas laid down on board – round:
104.1cm.
(Butterfield & Butterfield)   **£630 $1,100**

Attributed to DAVID COX (1783–1859) – Coastal
shipping in choppy conditions – with signature – pencil and
watercolour – 15.5 x 26cm.
(Christie's)   **£660 $1,175**

JACK COX – Unloading crab boats, North Norfolk coast –
signed – acrylic – 13 x 21in.
(GA Key)   **£340 $605**

Studio of CHARLES-ANTOINE COYPEL (1694–1752)
– Rebecca at the well – oil on canvas – 84.5 x 125.5cm.
(Sotheby's)   **£4,180 $7,524**

FLORENT NICOLAS CRABBELS (1829–1896) –
Lunch at the inn – signed and dated *1856* – oil on canvas –
42 x 57.1cm.
(Christie's)   **£4,400 $7,656**

LUCAS CRANACH the Elder (1472–1553) – Portrait of
a man in a small black cap – oil on paper – 25 x 19.5cm.
(Sotheby's)   **£88,000 $158,400**

137

WALTER CRANE, R.W.S. (1845–1915) – Sketch for The fate of Persephone – signed with monogram and dated *May 1877* – watercolour and bodycolour on paper – 21.5 x 45.5cm.
(Christie's) **£8,800 $14,256**

Studio of LUCAS CRANACH the Elder (German , 1472–1553) – Adam and Eve in paradise – oil on cradled panel – 76 x 58.5cm.
(Butterfield & Butterfield) **£5,673 $9,900**

GERARD ANTOINE CREHAY (1844–1936) – A tiger breaking cover in the jungle – signed and dated *1893* – oil on canvas – 63.5 x 101cm.
(Christie's) **£1,760 $2,886**

LUCAS CRANACH the Elder (1472–1553) – Portrait of a man in a red hat – oil on paper – 25 x 19.5cm.
(Sotheby's) **£187,000 $336,600**

GEORGES CROEGAERT (French, b. 1848) – The reader – signed, inscribed and dated *1887* – oil on cradled panel – 34.9 x 27.3cm.
(Butterfield & Butterfield) **£1,891 $3,300**

BENEDICT CROIX – By the Seine – signed – oil on canvas – 46 x 55cm.
(Duran)   £280 $493

GEORGES CROEGAERT (French, b. 1848) – A gentleman waiting in an interior – signed and inscribed – oil on panel – 26 x 19cm.
(Sotheby's)   £1,980 $3,505

RAY CROOKE – Islanders at rest – signed – oil on canvas – 61 x 51cm.
(Australian Art Auctions)   £1,326 $2,354

BENEDICT CROIX – In the park – signed – oil on board – 41 x 27cm.
(Duran)   £95 $168

RAY AUSTIN CROOKE (b. 1922) – In the shade – signed – oil on masonite – 31 x 37.8cm.
(Christie's)   £880 $1,549

JASPER FRANCIS CROPSEY (1823–1900) –Sunset – signed and dated *1894* – oil on canvas – 26 x 51cm.
(Christie's)   £5,104 $8,800

NICHOLAS JOSEPH CROWLEY – Stolen treasure –
signed and inscribed on reverse – oil on board –
33 x 43.2cm.
(Christie's)   £638 $1,030

**CHARLES COURTNEY CURRAN (American, 1861–
1942)** – The Supreme Temple – signed, dated and inscribed
1936 – oil on canvas mounted on masonite – 18 x 22in.
(Skinner Inc.)   £823 $1,430

**JAMES JACKSON CURNOCK (1839–1891) and
THOMAS FRANCIS WAINEWRIGHT (circa 1830–
circa 1900)** – Anglers on a river bank – signed and dated
1860 – and signed and inscribed *Cattle by T.F.
Wainewright* – pencil and watercolour heightened with
bodycolour – 363 x 533mm.
(Christie's)   £495 $802

JOHN STEUART CURRY (1898–1946) – The carnival –
signed – watercolour on paper – 48.2 x 61cm.
(Christie's)   £1,864 $3,300

140

FRANK DADD (1851–1929) – Her lawyer – signed and
dated *1892* – oil on canvas – 45.8 x 61cm.
(Christie's) £4,950 $8,762

JOHAN CHRISTIAN CLAUSEN DAHL (1788–1857) –
Rooks perched on a rock in a wooded winter landscape –
signed and dated *1836* – oil on canvas laid down on panel –
9.9 x 8.9cm.
(Christie's) £9,900 $17,325

PASCAL-ADOLPHE-JEAN DAGNAN-BOUVERET
(1852–1929) – Sancta Genovefa – signed and dated *1878* –
oil on canvas – 31 x 28cm.
(Christie's) £1,430 $2,488

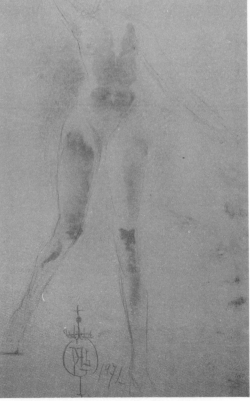

HANS DAHL (Norwegian, 1849–1937) – Returning from
harvesting – signed and dated *1881* – oil on canvas –
84 x 145cm.
(Sotheby's) £12,100 $21,417

SALVADOR DALI (1904–1989) – Floating female nude –
monogrammed and dated *1974* – watercolour, wax crayon
and pencil on stryafoam board – 152.5 x 101.6cm.
(Christie's) £11,000 $17,820

SALVADOR DALI (1904–1989) – Chocolat – signed and inscribed – watercolour and ballpoint pen on paper – 38.5 x 28.5cm.
(Christie's) £18,700 $32,912

GEORGE DANCE, Jun. R.A. (1741–1825) – Study of an architect – coloured chalks – inscribed oval – 300 x 240mm.
(Christie's) £418 $673

EMILIO POY DALMAU (b. 1876) – Driving the livestock – signed – oil on board – 23 x 44cm.
(Duran) £1,008 $1,775

EMILE VAN DAMME-SYLVA – Cattle watering at a pool – signed – oil on panel – unframed – 30.5 x 45.7cm.
(Christie's) £495 $851

School of NATHANIEL DANCE –A portrait of two huntsmen and a horse – oil on canvas – 97.8 x 73.6cm.
(Woolley & Wallis) £12,000 $20,570

WILLIAM DANIELL, R.A. – Jedburgh Abbey – signed –
watercolour – 7¹/₄ x 13in.
(Bearne's) **£900 $1,561**

LEON-MARIE DANSAERT (Belgian, 1830–1909) –
Matinée musicale – signed – oil on panel – 84.5 x 63cm.
(Sotheby's) **£12,100 $21,417**

WILLIAM DANIELL, R.A. (1769–1837) – The Jama
Masjid, Delhi – signed and inscribed on mount – pencil and
watercolour, watermark Strasburg Lily over GR –
473 x 753mm.
(Christie's) **£8,250 $14,520**

CHARLES-FRANÇOIS DAUBIGNY (1817–1878) –
Flock of sheep at the riverside – signed and dated *1875* –
oil on panel – 37.5 x 66cm.
(Christie's) **£18,700 $30,481**

DANISH SCHOOL – A figure shaded by a vine on a
Neapolitan coastal road – signed and dated *04* – oil on
canvas – 50.8 x 68.6cm.
(Christie's) **£715 $1,230**

HONORE DAUMIER – After the hearing – signed –
charcoal, pen and ink and watercolour on paper laid down
on paper – 29 x 35.8cm.
(Sotheby's) **£374,000 $661,980**

DAUMIER

HONORE DAUMIER – The parade – signed with initials
– charcoal, pen and ink, pastel and watercolour on paper
laid down on board – 44 x 33.4cm.
(Sotheby's)   £385,000 $681,450

HONORE DAUMIER – The drinking song – signed –
coloured crayons, pen and ink and watercolour –
25 x 35cm.
(Sotheby's)   £352,000 $623,040

ADRIEN DAUZATS (French, 1804–68) – Three Arabs
praying – stamped with the cachet de vente (Lugt 653) –
pencil and watercolour – 20.5 x 28cm.
(Sotheby's)   £1,100 $1,947

JACQUES-LOUIS DAVID (1748–1825) – Heads of a
soldier and a king and Two female heads – black chalk, pen
and grey ink, grey wash – 80 x 130mm. – a pair
(Christie's)   £11,167 $18,537

ALLAN DAVIDSON – Drawing room interior with a
child playing with toy bricks beside a window – indistinctly
signed – oil on board – 27 x 30cm.
(Spencer's) **£950 $1,653**

BESSIE DAVIDSON (1879–1965) – Fruit and a jug of
flowers on a table – signed – oil on board – 30.4 x 74.9cm.
(Christie's) **£7,700 $13,552**

ARTHUR B. DAVIES (1862–1928) – Six figures in a
landscape – watercolour on joined tissue laid down on
paper – 55.9 x 42.5cm.
(Sotheby's) **£1,262 $2,310**

ARTHUR BOWEN DAVIES (1862–1928) – The bathers
– oil on board – 29.5 x 40.6cm.
(Christie's) **£2,361 $4,180**

ARTHUR BOWEN DAVIES (American, 1862–1928) –
Female figures – oil on canvas – unframed – 20¼ x 42½in.
(Skinner Inc.) **£529 $935**

JAMES HEY DAVIES (British, 1848–1901) – A country
cottage – signed – oil on canvas – 61 x 50.2cm.
(Butterfield & Butterfield) **£630 $1,100**

RICHARD BARRET DAVIS, R.B.A. – Three feral horses standing in a rocky tropical landscape – signed and dated *1827* – oil on canvas – 63.5 x 76.2cm.
(Bonhams) £3,400 $5,406

FRED DAVIS – Young girls and poultry by cottage door – signed – oil on canvas – 11 x 15in.
(G.A Key) £260 $463

MONTAGUE DAWSON (1895–1973) – Constance, in full sail – signed – pencil, watercolour and bodycolour heightened with white – 43.2 x 68.6cm.
(Christie's) £12,650 $22,518

LOUIS B. DAVIS (1860–1941) – A child angel – signed with monogram, dated *1897* and inscribed – watercolour with bodycolour – 299 x 172mm.
(Christie's) £1,100 $2,002

DAWSON DAWSON-WATSON (1864–1939) – The hunter – signed and dated *1891* – oil on canvas – unframed – 170.2 x 131.4cm.
(Sotheby's) £1,322 $2,420

L. DEHESGHUES (French, 19th century) – At the fair –
signed and dated *1884* – oil on canvas – 102 x 125cm.
(Sotheby's) £11,000 $19,470

WALTER LOFTHOUSE DEAN (American, 1854–
1912) – Off Cape Ann – signed – watercolour and gouache
on paper – 14³/₄ x 10¹/₄in.
(Skinner Inc.) £538 $935

FRANCOIS B. DEBLOIS (Canadian, circa 1829–1913)
– The hay wagon – signed, dated and inscribed *1878* – oil
on canvas – 12 x 19in.
(Skinner Inc.) £506 $880

ADOLF ARTHUR DEHN (American, 1895–1968) – A
tropical village scene – signed and dated *42* – watercolour
and graphite on paper – 17¹/₄ x 23¹/₂in.
(Skinner Inc.) £747 $1,320

EDGAR DEGAS (1834–1917) – The racehorses, coming
out of the paddock – signed – oil on panel – 32.5 x 40.4cm.
(Christie's) £6,050,000 $9,922,000

ADOLF ARTHUR DEHN (American, 1895–1968) –
Beauty is where you find it – signed and dated *40* –
watercolour and graphite on paperboard – 18 x 24in.
(Skinner Inc.) £728 $1,265

147

EUGENE DELACROIX – By the Sebou – signed and
dated *1858* – oil on canvas – 50 x 60.7cm.
(Sotheby's)   **£396,000 $700,920**

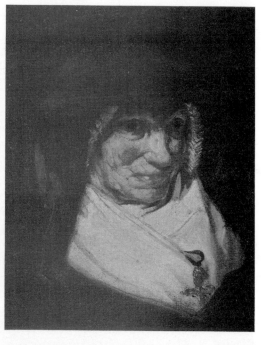

EUGENE DELACROIX – Study of the head of an Indian
woman – signed – oil on canvas – 60 x 49cm.
(Sotheby's)   **£792,000 $1,401,840**

EUGENE DELACROIX – Head of an old woman (Mme
Bornot?) – bears the artist's seal on stretcher – oil on canvas
– 40.5 x 32.3cm.
(Sotheby's)   **£93,500 $165,495**

Circle of WILLIAM DELAMOTTE – A wooded
landscape with barges and swimmers in a river – oil on
canvas – unframed – 91.5 x 123.2cm.
(Bonhams)   £3,200 $5,088

Attributed to ABRAHAM DELANOY (1742–1795) –
Portrait of Captain Harding Williams, circa 1785 – oil on
canvas – 32¼ x 26in.
(Christie's)   £15,312 $26,400

ALVARO DELGADO (b. 1922) – De los hombres del
Navia – signed and dated on reverse *1978* – oil on canvas –
46 x 38cm.
(Duran)   £1,950 $3,500

P. DELVAUX – The apparition – signed – etching
heightened with watercolour – 34.5 x 27cm.
(Hôtel de Ventes Horta) **£3,793 $6,600**

EMILE VICTOR AUGUSTIN DELOBRE (French, b.
1873) – Marthe in a shawl – oil on board – 32.4 x 23.5cm.
(Butterfield & Butterfield) **£2,049 $3,575**

PAUL DELVAUX (b. 1898) – The forest awakening –
signed and dated *8.39* – oil on canvas – 171 x 225.5cm.
(Christie's) **£715,000 $1,172,600**

JEAN DELVILLE (1867–1953) – Death – signed – pastel on card – 62 x 52cm.
(Hôtel de Ventes Horta) **£5,802 $9,922**

MAURICE DENIS (1870–1943) – Marthe and Noële at the green door – signed with monogram and dated *98* – oil on paper laid down on canvas – 45.5 x 39cm.
(Christie's) **£92,825 $164,300**

T. DENTZ (American, 20th century) – Down by the river, a New York scene – signed – oil on board – 5¹/₂ x 7in.
(Skinner Inc.) **£127 $220**

EDWARD JULIUS DETMOLD (1883–1957) – A blue tit and a wren – pencil and watercolour heightened with gum arabic – 177 x 216mm.
(Christie's) **£880 $1,426**

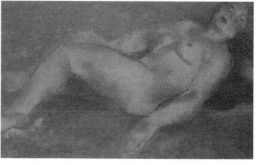

LEON DEVOS (Belgian, 1897–1974) – Ostende harbour – signed – oil on panel – 50 x 61cm.
(Hôtel de Ventes Horta) **£806 $1,370**

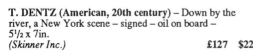

LEON DEVOS (Belgian, 1897–1974) – Reclining nude – signed – oil on panel – 30 x 50cm.
(Hôtel de Ventes Horta) **£3,065 $5,211**

THEOPHILE LOUIS DEYROLLE (French, 1844–1923) – Picking flowers – signed – oil on canvas – 71 x 100cm.
(Sotheby's) £4,620 $8,177

SIR FRANCIS BERNARD DICKSEE (1853–1928) – An offering – signed and dated *1898* – oil on canvas – 97.1 x 130.8cm.
(Christie's) £88,000 $149,600

ANTON H. DIEFFENBACH (German, 1831–1914) – A spoonful for baby – signed and dated *1865* – oil on canvas – 15½ x 13½in.
(Skinner Inc.) £2,849 $4,950

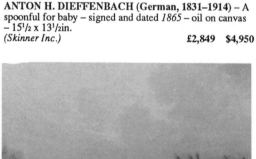

VIRGILIE NARCISSE DIAZ DE LA PENA (French, 1808–1876) – Flora and Cupids – signed – oil on canvas – 18 x 15in.
(Skinner Inc.) £2,489 $4,400

PRESTON DICKINSON (1891–1930) – Spring in the village – signed and dated *20* – oil, charcoal and watercolour on paper – 38.1 x 55.2cm.
(Christie's) £6,699 $11,550

ALWIN DIEHLE (b. 1854) – Boating in the bulrushes – signed and dated *1895* – oil on canvas – 107 x 66cm.
(Christie's) £4,620 $8,039

ADELHEID DIETRICH (b. 1827) – Morning glories –
signed and dated *1867* – oil on canvas – 31.8 x 24.8cm.
(Sotheby's)   **£17,111 $30,800**

JESSICA DISMORR (1885–1939) – The cafe, Cassis,
1925 – signed – watercolour – 38 x 26.5cm.
(Christie's)   **£1,210 $2,081**

FRANK DILLON (1823–1909) - Pylon at the end of the
Eastern Dromos, Karnac, Thebes – signed – oil on canvas –
88.9 x 156.2cm.
(Christie's)   **£3,300 $6,006**

JOHN BENTHAM DINSDALE – Driven hard, the
Windsor Castle – signed – oil on canvas – 91.4 x 122cm.
(Bonhams)   **£400 $660**

OTTO DIX (1891–1969) – Portrait of the painter Görtitz –
oil on paper – 47 x 34.2cm.
(Lempertz)   **£6,228 $9,934**

153

DIXON

CHARLES DIXON (English, 1872–1934) – Off Deptford – signed and inscribed – watercolour heightened with white – 26.6 x 76.2cm.
(Bonhams) £2,600 $4,290

CHARLES DIXON – Greenwich Reach - signed and dated *1918* – watercolour – 11 x 30in.
(G.A. Key) £2,000 $3,540

CHARLES DIXON (English, 1872–1934) – The Pool – signed and dated *1901* – watercolour – 26.3 x 76.5cm.
(Bonhams) £3,600 $5,940

CHARLES EDWARD DIXON (1872–1934) – Above Woolwich – signed and dated *06* – pencil and watercolour heightened with white – 280 x 782mm.
(Christie's) £3,080 $5,205

JOHN DOBBIN – A view on Cockerbeck, near Darlington – signed and dated *1842* - watercolour – 21 x 26in.
(G.A. Key) £450 $878

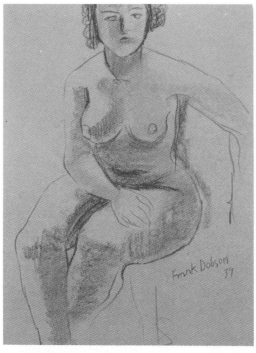

FRANK DOBSON – Seated female nude – signed and dated *39* – coloured chalks and charcoal – 30.5 x 24.1cm.
(Christie's) £385 $612

LOUIS DODD (b. 1943) – The Yacht Royal Charlotte, off Greenwich Hospital, 1765 – signed – oil on panel – 39.3 x 59.7cm.
(Christie's) £3,080 $5,482

LOUIS DODD (b. 1943) – A view of the English Harbour, Antigua, from the Careening Wharf of St Helena 1788 – signed – oil on panel – 54.6 x 90.3cm.
(Christie's) £6,050 $10,769

LOUIS DODD (b. 1943) – Dogana da Mar, Venice –
signed – oil on panel – 39.3 x 59.7cm.
(Christie's) **£1,760 $3,133**

STEVAN DOHANOS (American, b. 1907) – Mail early –
signed – mixed media including watercolour, ink, graphite
and tempera on board – 25¼ x 19½in.
(Skinner Inc.) **£1,013 $1,760**

Follower of CARLO DOLCI (18th century) – A female
saint – oil on canvas – 30.1 x 24.9cm.
(Sotheby's) **£2,200 $3,960**

FRANCISCO DOMINGO (1842–1920) – Velázquez –
signed – charcoal drawing – 23 x 28cm.
(Duran)   **£257 $453**

CORNELIS CHRISTIAN DOMMERSEN (Dutch,
1842–1928) – The flower market, Brussels – signed and
dated *1886* – oil on canvas – unframed – 65 x 55.5cm.
(Sotheby's)   **£7,920 $14,018**

CORNELIS CHRISTIAN DOMMERSEN (Dutch,
1842–1928) – Dutch canal scenes – both signed and dated
1876 – oil on canvas – 37 x 29.5cm. – a pair
(Sotheby's)   **£11,000 $19,470**

Follower of CORNELIS CHRISTIAN DOMMERSEN –
Fishing boats and other shipping in choppy seas off a jetty –
oil on canvas – 33 x 48.3cm.
(Christie's) £935 $1,608

WILLIAM DOMMERSEN (d. 1927) – Amalfi, Italy –
signed – oil on canvas – 45.7 x 81.2cm.
(Fraser–Pinneys) £1,905 $3,305

WILLIAM DOMMERSEN – Tholen on the Scheldt,
Holland – signed – oil on canvas – 50.8 x 76.2cm.
(Christie's) £1,980 $3,421

WILLIAM DOMMERSEN – Enkhuizen on the Zuider
Zee, Holland – signed – oil on canvas – 30.5 x 40.7cm.
(Christie's) £1,100 $1,892

WILLIAM RAYMOND DOMMERSEN (d. 1927) – At
the fish market – signed and dated *1884* – oil on panel –
37 x 31cm.
(Sotheby's) £3,080 $5,452

WILLIAM RAYMOND DOMMERSON (d. 1927) – The
Amalfitan coast – signed – oil on canvas – 45.7 x 81.2cm.
(Christie's) £2,750 $4,785

STEFANO DONADONI (1844–1911) – Fishermen on the
Tiber by Castel Sant'Angelo, Rome – signed and dated
1893 – pencil and watercolour on card laid down on board
– 56 x 78.7cm.
(Christie's) £2,420 $4,211

DIONYS VAN DONGEN (1748–1819) – A landscape with shepherdesses bathing – signed and dated 1775 on paper pasted to reverse – oil on panel – 21.2 x 29.7cm.
(Glerum)   £5,280 $9,504

PIERO DORAZIO (b. 1927) – Borealis V – signed and dated *1986* on reverse – oil on canvas – 85 x 110cm.
(Finarte)   £11,155 $19,019

KEES VAN DONGEN (1877–1968) – The Models – signed – gouache, watercolour, brush and black ink on paper – 60 x 45cm.
(Christie's)   £27,500 $48,400

GUSTAVE DORÉ (1832–1883) – The monk's dream – signed and dated *1880* – oil on canvas – 243.8 x 304.7cm.
(Christie's)   £15,400 $26,950

**PAUL-GUSTAVE-LOUIS-CHRISTOPHE DORE
(1832–1883)** – A mountain torrent in the Highlands –
signed – oil on canvas – 52.7 x 78.1cm.
(Christie's) £9,900 $16,137

EDWIN DOUGLAS (1848–1914) – A Collie, the guardian
of the flock – signed and dated *1908* – oil on canvas –
66.1 x 55.8cm.
(Christie's) £3,300 $5,412

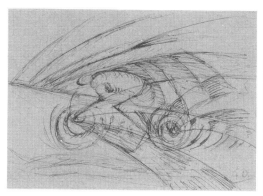

GERARDO DOTTORI (1889–1977) – Speed – signed
with initials – pen and ink on paper – 11 x 16.5cm.
(Christie's) £4,620 $8,131

JOHN PATRICK DOWNIE (Scottish, 1871–1945) – The
midday meal – signed and inscribed on reverse – oil on
canvas – 25.4 x 35.6cm.
(Bonhams) £260 $414

PARKE CUSTIS DOUGHERTY (b. 1867) – Winter
morning: Quai Voltaire – signed and dated *09* – oil on
canvas – 66 x 81cm.
(Christie's) £3,828 $6,600

JOHN DOWNMAN, A.R.A. (1750–1824) – Portrait of a
young girl playing a mechanical zither – signed and dated
1784 – black and white chalk, stump and watercolour on
paper laid on linen – oval – 280 x 387mm.
(Christie's) £1,210 $1,948

DOWNMAN

JOHN DOWNMAN, A.R.A. (1750–1824) – Portrait of Mrs. John Langston (?), half length, wearing a white and blue striped hat – signed and dated *1790* – black and white chalk, stump and watercolour – oval – 242 x 190mm.
(Christie's) **£715 $1,258**

JOHN DOWNMAN (1750–1824) – Portrait of Mrs. Hartop and her child – signed with initials, and dated *1780* – black and white chalk, stump and watercolour – oval – 210 x 178mm.
(Christie's) **£3,850 $6,776**

JOHN DOWNMAN, A.R.A. (1750–1824) – Portrait of Queen Charlotte, seated by a table with a landscape beyond – signed and dated *1784* – black and white chalk, stump and watercolour, paper laid on linen – 527 x 337mm.
(Christie's) **£7,150 $11,511**

JOHN DOWNMAN (1750–1824) – Portrait of Sarah Whitmore, seated by a column – signed and dated *1787* – black chalk, stump and watercolour – oval – 206 x 172mm.
(Christie's) **£1,870 $3,291**

Follower of FRANCOIS-HUBERT DROUAIS – Portrait of a lady, seated half length, in a blue dress with a lace collar and sleeves, embroidering a cushion – oil on canvas – 91.4 x 71.2cm.
(Christie's) £1,100 $1,716

JAMES DRUMMOND (1816–1877) – The day's bag – signed – pencil and watercolour heightened with white – 572 x 445mm.
(Christie's) £1,210 $2,045

ARTHUR DRUMMOND (1871–1951) – Blossoms – signed and dated *1890* – oil on canvas – 76 x 55.5cm.
(Christie's) £12,100 $19,602

WILLIAM DRUMMOND – Three boys on a balcony – watercolour, gum arabic and bodycolour – arched – 22 x 17¹/₂in.
(David Lay) £450 $809

PIERRE LOUIS DUBOURCQ (1815–1873) – L'Agro
Romano – signed and dated *1849* - oil on panel –
83 x 120.5cm.
(Christie's) £15,400 $25,102

WILLIAM DRUMMOND – Father and daughter on a
terrace, beside them a river meandering to a distant town –
signed and dated *1848* – watercolour, gum arabic and
bodycolour – arched – 21 x 17in.
(David Lay) £350 $629

WILLIAM DRUMMOND – A young lady seated at a
table – signed and dated *1848* – watercolour, gum arabic
and bodycolour – arched – 20^1/$_2$ x 16in.
(David Lay) £280 $503

JEAN DUBUFFET (1901–1985) – Tricoloured landscape
with a view of the rear of the Grand Hotel des Bains –
signed with initials and dated *74* – vinyl on canvas –
203.5 x 129.7cm.
(Christie's) £88,550 $156,733

JEAN DUFY (1888–1964) – Rue de l'Abreuvoir,
Montmartre – signed – oil on canvas – 38.1 x 46.3cm.
(Christie's) £12,100 $21,296

JEAN DUBUFFET (1901–1985) – View of Paris with
four trees and four figures (Place de l'Estrapade) – signed
and dedicated – gouache on paper – 37 x 30cm.
(Christie's) £39,600 $64,152

JEAN DUFY (1888–1964) – Le Havre – signed and dated
30 – oil on canvas – 65 x 81cm.
(Christie's) £24,200 $39,204

JACOB DUCK – A guardroom scene, with soldiers
playing cards and smoking at a table – oil on canvas –
62.2 x 72.5cm.
(Bonhams) £17,500 $27,825

CHARLES DUDLEY – After the day's shoot – oil on
canvas – unframed – 51 x 75cm.
(David Dockree Fine Art) £560 $985

RAOUL DUFY (1877–1953) – Reception – signed – oil on
panel – 23 x 38cm.
(Christie's) £82,500 $135,300

163

DUFY

RAOUL DUFY (1877-1953) – Haystacks in Normandy – signed – gouache on paper – 47.5 x 61cm.
(Christie's) **£15,400 $27,104**

ALFRED DUKE (d. circa 1905) – In full cry – signed – oil on canvas – 30.4 x 40.6cm.
(Christie's) **£880 $1,443**

RAOUL DUFY (1877–1953) – In the studio – signed and dated *1944* – gouache on paper – 26.9 x 20.5cm.
(Christie's) **£8,800 $14,256**

RAOUL DUFY (French, 1877–1953) – Seated nude – signed – pen and brown ink – 58.5 x 41cm.
(Butterfield & Butterfield) **£1,576 $2,750**

EDMOND DULAC (French, 1882–1953) – Fairyland Lovers/the fairy Dari-Banov – signed – watercolour and gouache on paperboard – 17 x 14in.
(Skinner Inc.) **£3,165 $5,500**

ROMEO DUMOULIN (Belgian 1883–1944) – Afternoon at Granada – signed and dated 1935 – oil on canvas – 41 x 60cm.
(Hôtel de Ventes Horta)   **£3,103 $5,400**

Attributed to R.O. DUNLOP – Head and shoulders portrait of a lady in feather trimmed dress and hat – oil on canvas – 16 x 10in.
(G.A. Key)   **£430 $761**

EDWARD DUNCAN (British, 1802–1882) and PHILIP CONNARD (British, b. 1875) – Morning walk in the glade; Reflections on the bay (two drawings) – one signed *Philip Connard* – one: pencil and watercolour heightened with white on paper; one: watercolour on paper – 14 x 16.5cm. and 22.5 x 29.5cm.
(Butterfield & Butterfield)   **£315 $550**

THOMAS R. DUNLAY - Still life of Staffordshire bowl and fruit – signed – oil on canvas – 45.7 x 61cm.
(Sotheby's)   **£511 $935**

BERNARD DUNSTAN (b. 1920) – Self portrait with nude model – signed with initials – oil on board – 28 x 30.8cm.
(Christie's)   **£2,860 $4,748**

JULES DUPRE (French, 1811–89) – A seascape – signed
– oil on panel – 29 x 47.5cm.
(Sotheby's)   **£3,850 $6,814**

BERNARD DUNSTAN (b. 1920) – The Artist's family at
tea – signed with initials – oil on board – 21 x 31cm.
(Christie's)   **£1,650 $2,739**

BERNARD DUNSTAN, R.A. (b. 1920) – Two bathers –
signed – oil on canvas laid over board – 21.5 x 30.5cm.
(Christie's)   **£1,320 $2,270**

JULIEN DUPRE (French, 1851–1910) – The milkmaid –
signed – oil on canvas – 47 x 61.6cm.
(Butterfield & Butterfield)   **£6,934 $12,100**

BERNARD DUNSTAN (b. 1920) – Dinner at Limoux –
signed with initials – oil on board – 30.5 x 35cm.
(Christie's)   **£2,860 $4,748**

RAFAEL DURANCAMPS (1891–1979) -- Landscape
with figures – signed – oil on canvas – 38 x 46cm.
(Duran)   **£7,799 $13,999**

DUTCH SCHOOL in the manner of Adrien Pietersz van de Venne – Interior of a school room with numerous figures studying at tables, a dunce in the foreground – oil on panel – 30 x 34cm.
(Spencer's) £1,900 $3,031

Attributed to ASHER BROWN DURAND (1796–1886) – Portrait of Miss Leupp in childhood – oil on canvas – 53.3 x 45.1cm.
(Christie's) £932 $1,650

DUTCH SCHOOL (late 19th century) – Sailing on the stormy Zuiderzee; Preparing the boats – oil on canvas – 23.5 x 30.5cm. – a pair
(Butterfield & Butterfield) £1,418 $2,475

DUTCH SCHOOL (19th century) – Still life of roses, tulips and irises in a decorative vessel with a bird's nest and a butterfly above – signed with monogram *KO* – oil on panel – 39.4 x 29.2cm.
(Butterfield & Butterfield) £1,261 $2,200

DUTCH SCHOOL (19th century) – The rude awakening – indistinctly monogrammed and dated *18* – oil on canvas – 95.9 x 135.9cm.
(Butterfield & Butterfield) £3,152 $5,500

DUTCH SCHOOL (17th century), after Pieter Brueghel the Younger – The Adoration of the Magi – oil on panel – 43.8 x 59cm.
(Bonhams) £1,000 $1,590

167

THEOPHILE EMMANUEL DUVERGER (French, b. 1821) – The visit party at Grandmother's – signed and dated *1857* – oil on panel – 15 x 18³/₄in.
(Skinner Inc.) £4,432 $7,700

HENRI DUVIEUX (fl. 1880–1882) – The Rialto Bridge, Venice – signed – oil on paper laid down on panel – 22.2 x 31.1cm.
(Christie's) £1,650 $2,871

Manner of SIR ANTHONY VAN DYCK – Portrait of a lady, standing half length in a black dress with gold embroidered sleeves and bodice and lace collar and cuffs, on a terrace – oil on canvas – 100.3 x 92.7cm.
(Christie's) £1,210 $1,888

MARCEL DYF (French, 1899–1985) – Before the ball – signed – oil on canvas – 73 x 60.3cm.
(Butterfield & Butterfield) £2,521 $4,400

Follower of VAN DYCK – Portrait of a lady – oil on canvas – 53 x 40cm.
(Duran) £1,253 $2,249

MARCEL DYF (French, 1899–1985) – Flowers – signed – oil on canvas – 65.4 x 54.6cm.
(Butterfield & Butterfield) £6,934 $12,100

ALEX DZIGURSKI (American, b. 1910) – Seascape at
sunset – signed – oil on canvas – 24 x 36in.
(Du Mouchelles)   **£1,226 $2,100**

SIR ALFRED EAST (1849–1913) – Shepherd with his
sheep in a river landscape – oil on canvas – 91.5 x 132cm.
(Christie's)   **£704 $1,169**

ANTON EBERT (Bohemian, 1845–1896) – The broken
pitcher – signed and inscribed – oil on canvas –
105.4 x 73.7cm.
(Butterfield & Butterfield)   **£5,673 $9,900**

CHARLES EARLE (1832–1893) – Evening: Elegant
figures by a country house – signed – pencil and
watercolour with touches of white heightening –
560 x 343mm.
(Christie's)   **£1,980 $3,208**

ANTON EBERT – Spring; and Autumn – both signed and
dated *1869* – oval – oil on canvas – 79 x 63cm. – a pair
(Christie's)   **£4,620 $7,983**

EBERT

MARY ROBERTS EBERT (b. 1873–1956) – Mohegan
Island, Maine – signed – oil on canvas – 63.5 x 76.2cm.
(Christie's) **£5,593 $9,900**

Attributed to FRANCIS WILLIAM EDMONDS (1806–
1863) – George Washington – bears signature *F.W. Edmons*
– oil on board – 16.5 x 14cm.
(Butterfield & Butterfield) **£504 $880**

FREDERICK CHARLES VIPOND EDE (1865–1907) –
Lady with a parasol – signed and dated *1888* – watercolour
– 27.2 x 40.6cm.
(Fraser-Pinneys) **£340 $598**

MAY DE MONTRAVEL EDWARDES – Menton from
the hills above – signed with initials and dated *III 1921* –
watercolour – 7³/₄ x 9³/₄in. – and three others
(Christie's) **£165 $283**

LIONEL DALHOUSIE ROBERTSON EDWARDS – A
check; Scent failed. The Dulverton at Bampfylde Clump,
South Molton, Devon – signed – gouache – 13¹/₂ x 9³/₄in.
(Bearne's) £2,400 $4,248

DIETZ EDZARD (1893–1963) – The little girl with roses
– signed – oil on canvas – 61 x 50.2cm.
(Fraser–Pinneys) £4,010 $6,957

AUGUSTUS LEOPOLD EGG, R.A. (1816–1863) – The
Cartoon Gallery, Knowle – signed and inscribed on reverse
– oil on canvas – 25.5 x 31cm.
(Christie's) £1,650 $2,673

NICK EGGENHOFER (1897–1976) – Riders of the
purple sage – signed – watercolour and gouache on paper –
24.1 x 31.8cm.
(Butterfield & Butterfield)   £2,206 $3,850

GEORG DIONYSIUS EHRET (1708–1770) – An old
English rose – signed and dated *1760* – pencil and
watercolour on vellum – unframed – 235 x 184mm.
(Christie's)   £2,420 $4,259

GEORG DIONYSIUS EHRET (1708–1770) – Magnolia
– signed and inscribed – pencil, watercolour and
bodycolour on vellum – 522 x 368mm.
(Christie's)   £71,500 $115,115

CHARLES EISEN (1720–1778) – An Allegory of the Arts
– oil on canvas – 84.5 x 134cm.
(Christie's) **£8,934 $14,830**

E. EICHINGER (German, 20th century) – Bavarian man
holding a wine glass – signed – oil on board – 10¹/₂ x 8in.
(Du Mouchelles) **£637 $1,100**

FERENCZ EISENHUT (Hungarian, 1857–1903) – The
armourer – signed and dated *87* – oil on canvas –
71 x 54cm.
(Sotheby's) **£12,100 $21,417**

GEORGE SAMUEL ELGOOD (1851–1943) – Compton
Wynyates, Warwickshire – signed and dated *1890* – pencil
and watercolour – 362 x 534mm.
(Christie's) **£12,100 $19,602**

E. EICHINGER (German, 20th century) – Bavarian man
holding a pipe – signed – oil on board – 10¹/₂ x 8in.
(Du Mouchelles) **£463 $800**

ELIZABETHAN SCHOOL (attributed to the Master of the Countess of Warwick) – A three-quarter length portrait of Sir Gabriel Poyntz, aged 36 – oil on panel – 38 x 28in.
(Boardman) £10,500 $17,850

ARTHUR JOHN ELSLEY (b. 1861) – The piggy-back ride – signed and dated *1900* – oil on canvas – 91.4 x 71.2cm.
(Christie's) £22,000 $37,400

H. ELLIOT (English?, 19th century) – Over the fence – signed – oil on panel – 15.9 x 36.8cm. – and companion – a pair
(Bonhams) £900 $1,431

TRISTRAM JAMES ELLIS (1844–1922) – Sintra, Portugal – signed and dated *1894* – pencil and watercolour – 357 x 528mm.
(Christie's) £880 $1,487

ARTHUR WEBSTER EMERSON (American, b. 1885) – The wharf – signed and dated *37* – oil on canvas – 28 x 22in.
(Skinner Inc.) £253 $440

JOHN EMMS (English, 1843–1912) – A horse in a stable
interior – signed and dated *94* – 61 x 76.2cm.
(Bonhams) **£1,200 $1,908**

JOHN EMMS (1841–1912) – Shot and his friends, three
Irish red and white setters – signed and dated *76* – oil on
canvas – 38.1 x 55.9cm.
(Christie's) **£4,180 $6,855**

JOHN EMMS – Two foxhounds Barmaid and Ringlet –
signed, dated and inscribed *1892* – oil on canvas –
40 x 60.3cm.
(Woolley & Wallis) **£5,600 $9,968**

JOHANN-NEPOMUK ENDER (Austrian, 1793–1854) –
King David – signed and dated *'845* – oil on panel –
unframed – 125 x 95cm.
(Sotheby's) **£2,860 $5,062**

ENGLISH SCHOOL (19th century) – A portrait group of
three children of the Bennett family with a black
Newfoundland dog – oil on canvas – 127 x 101.6cm.
(Woolley & Wallis) **£3,300 $5,874**

175

ENGLISH SCHOOL (early 20th century) – Portrait of a
woman, bust length, wearing a turban – signed with initials
F.H.S. – tempera on panel – 39.3 x 29.2cm.
(Christie's)   £1,430 $2,531

ENGLISH SCHOOL (circa 1830) – A group portrait of
Master William Orme Foster and his brother Percival
Foster, in an interior – oil on canvas – 114.4 x 96.5cm.
(Christie's)   £1,320 $2,340

ENGLISH SCHOOL (mid 19th century) – Portrait of
John Leon Francis Paul seated half length, holding a St.
Bernard – signed with monogram and dated *A.D. 1850* – oil
on canvas – 80.8 x 63cm.
(Christie's)   £3,300 $5,346

ENGLISH SCHOOL (19th century) – Roses and other
flowers in a glass bowl on a ledge – oil on canvas –
40.6 x 30.5cm.
(Christie's)   £825 $1,462

ENGLISH SCHOOL (19th century) – A Bichon Frisé –
oil on canvas – unframed – 63.5 x 81.3cm.
(Christie's) £4,180 $6,855

ENGLISH SCHOOL (early 19th century) – Portrait of a
boy, standing small full length in a landscape – oil on
canvas – 65 x 47cm.
(Christie's) £715 $1,155

ENGLISH SCHOOL (19th century) – On the Grand
Canal, Venice – with signature and the date *1850* – oil on
canvas – 50.8 x 76.2cm.
(Christie's) £770 $1,365

ENGLISH SCHOOL (circa 1770) – Farm labourers
harvesting, Langharne, Carmarthen – inscribed in margin –
pencil, pen and brown ink and watercolour – 368 x 520mm.
(Christie's) £880 $1,549

ENGLISH SCHOOL (19th century) – Lord Howe's
Victory – oil on canvas – 99 x 151.8cm.
(Bonhams) £1,500 $2,475

ENGLISH SCHOOL (19th century) – A Cavalier King
Charles spaniel on a runner – oil on canvas –
50.8 x 60.9cm.
(Christie's) £550 $902

ENGLISH SCHOOL (19th century) – Shipping off the
South coast – with traces of a signature and the date *1873?*
– oil on canvas – 71 x 91.5cm.
(Christie's) £1,540 $2,741

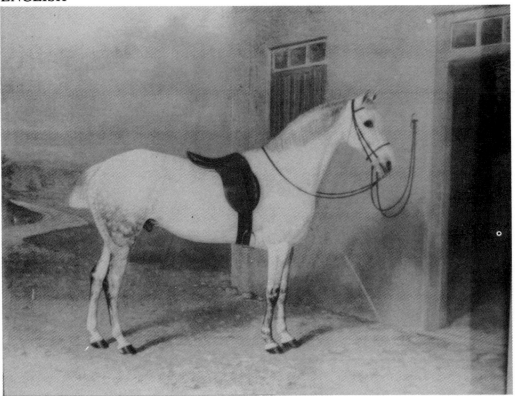

ENGLISH SPORTING SCHOOL (early 19th century) –
Portrait of a grey horse standing saddled by a stable door
with a landscape in the distance – 20 x 24in.
(Boardman)   **£1,000 $1,700**

ENGLISH SYMBOLIST SCHOOL – Femme fleur –
signed with monogram *CW* – oil on canvas – 128 x 106cm.
(Hôtel de Ventes Horta)   **£2,580 $4,386**

DELPHIN ENJOLRAS (French, b. 1857) – A nude by
firelight – signed – pastel – 71 x 51cm.
(Sotheby's)   **£4,180 $7,399**

JOHN JOSEPH ENNEKING (1841–1916) – Spring
blossoms – signed and dated *05* – oil on canvas –
45.7 x 61cm.
(Christie's) £6,380 $11,000

JOSEPH ELIOT ENNEKING (American, 1881–1942) --
The harbour – signed – oil on canvasboard – 8 x 10in.
(Skinner Inc.) £373 $660

JAMES ENSOR (1860–1940) – Rayons de Palette –
signed – oil on canvas – 60.3 x 50.2cm.
(Christie's) £51,700 $90,992

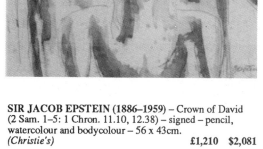

JAMES ENSOR (1860–1940) – Study of a young boy –
signed and dated *90* – charcoal, watercolour and grey wash
on paper – 56.6 x 47cm.
(Christie's) £19,800 $32,076

SIR JACOB EPSTEIN (1886–1959) – Crown of David
(2 Sam. 1–5: 1 Chron. 11.10, 12.38) – signed – pencil,
watercolour and bodycolour – 56 x 43cm.
(Christie's) £1,210 $2,081

PAINTINGS PRICE GUIDE

RUDOLF ERNST (Austrian, 1854–1932) – The manicure - signed – oil on panel – 64 x 82.5cm.
(Sotheby's) **£33,000 $58,410**

MAX ERNST (1898–1976) – Eskimo sun – signed and dated *56* – oil on canvas – 55 x 46cm.
(Christie's) **£143,000 $231,660**

LUIS ESPINOS (19th century) – Little girl in blue – signed and dated *1890* – pastel – 41 x 33cm.
(Duran) **£223 $400**

RUDOLF ERNST (Austrian, 1854–1932) – The harem guard – signed – oil on panel – 38.7 x 28.6cm.
(Butterfield & Butterfield) **£4,727 $8,250**

LUIS ESPINOS (19th century) – Little girl in red – signed and dated *1890* – pastel – 41 x 32cm.
(Duran) **£200 $359**

FREDERICK ETCHELLS (1886–1973) – Cellular composition – signed and inscribed on reverse – oil on panel – 26 x 34cm.
(Christie's) **£1,980 $3,287**

EMLEN ETTING (b. 1905) – Gentleman standing with nude in the background – signed – oil on board – 40.6 x 30.5cm.
(Sotheby's) **£391 $715**

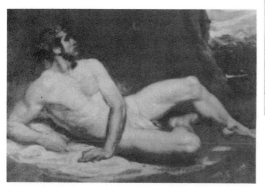

WILLIAM ETTY (British, 1787–1849) – Reclining male nude with laurel wreath – unsigned – oil on board mounted on canvas – 16¹/₂ x 23¹/₂in.
(Skinner Inc.) **£1,266 $2,200**

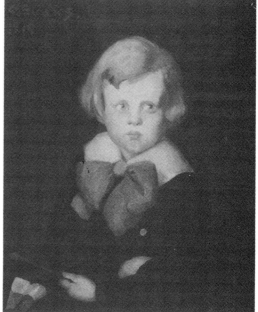

GRACE LYDIA EVANS (b. 1877) – The little Alley – signed and dated *1919* – oil on canvas – 55.8 x 45.7cm.
(Christie's) **£298 $528**

JESSIE BENTON EVANS (American, 1866–1954) – Road through the desert – signed – oil on canvas – 14 x 14in.
(Skinner Inc.) **£95 $165**

JEAN EVE (French, 1900–1968) – Springtime, Vincelles (Yonne) – signed – oil on canvas – 46.4 x 55.2cm.
(Butterfield & Butterfield) **£2,206 $3,850**

ADRIANUS EVERSEN (1818–1897) – View of a Dutch town – signed – oil on board – 43.8 x 35.5cm.
(Fraser–Pinneys) **£8,271 $14,350**

CESAR BOETIUS VAN EVERDINGEN (1617–1678) – Allegory of Winter – oil on canvas – 95 x 79.5cm.
(Glerum) **£204,082 $360,715**

CHARLES VAN DEN EYCKEN (1859–1923) – Circus entertainers – signed and dated *1890* – oil on canvas – 43.3 x 45.7cm.
(Christie's) **£6,600 $10,824**

PHILIP EVERGOOD (American, 1901–1973) – Susanna and the Elders, 1958 – signed – oil on canvas – 24 x 18in.
(Skinner Inc.) **£2,058 $3,575**

CHARLES VAN DEN EYCKEN (1859–1923) – A tabby cat – signed and dated *1920* – oil on canvas – 38.1 x 49.6cm.
(Christie's) **£6,050 $9,922**

L. FAILLE - Odalisque – signed – 21¹/₄ x 35in.
(*Bearne's*)   **£680 $1,179**

Follower of ANIELLO FALCONE – Muleteers on a
track, a hilltop village beyond – oil on canvas –
55.8 x 71.2cm.
(*Christie's*)   **£3,300 $5,148**

FABIO FABBI (Italian, 1861–1946) – The slave market –
signed – oil on canvas – 76.8 x 47cm.
(*Butterfield & Butterfield*)   **£1,891 $3,300**

FABIO FABBI (1861–1946) – In the harem – signed – oil
on canvas – 72.4 x 110.5cm.
(*Christie's*)   **£15,950 $27,912**

CAREL VAN FALENS (Belgian 1683–1733) – The farrier – oil on panel – 29.6 x 37.7cm.
(Hôtel de Ventes Horta)   £7,241 $12,599

JOHN LA FARGE (1835–1910) - Apple blossoms and butterfly – watercolour on paper laid down on board – 12 x 12cm. – (in a painted circle)
(Christie's)   £5,104 $8,800

HENRI FANTIN-LATOUR (1836–1904) – Bouquet of flowers–Pansies – signed and dated 83 – oil on canvas – 26 x 30.5cm.
(Christie's)   £82,500 $135,300

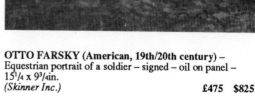

HENRI FANTIN-LATOUR – Still life, roses, grapes and peaches – signed and dated '74 – oil on canvas – 30 x 58cm.
(Sotheby's)   £385,000 $681,450

OTTO FARSKY (American, 19th/20th century) – Equestrian portrait of a soldier – signed – oil on panel – 15¼ x 9¾in.
(Skinner Inc.)   £475 $825

Attributed to GIOVANNI FATTORI (Italian, 1825–1908) – Washer woman – oil on canvas – 41.9 x 69.9cm.
(Butterfield & Butterfield) **£883 $1,540**

Studio of GIACOMO FAVRETTO (1849–1887) – El Liston, Piazza San Marco, Venice – with signature – oil on canvas – 87 x 170.2cm.
(Christie's) **£10,120 $17,609**

JEAN FAUTRIER (1898–1964) – Portrait – signed – oil on canvas – 34.6 x 26.9cm.
(Christie's) **£24,200 $40,172**

MARY FEDDEN (b. 1915) – Nightjars – signed and dated *58* – oil on canvas – 38.5 x 49cm.
(Christie's) **£770 $1,278**

L. FAVARD (French, 19th–20th century) – Early morning sail – signed – oil on canvas – 71 x 91.5cm.
(Butterfield & Butterfield) **£1,418 $2,475**

MARY FEDDEN (b. 1915) – Suzi – signed and dated *1988* – watercolour and bodycolour – 17 x 20cm.
(Christie's) **£638 $1,097**

FEDDEN

MARY FEDDEN (b. 1915) – The black cat – signed and
dated *1991* – oil on canvas – 28.5 x 33cm.
(Christie's) £770 $1,278

MARY FEDDEN (b. 1915) – Isle of Gozo – signed and
dated – oil on canvas – 48 x 58.5cm.
(Christie's) £1,078 $1,789

PAUL FELGENTREFF (German, 1854–1933) – The
young girl's lesson – signed – oil on canvas – 21 x 17.8cm.
(Butterfield & Butterfield) £1,261 $2,200

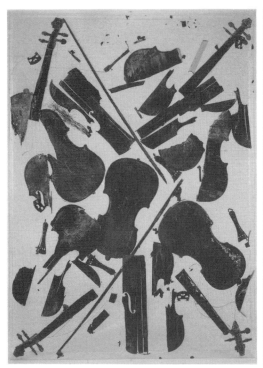

ARMAN (Arman Fernandez) (b. 1928) – Untitled –
signed – accumulation of burnt and broken violins in
polyester and plexiglas – 120 x 90 x 11cm.
(Christie's) £33,000 $53,460

BERNARDO FERRANDIZ Y BADENES (1835–1885) –
In the courtyard – signed – oil on canvas – 46.3 x 71.1cm.
(Christie's) £24,200 $39,446

FERRARESE SCHOOL (16th century) – The Nativity –
oil on panel – 62 x 44cm.
(Sotheby's) £2,200 $3,960

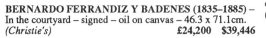

RAINER FETTING (b. 1949) – Ironer VII – signed and
dated *83* – acrylic on canvas – 230 x 200cm.
(Christie's) **£15,500 $25,110**

FELICE FICHERELLI, called Il Riposo (1605–1669) –
Salome with the head of John the Baptist – oil on canvas
(originally octagonal) – 97 x 123cm.
(Sotheby's) **£27,500 $49,500**

AUGUSTE FERVEL (French, 19th/20th century) –
Elegant couples in Venice – both signed – watercolour –
each 40.5 x 29cm. – a pair
(Sotheby's) **£1,870 $3,310**

WALTER FIELD (1837–1901) – The gentle wind
bloweth ... – signed and dated *1870* – oil on canvas –
76 x 122cm.
(Christie's) **£4,180 $6,772**

Circle of FRANCESCO FIERAVINO, il Maltese – Still life with baskets of fruit and flowers on a trestle – oil on canvas – 69.3 x 95.5cm. – a pair
(Christie's) **£6,700 $11,122**

EMIL FILLA (1882–1953) – Still life with pears – signed and dated 27 – oil on panel – 32.5 x 41cm.
(Christie's) **£14,300 $25,168**

ERNEST FIENE (American, 1894–1965) – White lilacs in Japanese vase – signed – oil on canvas – 30 x 22in.
(Skinner Inc.) **£823 $1,430**

HAZEL FINCK (b. 1894) – Rendezvous on the bridge – signed – oil on canvas – 41.3 x 52.1cm.
(Sotheby's) **£1,563 $2,860**

LEONOR FINI (b. 1908) – Petit Sphinx Gardien – signed and dated *1943* – oil on canvas – 20.3 x 35.8cm.
(Christie's) £18,700 $32,912

HUGO FISHER (1854–1916) – Shepherd and flock –
signed – watercolour on paper – 66 x 88.9cm.
(Butterfield & Butterfield) £315 $550

PAUL FISCHER (Danish, 1860–1934) – The three
bathers – signed – oil on canvas – 55.5 x 73.5cm.
(Sotheby's) £20,900 $36,993

CHARLES FISHER – Coastal scene loading a hay barge
– signed and dated *89* – watercolour – 29.2 x 44.5cm.
(Woolley & Wallis) £380 $676

PERCY HARLAND FISHER (1865–1944) – A wire-
haired Fox Terrier – oil on canvas – 50.7 x 40.6cm.
(Christie's) £528 $866

ROWLAND FISHER – On Fritton marshes – signed – oil – 12 x 14in.
(G.A. Key) £170 $271

JOHN FLAXMAN, R.A. (1755–1826) – Charity – pencil, pen and grey ink, grey wash – 285 x 473mm.
(Christie's) £1,210 $1,948

FLEMISH SCHOOL – Musical gathering – signed *D. Ryckaert* – oil on canvas – 36 x 48¹/₂in.
(Du Mouchelles) £9,340 $16,000

GERTRUDE FISKE (1879–1961) – Old seated woman – oil on canvasboard – 25.4 x 20.3cm.
(Butterfield & Butterfield) £693 $1,210

JOHN AUSTEN FITZGERALD (1832–1906?) – The original sketch for 'The Fairy's Banquet' (recto); Giving alms (verso) – signed and inscribed – oil on board – 23 x 28cm.
(Christie's) £28,600 $46,332

FLEMISH SCHOOL – The rat catcher – oil on canvas – 76 x 64cm.
(Hôtel de Ventes Horta) £3,276 $5,700

191

FLEMISH

FLEMISH SCHOOL (circa 1700) –A fox caught in a trap with a wild dog pursuing – oil on canvas – 50.8 x 70.5cm. *(Butterfield & Butterfield)* £504 $880

FLEMISH SCHOOL (19th century) – St. Jerome – oil on panel – 92 x 68cm.
(Duran) £1,008 $1,774

EDWIN FLETCHER – A fishing boat off Greenwich – signed – oil on canvas – 91.4 x 71.1cm.
(Bonhams) £1,000 $1,650

FLEMISH SCHOOL (17th century) – The Flight into Egypt – oil on copper – 25.4 x 20.2cm.
(Sotheby's) £4,400 $7,920

PAUL FRANZ FLICKEL (1852–1903) – A huntsman on a wooded path by a lake – signed and dated *1895* – oil on canvas – 95.2 x 140.3cm.
(Christie's) £11,000 $19,250

FRANCIS RUSSELL FLINT (b. 1915) – Shipbuilding –
signed – watercolour and bodycolour – 54.5 x 76cm.
(Christie's) **£1,100 $1,826**

SIR WILLIAM RUSSELL FLINT (1880–1969) – The
mill, St. Martin d'Ardeche – signed – watercolour –
17.5 x 28cm.
(Christie's) **£5,060 $8,400**

JOSEPH FLOCH (1895–1977) – In my studio – signed –
oil on canvas – 55.2 x 38.7cm.
(Sotheby's) **£1,142 $2,090**

SIR WILLIAM RUSSELL FLINT, R.A. (1880–1969) –
Tristram and Isolde – signed and dated *MCMX* –
watercolour and bodycolour – 28 x 23cm.
(Christie's) **£4,950 $8,514**

SIR WILLIAM RUSSELL FLINT (1880–1969) –
Gabrielle – signed – tempera – 42 x 67cm.
(Christie's) **£27,500 $45,650**

FLORENTINE SCHOOL (18th century) – A putto
playing with a dog; Putti playing with fruit in landscapes –
both oil on canvas, oval – 58 x 70.5cm. – a pair
(Sotheby's) **£5,500 $9,900**

PAINTINGS PRICE GUIDE

FLORENTINE SCHOOL (17th century) – Saint Cecilia
– oil on canvas – 100 x 125cm.
(Sotheby's) **£5,720 $10,296**

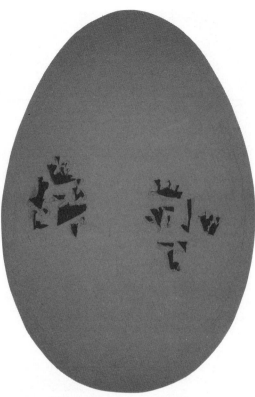

LUCIO FONTANA (1899–1968) – La Fine di Dio, La
Genesi – signed – oil on canvas – 178 x 123cm.
(Christie's) **£143,000 $253,110**

JOHN F. FOLINSBEE (1892–1972) – The frozen
Delaware River – signed – oil on canvas – 50.8 x 76.2cm.
(Christie's) **£1,181 $2,090**

GUSTAVE FONTAINE (French, 19th century) – The
courtship – signed – oil on canvas – 61 x 50.8cm.
(Butterfield & Butterfield) **£1,261 $2,200**

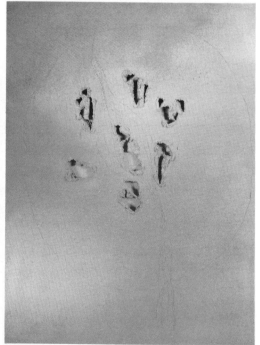

LUCIO FONTANA (1899–1968) – Concetto spaziale –
signed – oil on canvas – 146.5 x 114.5cm.
(Christie's) **£154,000 $249,480**

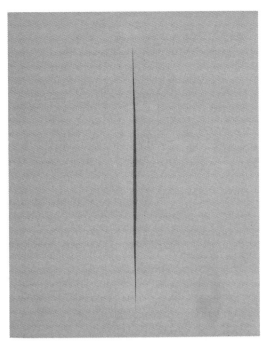

STANHOPE ALEXANDER FORBES, R.A. (1857–1947) – A Cornish village – signed and dated *1925* – oil on canvas – 60 x 75cm.
(Christie's) £20,900 $34,694

LUCIO FONTANA (1899–1968) – Concetto spaziale – signed – waterbased paint on canvas – 61.3 x 50cm.
(Christie's) £34,100 $56,606

ELIZABETH ADELA STANHOPE FORBES (nee Armstrong) A.R.W.S. – The maids were in the garden, hanging out the clothes – signed with monogram – pastel – 28 x 38in.
(Bearne's) £48,000 $83,280

FORD

HENRY JUSTICE FORD (1860–1941) – Psyche loses
Cupid – signed – pencil and watercolour – 280 x 165mm.
(Christie's) £770 $1,301

HELENE FORESTIER – Annabella – signed – pastel –
23 x 19in.
(G.A. Key) £215 $343

**WILLIAM BANKS FORTESCUE, R.W.A., R.B.S.A.
(circa 1855–1924)** – A view into the harbour, St. Ives –
signed – watercolour – 5 x 7¹/₂in.
(David Lay) £330 $525

ETTORE FORTI (Italian, 19th century) – At the
antiquarians – signed and inscribed – oil on canvas –
59 x 100cm.
(Sotheby's) £24,200 $42,834

MARC-AURELE FORTIN (1888–1970) – Montreal
harbour, building the Jacques Cartier bridge – signed – oil
on board – 55.8 x 71.2cm.
(Fraser–Pinneys) £9,022 $15,653

MARC-AURELE FORTIN (1888–1970) – Shadows on Hochelaga – signed – oil on board – 42.5 x 64.7cm.
(Fraser–Pinneys) £15,037 $26,089

MYLES BIRKET FOSTER (1825–1899) – Auchenellan, Argyll – signed with monogram and inscribed – pencil and watercolour heightened with white – 260 x 210mm.
(Christie's) £6,600 $12,012

BEN FOSTER (1852–1926) – Landscape and stream – signed – oil on canvas – 61 x 61cm.
(Butterfield & Butterfield) £1,576 $2,750

MYLES BIRKET FOSTER (1825–1899) – First of May, Garland Day – signed with monogram – pencil and watercolour with touches of white heightening – 206 x 270mm.
(Christie's) £8,250 $15,015

MYLES BIRKET FOSTER – The bird cage – signed with monogram – watercolour over traces of pencil – 19.75 x 15.9cm.
(Woolley & Wallis) £5,100 $8,721

FOSTER

MYLES BIRKET FOSTER – At the cottage door –
signed with monogram – pencil and watercolour –
10.8 x 14.6cm.
(Bonhams) **£1,400 $2,226**

MYLES BIRKET FOSTER (1825–1899) – By the duck
pond – signed with monogram – pencil, watercolour and
bodycolour – 235 x 344mm.
(Christie's) **£10,450 $17,660**

MYLES BIRKET FOSTER, R.W.S. (1825–1899) – The
vegetable market by Le Fabriche Vecchie Di Rialto, Venice
– signed with monogram – pencil and watercolour
heightened with bodycolour – 559 x 477mm.
(Christie's) **£6,050 $10,225**

MYLES BIRKET FOSTER (1825–1899) – Shipping on
the Bacino near the Salute, Venice – signed with monogram
– pencil and watercolour with touches of bodycolour –
356 x 533mm.
(Christie's) **£19,800 $36,036**

MYLES BIRKET FOSTER (1825–1899) – The young angler – signed with monogram – pencil and watercolour heightened with bodycolour – 215 x 280mm.
(Christie's) £5,500 $8,910

ALBERT AUGUSTE FOURIE (French, b. 1854) – Afternoon tea in the garden – signed – oil on canvas – 38.1 x 46.4cm.
(Butterfield & Butterfield) £3,467 $6,050

HENRY CHARLES FOX – Bringing in the hay – signed and dated *1910* – watercolour – 36.8 x 54.6cm. – and companion – a pair
(Bonhams) £1,150 $1,829

Attributed to NICOLAS FOUCHE (1650–1733) – The Allegory of Youth and the Allegory of Fortune – oil on canvas – 63cm. diam. – a pair
(Christie's) £21,217 $35,220

HENRY CHARLES FOX (1860–circa 1930) – A traveller on a country lane – signed and dated *1910* – pencil and watercolour heightened with white – 372 x 547mm. – and a watercolour of cart horses at a straw stack, by the same hand – a pair
(Christie's) £1,430 $2,603

HENRY CHARLES FOX – Shepherd and sheep in a
country lane in autumn – signed and dated *1901* –
watercolour – 29 x 20in.
(G.A. Key) £1,050 $1,859

ROSSELLO DI JACOPO FRANCHI (1377–1456) –
Madonna and Child – oil and tempera on panel, arched top,
gold ground – unframed – 64.3 x 43.2cm.
(Sotheby's) £35,200 $63,360

**Attributed to JEAN-HONORE FRAGONARD (1732–
1806) and his studio** – Sappho inspired by Love – oil on
canvas – 55 x 45cm.
(Christie's) £9,492 $15,757

ALEXANDRE T. FRANCIA – A French harbour at
sunset – signed – oil on canvas – 42 x 66cm.
(Christie's) £3,630 $6,244

SAM FRANCIS (b. 1923) – Untitled – signed and dated
on the reverse *1978* – acrylic on canvas – unframed –
229 x 167cm.
(Christie's)   £110,000 $194,700

Circle of **FRANS FRANCKEN II** – Christ at supper with
Simon the Pharisee – oil on canvas – 116.2 x 159cm.
(Christie's)   £3,080 $4,805

FRANS FRANCKEN II (1581–1642) – The legend of
Virgil and the Emperor's daughter – oil on panel –
58.8 x 80cm.
(Christie's)   £18,984 $31,513

SAM FRANCIS (b. 1923) – Untitled – acrylic on canvas –
134 x 52cm.
(Christie's)   £33,000 $58,410

Circle of **FRANS FRANCKEN the Younger** –
Cleopatra's banquet – oil on copper – 48.5 x 61.5cm.
(Sotheby's)   £6,600 $11,880

FRANCO-ITALIAN SCHOOL (late 17th/early 18th century) – The finding of Moses among the bulrushes – oil on panel – 14 x 16³/₄in.
(Skinner Inc.)   £8,091 $14,300

ELLEN A. FRANK (English, Exh. 1889–1912) – A gossip in the 'thirties – signed – oil on canvas – 26 x 38.1cm.
(Bonhams)   £500 $795

PIERRE JOSEPH CELESTIN FRANÇOIS (1759–1851) – The death of Marcus Curtius – signed – oil on panel – 66 x 51cm.
(Christie's)   £7,150 $11,654

BENGT FRANSSON (b. 1935) – View of Stockholm – signed – oil on canvas – 79 x 98cm.
(AB Stockholms Auktionsverk)   £640 $1,096

ROBERT WINCHESTER FRASER – On the Bure –
signed and dated *90* – pencil and watercolour heightened
with white – 9³/₄ x 19¹/₂in.
(Christie's) £792 $1,404

FRENCH SCHOOL (circa 1740) - A scene of sacrifice --
bears inscription – red chalk on watermarked Strasbourg
paper – 270 x 332mm.
(Christie's) £1,005 $1,668

FRENCH SCHOOL – King – oil on canvas – 120 x 69cm.
(Duran) £269 $473

FRENCH SCHOOL (circa 1800) – Portrait of a woman
wearing a white dress – oil on canvas laid down on board –
30.5 x 25.4cm.
(Butterfield & Butterfield) £504 $880

FRENCH SCHOOL – A noble family in the grounds of a
chateau – oil on canvas – 76.2 x 91.4cm.
(Christie's) £1,870 $2,917

FRENCH SCHOOL (mid-16th century) – Portrait of a lady, aged 36, bust length, wearing a black dress and head-dress embroidered with pearls – inscribed and dated *1559* – oil on panel – 21 x 16.5cm.
(Bonhams)   **£800 $1,272**

FRENCH SCHOOL – Woman with Cupid – oil on canvas – 120 x 88cm.
(Duran)   **£280 $493**

FRENCH SCHOOL (mid-18th century) – Portrait of a young girl, half length, standing at a stone ledge holding a basket of flowers – indistinctly signed and dated *1768* – oil on canvas – 52 x 43.8cm.
(Bonhams)   **£2,200 $3,498**

FRENCH SCHOOL – Classical ruins with a sailing vessel – bears date *1705* – oil on wood panel – 29 x 42in.
(Du Mouchelles)   **£1,459 $2,500**

FRENCH SCHOOL (19th century) – A Turkish
gentleman smoking a cigarette – oil on canvas – 63 x 45cm.
(Sotheby's)   **£2,420 $4,283**

FRENCH SCHOOL (17th century) – Portrait of Madame
de Chevreuze, full length, wearing a red and gold
embroidered dress – inscribed – oil on canvas, arched top –
189.3 x 111.8cm.
(Bonhams)   **£900 $1,431**

FRENCH SCHOOL (early 20th century) – Girls by a
flower stall – signed – oil – 17 x 22in.
(G.A. Key)   **£520 $829**

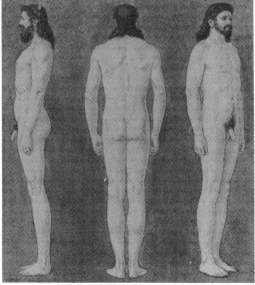

FRENCH SCHOOL (circa 1840) – Sketch for an
allegorical painting – oil on canvas – 34.9 x 61cm.
(Butterfield & Butterfield)   **£630 $1,100**

JARED FRENCH (b. 1905) – One man, three views –
signed – India ink and wash on paper – 20.3 x 19.1cm.
(Sotheby's)   **£1,382 $2,530**

FRENCH

CHARLES THEODORE FRERE (French, 1814–1888)
– Arab encampment – signed – oil on panel –
16.5 x 29.2cm.
(Butterfield & Butterfield)   £1,576 $2,750

LEONARD FRENCH (b. 1928) – The merry-go-round –
signed – enamel on board – 135.9 x 120cm.
(Christie's)   **£11,000 $19,360**

CHARLES-THEODORE FRERE (1814–1888) – A
street in Beirut – signed – oil on canvas – 61 x 49.2cm.
(Christie's)   **£6,160 $10,718**

CHARLES THEODORE FRERE (French, 1814–1888)
– Caravan entering an oasis, sunset – signed – oil on panel
– 7 x 5¼in.
(Skinner Inc.)   £809 $1,430

EDOUARD FRERE (1819–1886) – At grandmother's –
signed – oil on canvas – 65.5 x 54cm.
(Christie's)   **£3,960 $6,890**

LUCIAN FREUD (b. 1922) – Portrait of a man – oil on canvas – 24 x 19cm.
(Christie's) £126,500 $221,375

ARTHUR A. FRIEDENSON (1872–1955) – The artist's followers – signed and dated *81* – oil on canvas – 56 x 40.7cm.
(Christie's) £3,080 $5,452

ARNOLD FRIBERG (American, b. 1913) – In the land of the shining mountains – signed – oil on canvas – 32 x 26in.
(Skinner Inc.) £1,899 $3,300

FRIEDRICH FRIEDLANDER (1825–1901) – A good vintage – signed – oil on panel – 39.5 x 31.6cm.
(Christie's) £3,740 $6,508

RICHARD BERNHARDT LOUIS FRIESE (1854–1918)
– A polar bear in an Arctic landscape – signed and dated *99*
– oil on canvas – 89 x 162.5cm.
(Christie's) £6,600 $10,758

EMILE OTHON FRIESZ (1879–1949) – Fishing boats
putting into Honfleur – signed – watercolour on paper laid
down on card – 30.5 x 38.8cm.
(Christie's) £4,400 $7,128

ARNOLD FRIEDMAN (1879–1946) – Self portrait: and
three other works – the first, pencil on tan paper, unframed
– the second, pencil on brown paper, unframed – the third,
pen and ink on paper, unframed – the fourth, signed,
watercolour on paper (illustrated) – 48.8 x 36.3cm. and
smaller – four
(Christie's) £2,424 $4,180

DONALD FRIEND – Fruit and flowers – signed and dated
86 – watercolour – 57 x 75cm.
(Australian Art Auctions) £2,431 $4,315

FREDERICK TRAP FRIIS (1865–1909) – Santa Maria
Novella – bears artist's estate stamp on the stretcher – oil on
canvas – 53 x 53cm.
(Christie's) £3,509 $6,050

WILLIAM POWELL FRITH, R.A. (1819–1909) –
Norah Creina – signed and dated *1846* – oil on canvas –
oval – 33 x 26cm.
(Christie's) £3,850 $6,237

R. FRIGERIO – Man with pipe; Sicilian fisherman – oil
on canvas – 15 x 11in. – a pair
(Du Mouchelles) £195 $325

Attributed to WILLIAM POWELL FRITH – An elderly
gentleman and his two grandchildren, one holding his hat
for alms – 18 x 23cm.
(Spencer's) £420 $670

209

FRITH

WILLIAM POWELL FRITH (English, 1819–1909) – The family lawyer – signed – oil on canvas – 25 x 25in.
(Du Mouchelles) **£6,761 $12,000**

JESUS FUERTES (b. 1938) – Watermelon with limes – signed and dated *86* – oil on canvas – 50 x 70cm.
(Duran) **£2,786 $5,000**

ALBERT HENRY FULLWOOD – Peel Valley – signed – oil on board – 15 x 20cm.
(Australian Art Auctions) **£663 $1,177**

TERRY FROST (b. 1915) – Umber and grey figure – signed – oil on board – 88.5 x 43cm.
(Christie's) **£2,750 $4,812**

JOHANN HEINRICH FUSELI, HENRY FUSELI, R.A. (1741–1825) – An old prophet preaching – inscribed on the mount – pencil, grey and pale green wash – 160 x 130mm. – and seven other studies
(Christie's) **£3,300 $5,313**

PIETRO GABRINI (1865–1926) – Home again, Naples – signed and dated *1907* – oil on canvas – 64.1 x 111.1cm.
(Christie's) **£7,920 $13,781**

FRANS GAILLIARD (Belgian, 1861–1932) – The Madeleine, Paris – signed – oil on canvas – 65.5 x 50cm.
(Hôtel de Ventes Horta) **£4,194 $7,130**

CARL F. GAERTNER (b. 1898) – The ladle – signed and dated *1929* – oil on canvas – 101.5 x 101.5cm.
(Christie's) **£2,871 $4,950**

F. GAILLIARD (Belgian, 1861–1932) – The passage of Time – signed – oil on canvas – 55 x 68cm.
(Hôtel de Ventes Horta) **£3,065 $5,211**

THOMAS GAINSBOROUGH, R.A. (1727–1788) – A lady walking in a garden, holding her small child by the hand, possible a study for The Richmond Water-walk – black chalk and stump, heightened with white (partly in oil paint) on buff paper – 505 x 320mm.
(Christie's) **£616,000 $991,760**

GAINSBOROUGH

Follower of THOMAS GAINSBOROUGH – Elegant figures resting in a landscape; and Elegant figures on a terrace – oil on canvas – 29.3 x 34.4cm. – a pair
(Christie's) £660 $1,096

SIMON GALES – The college – signed and dated *Jan 1990* – polyptych – 61 x 53.3cm. opened
(Christie's) £2,200 $3,498

GALIEN LALOUE – By the Seine – bears signature – gouache – 19 x 30cm.
(Duran) £840 $1,479

EUGENE GALIEN-LALOUE (1854–1941) – Quai Malaquais, Paris – signed – charcoal and bodycolour on paper – 20 x 35cm.
(Christie's) £4,400 $7,700

EUGENE GALIEN-LALOUE (1854–1941) – The Quai du Louvre, Paris – signed – pencil and water colour heightened with white on paper – 27.6 x 35.2cm.
(Christie's) £5,500 $9,570

EUGENE GALIEN-LALOUE (1854–1941) – The Rive Gauche, Paris with Notre Dame beyond – signed – charcoal and bodycolour on card – 19.1 x 31.2cm.
(Christie's) £6,050 $10,527

EUGENE GALIEN-LALOUE (1854–1941) – Place de la République, Paris – signed – charcoal and bodycolour on paper – 19 x 30cm.
(Christie's) £6,380 $11,165

EUGENE GALIEN-LALOUE (French, 1854–1941) – La Madeleine; The flower market at the Madeleine, Paris – both signed – gouache – each 18 x 31cm. – a pair
(Sotheby's) **£13,200 $23,364**

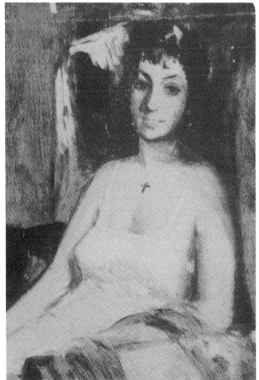

FRANÇOIS GALL (b. 1912) – Picture of a young woman – signed – oil on wood – 24 x 16cm.
(Lempertz) **£623 $994**

ROBERT GALLON (1845–1925) – A sailing boat on an estuary – signed – oil on canvas – 60.5 x 101cm.
(Christie's) **£3,300 $5,346**

ROBERT GALLON (1845–1925) – Feeding the chickens – signed – oil on canvas – 51 x 76cm.
(Christie's) **£4,950 $8,019**

ROBERT GALLON (1845–1925) – Children playing by a river – signed and dated *1882* – oil on canvas – 61 x 101.5cm.
(Christie's) **£6,050 $9,801**

EMIL GANSO (1895–1941) – Reclining female nudes – each signed – the first pencil on paper, the second pastel and pencil on paper – each unframed – 40.6 x 55.9cm. and 39.4 x 62.9cm. – two
(Sotheby's) **£481 $880**

GARDELL-ERICSON

ANNA GARDELL-ERICSON (Swedish, 1853–1939) –
In the Bois de Boulogne, Paris – signed and dated *1883* –
watercolour – 26 x 36cm.
(Sotheby's) £5,280 $9,346

WILLIAM FRASER GARDEN – The old sheepwash at
Bedford – signed – watercolour heightened with white –
11 x 15in.
(Christie's) £770 $1,364

WILLIAM FRASER GARDEN (1856–1921) – In the
wood; and The wood at dusk – both signed and dated *1885*
and *1884* respectively – watercolour and gum arabic –
273 x 382mm. – a pair
(Christie's) £11,000 $18,590

DEREK GEORGE MONTAGUE GARDNER – Golden
Fleece – signed, inscribed on reverse – oil on canvas –
61 x 91.4cm.
(Bonhams) £3,100 $5,115

WILLIAM FRASER GARDEN – The Ferry Boat Inn,
Holywell – signed and dated *1908* – watercolour –
18.4 x 26.8cm.
(Bonhams) £920 $1,463

DEREK GEORGE MONTAGUE GARDNER – Driving
hard, the Cutty Sark – signed and dated *1965* – oil on
canvas – 61 x 76.2cm.
(Bonhams) £1,600 $2,640

VALENTINE THOMAS GARLAND (fl. 1884–1903) –
A fox terrier puppy with a ball – signed and dated *1895* –
oil on panel – 24.2 x 33cm.
(Christie's)   **£1,100 $1,947**

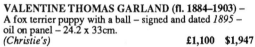

ALETHEA GARSTIN (1894–1978) – Guiness's boat,
Dublin – signed – oil on panel – 9¹/₂ x 13in.
(David Lay)   **£2,500 $3,975**

JULES-ARSENE GARNIER (1847–1889) – In the park –
signed and dated *1880* – oil on canvas – 97.5 x 76.5cm.
(Christie's)   **£5,500 $9,570**

NORMAN GARSTIN, N.E.A. (1847–1926) – A winter's
day street scene – signed – watercolour – 7 x 10in.
(David Lay)   **£650 $1,168**

Follower of HENRI GASCARS – Portrait of a sportsman, standing three-quarter length in a red tunic a blue coat and a feathered hat, holding a musket – oil on panel – 29.2 x 22.8cm.
(Christie's)   **£1,045 $1,630**

HENRY GASSER (1909–1981) – A side balcony – signed – watercolour on paper – 36.9 x 21.6cm.
(Christie's)   **£497 $880**

LEON GASPARD (1882–1964) – Ergeyevsky Lavore, monastery – signed – oil on board – 55.9 x 45.7cm.
(Butterfield & Butterfield)   **£14,183 $24,750**

HENRY GASSER (1909–81) – Feeding the chickens – signed – oil on canvas – 50.8 x 61cm.
(Sotheby's)   **£1,262 $2,310**

HENRY GASSER (1909–1981) – Mountain road – signed – oil on board – 22.9 x 30.5cm.
(Christie's) **£994 $1,760**

HENRY MARTIN GASSER (American, 1909–1981) – Winter harbour – signed – watercolour and gouache on paper/board – 19 x 23³/₄in.
(Skinner Inc.) **£669 $1,182**

HENRY GASSER (1909–1981) – Hoboken, New Jersey – signed – oil on canvas laid down on masonite – 58.5 x 92.8cm.
(Christie's) **£1,554 $2,750**

HENRY GASSER (1909–81) – The house by the tracks – signed – watercolour on paper – 38.1 x 55.9cm.
(Sotheby's) **£571 $1,045**

HENRY GASSER (1909–81) – After the storm – signed – watercolour on paper laid down on board – 60.3 x 81.3cm.
(Sotheby's) **£721 $1,320**

A. GATES – The Snaicow – signed – oil on canvas – 34¹/₄ x 57¹/₂in.
(Christie's) **£3,062 $5,280**

GAUDIER-BRZESKA

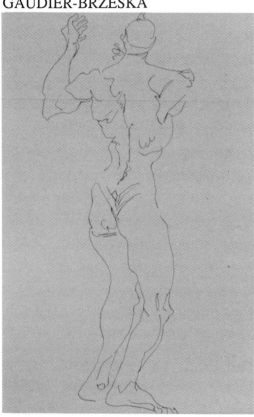

HENRI GAUDIER-BRZESKA (1891–1915) – Seated
female study – pen and black ink – unframed –
25.3 x 38.5cm.
(Christie's) £1,210 $2,009

HENRI GAUDIER-BRZESKA (1891–1915) – Standing
nude, arms raised – pen and black ink – unframed –
38.5 x 25.5cm.
(Christie's) £935 $1,552

MALCOLM GAVIN (b. 1874) – Young ladies arranging
daffodils – signed – oil on canvas – 76.8 x 63.5cm.
(Fraser–Pinneys) £1,805 $3,132

CLAUDE GAUTHEROT (French, 1796–1825) –
Napoléon wounded before Ratisbonne – inscribed on
reverse – oil on canvas – 28 x 43cm.
(Sotheby's) £7,700 $13,629

WALTER GAY (1856–1937) – The recital – signed – oil on canvas – 46.4 x 38.1cm.
(Sotheby's) **£2,164 $3,960**

EDOUARD GELHAY – In the park – signed – oil on canvas – 33 x 42cm.
(Christie's) **£1,100 $1,901**

OTTO FRIEDRICH GEBLER (1838–1917) – A shepherdess with sheep and cattle by a pool – signed and dated *1882* – oil on panel – 55 x 68cm.
(Christie's) **£16,500 $28,875**

JULES VICTOR GENISSON (Belgian, 1805–60) – Figures in the choir of a cathedral – signed and dated *1849* – oil on canvas – 119 x 98cm.
(Sotheby's) **£1,980 $3,505**

AUGUST GEIGER (1847–1910) – The visiting salesman – signed and dated *1878* – oil on canvas laid down on board – 57.8 x 35.6cm.
(Christie's) **£5,500 $9,570**

CESARE GENNARI (1637–1688) – Saint John the Baptist – oil on canvas, in an elaborate baroque carved and gilt wood frame – 70 x 60cm.
(Sotheby's) **£9,900 $17,820**

LILLIAN GENTH (1876–1953) – In a Spanish garden –
signed – oil on canvas – 73.7 x 88.9cm.
(Butterfield & Butterfield)   £5,358 $9,350

LILLIAN GENTH (1876–1953) – Springtime – signed – oil
on canvas – 99 x 127cm.
(Christie's)   £1,864 $3,300

After ORAZIO GENTILESCHI (Italian, 1562–1647) –
The finding of Moses – oil on canvas laid down on panel –
104.1 x 128.3cm.
(Butterfield & Butterfield)   £4,413 $7,700

THEODORE GERARD – A Continental town square,
with figures and animals beside a well, a dog in the
foreground, and the village beyond – signed and dated 1882
– 102 x 64cm.
(Spencer's)   £2,700 $4,698

GERMAN SCHOOL (1894–1895) – A fan decorated with
figure studies by Theodore Esser (1868–1937), and others –
all signed and some dated 1894/5 – oil on panel – the board
on which the fan is mounted 61.5 x 61.5cm.
(Christie's)   £2,750 $4,785

GERMAN SCHOOL (19th century) – A family portrait –
oil on canvas – 126 x 168cm.
(Sotheby's) **£4,180 $7,399**

GERMAN SCHOOL, late 17th century – Portrait of
Cardinal Lothar Heinrich von Offernich, standing three-
quarter length, holding a letter – oil on canvas –
150 x 112cm.
(Christie's) **£1,045 $1,630**

GERMAN SCHOOL (circa 1740) – A conversation piece
of a large family in a palace interior – oil on canvas –
65 x 80.5cm.
(Sotheby's) **£10,450 $18,810**

GERMAN SCHOOL (19th century) – An extensive
landscape with children at a well – oil on canvas –
57.2 x 90.2cm.
(Christie's) **£1,045 $1,797**

GERMAN SCHOOL (circa 1770–1780) – Venus rising –
gouache on vellum – 360 x 280mm.
(Christie's) **£5,583 $9,268**

GERMAN/AUSTRIAN

GERMAN/AUSTRIAN SCHOOL (circa 1850–1860) –
Les amateurs musiciens – oil on canvas – 42 x 49.5cm.
(Butterfield & Butterfield) £2,206 $3,850

FRANCOIS GEROME (French, 20th century) – A cafe
in St. Germain des Pres – signed and inscribed – oil on
canvas – 50.8 x 61cm.
(Butterfield & Butterfield) £2,049 $3,575

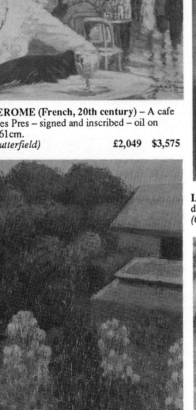

MARK GERTLER (1891–1939) – A summer garden –
signed and dated *37* – oil on canvas – 61 x 50.9cm.
(Christie's) £6,050 $10,043

LEO GESTEL (1881–1944) – On the stage – signed and
dated *04* – oil on canvas – 50 x 25.5cm.
(Christie's) £6,183 $10,952

LEO GESTEL (1881–1944) – A reclining nude – stamped
– gouache on paper – 69 x 98.5cm.
(Christie's) £2,750 $4,868

222

Circle of MARCUS GHEERAERTS (British, 1561–1636) – Portrait of a nobleman – oil on canvas – 105.4 x 80.6cm.
(Butterfield & Butterfield) £1,576 $2,750

Attributed to ANGELOS GIALLINA (b. 1857) – Pondikonísi and Vlakherné off Kanóni, Corfu – with inscription – pencil and watercolour on paper – 19 x 28cm.
(Christie's) £1,760 $3,062

GIUSEPPE GIARDIELLO (late 19th century) – Preparing the nets, Naples; and The return from fishing, Naples – both signed – oil on canvas – 26.7 x 43.2cm. – a pair
(Christie's) £5,500 $9,570

W. GIBBONS (circa 1875) – After the battle – signed and dated *1875* – oil on canvas – 88.8 x 112.4cm.
(Christie's) £1,650 $2,937

CHARLES GIBBS (fl. 1878–1899) – On the hill – signed and dated *1892* – oil on canvas –76.2 x 57.2cm.
(Christie's) £3,080 $4,990

JOHN GIBSON, R.A. (1790–1866) – Cupid and Psyche – pen and brown ink heightened with white on brown paper – unframed – 190 x 300mm.
(Christie's) £1,760 $2,834

GIACINTO GIGANTE (1806–1876) – Lago Il Fusaro,
Naples – signed and dated *1833* – bodycolour on paper –
unframed – 18.7 x 26.6cm.
(Christie's) £3,520 $6,125

Attributed to RICHARD GIBSON – A lady, believed to
be Queen Anne, seated in an open classical landscape by a
tree with armour in the foreground – inscribed – 72 x 44in.
(Boardman) £3,700 $6,290

**REGIS FRANCIS GIGNOUX (French/ American,
1816–1882)** – Hudson River – signed and dated *1858* – oil
on canvas – 14 x 20in.
(Skinner Inc.) £8,230 $14,300

JOHN GIFFORD – Gun dogs at rest – signed – oil on
canvas – 35¹/₂ x 27¹/₂in.
(The Auction Galleries, Berwick) £1,700 $2,890

SIR JOHN GILBERT, R.A., P.R.W.S. – Scenes from Gil
Blas – both signed with monogram – watercolour –
5³/₄ x 8in. – a pair
(Bearne's) £370 $642

GILBERT and GEORGE (b. 1934 and 1942) – Helping Hands – signed, inscribed and dated *1982* – hand-dyed photographs mounted on masonite frames – 241 x 201cm.
(Christie's) **£35,200 $62,304**

MINNIE F.W. GILBERT (fl. 1889) – Arranging flowers – signed – oil on canvas – 38 x 30.5cm.
(Christie's) **£1,650 $3,003**

VICTOR GABRIEL GILBERT (1847–1933) – A vegetable stand, at Les Halles Centrales, Paris – signed and dated *1878* – oil on canvas – 46 x 54.5cm.
(Christie's) **£30,800 $50,204**

JACOB GILDOR (Israeli, 20th century) – Cafe scene –
signed – gouache and oil on paper laid down on canvas –
69.9 x 77.5cm.
(Butterfield & Butterfield)   **£946 $1,650**

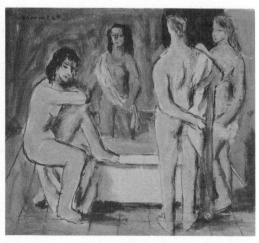

J. WILLIAM GILROY – The farm children – signed – oil
on canvas – 23¹/₂ x 27¹/₂in.
(The Auction Galleries, Berwick)   **£3,000 $5,100**

WILHELM GIMMI (Swiss, 1886–1965) – Women in a
bath – signed and dated *1964* – oil on paper –
43.5 x 53.5cm.
(Germann)   **£2,367 $4,000**

LUCA GIORDANO (1632–1705) – A philosopher – oil on canvas – 121.5 x 96cm.
(Sotheby's) **£11,000 $19,800**

CHARLES GINNER, A.R.A. (1878–1952) – The corner of the kitchen – signed – pen, black ink and watercolour – 35 x 23cm.
(Christie's) **£2,200 $3,652**

FRANCESCO GIOLI – Crossing the stream – signed and dated *1873* – oil on canvas – unframed – 66.1 x 39.3cm.
(Christie's) **£14,300 $24,710**

SEBASTIEN-CHARLES GIRAUD (1819–1892) – Preparing the hookah – signed – oil on panel – 53.3 x 39.4cm.
(Christie's) **£25,300 $41,239**

GLACKENS

WILLIAM GLACKENS (1870–1938) – Colonel Roosevelt and the Charge of the Rough Riders – pencil on paper – 29.1 x 39.5cm.
(Christie's) **£808 $1,430**

WILLIAM J. GLACKENS (1870–1938) – The attack of the blockhouse at El Caney – signed – pen and wash heightened with china white on paper, en grisaille – 43.2 x 33.7cm.
(Christie's) **£1,180 $2,090**

FRITZ GLARNER (Swiss, b. 1899) – The pink scarf – signed and dated *1929* – oil on canvas – unframed – 96 x 81cm.
(Butterfield & Butterfield) **£4,728 $8,250**

WILLIAM JAMES GLACKENS (1870–1938) - The Princess – signed – crayon on paper – 34 x 21.9cm.
(Christie's) **£1,276 $2,200**

HUGH DE TWENEBROKES GLAZEBROOK (1855–1937) – Rosaline – signed, inscribed and dated *1900* – oil on canvas – 57.1 x 41.9cm.
(Christie's) **£6,600 $12,012**

WILFRID GABRIEL DE GLEHN, R.A. (1870–1951) –
Summer meadow – signed – oil on canvas – 53 x 69cm.
(Christie's) **£2,310 $3,973**

ALBERT GLEIZES (1881–1953) – Domestic painting –
signed and dated *24* – oil on canvas – 102.5 x 77.5cm.
(Lempertz) **£138,408 $220,761**

ALBERT GLEIZES (1881–1953) – Toul landscape –
signed and dated *14* – gouache on paper – 29.7 x 23.5cm.
(Christie's) **£25,300 $44,528**

ALBERT GLEIZES (1881–1953) – Riverside – signed
and dated *06* – oil on canvas – 48.5 x 65cm.
(Christie's) **£12,100 $19,602**

ALBERT GLEIZES (1881–1953) – Composition – signed
and dated *22* – gouache on paper – 42 x 31cm.
(Christie's) **£17,600 $30,976**

ALFRED AUGUSTUS GLENDENING (1861–1907) –
Summer flowers – signed with monogram and dated *1903* –
pencil and watercolour heightened with white –
533 x 762mm.
(Christie's) £5,500 $9,295

HENRY GILLARD GLINDONI (1852–1913) – Fan
flirtation – signed and dated *1908* – oil on canvas –
86.2 x 111.5cm.
(Christie's) £6,050 $9,801

JOHN GLOVER – Greenwich, a panoramic view of the
hospital, river and London – watercolour over traces of
pencil – 41.3 x 58.9cm.
(Woolley & Wallis) £4,500 $7,695

ALFRED AUGUSTUS GLENDENING (fl. 1861–1903)
– A view in Kent – signed and dated *1870* – oil on canvas –
61 x 106.7cm.
(Christie's) £7,480 $13,240

ALFRED AUGUSTUS GLENDENING (fl. 1861–1903)
– Changing pasture – signed with initials and dated *74* – oil
on canvas – 30.5 x 40.6cm.
(Christie's) £2,200 $4,004

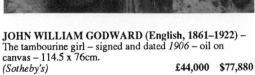

ALFRED AUGUSTUS GLENDENING (fl. 1861–1903)
– A view of Wrexham, North Wales – signed – oil on
canvas – 45.5 x 76cm.
(Christie's) £6,600 $10,692

JOHN WILLIAM GODWARD (English, 1861–1922) –
The tambourine girl – signed and dated *1906* – oil on
canvas – 114.5 x 76cm.
(Sotheby's) £44,000 $77,880

FREDERICK E.J. GOFF – Shipping before Tower
Bridge – signed and inscribed – watercolour –
11.4 x 15.3cm.
(Bonhams) £750 $1,193

JOHN WILLIAM GODWARD (1861–1922) – Lucilia –
signed and dated*1917* – oil on canvas, painted in a circle –
49.5 x 49.5cm.
(Christie's) £17,600 $29,920

ELLING WILLIAM GOLLINGS (American, 1878–
1932) – Cowboy on a horse with steer – signed and dated
1911 – watercolour – 12 x 10in.
(Du Mouchelles) £2,402 $4,000

FREDERICK E.J. GOFF (1855–1931) – Saint Paul's
from Bankside; Blackfriar's Bridge; and Westminster
Abbey – all signed – pencil and watercolour with touches
of white heightening – 118 x 156mm. and slightly smaller –
three
(Christie's) £3,300 $6,006

EDWARD ALFRED GOODALL – Venetian scene with
sailing barges – impressed signature – watercolour over
pencil – 28 x 46.6cm.
(Woolley & Wallis) £520 $926

EDWARD ANGELO GOODALL, (1819–1908) – Army officers playing cards – signed and dated *1863* – pencil and watercolour – 372 x 562mm.
(Christie's) £825 $1,501

FREDERICK GOODALL, R.A. (1822–1904) – The way from the village, Time of Inundation – signed with monogram and dated *1883* – oil on panel – 50.1 x 76.2cm.
(Christie's) £1,540 $2,726

FREDERICK GOODALL, R.A. (1822–1904) – Rachel and her flock – signed with monogram and dated *1893* – pencil and watercolour heightened with white – 330 x 749mm.
(Christie's) £825 $1,394

EDWARD ANGELO GOODALL (1819–1908) – Notre Dame from the Left Bank by moonlight – signed and dated *1864* – pencil and watercolour heightened with bodycolour – 369 x 572mm.
(Christie's) £1,650 $2,673

FREDERICK GOODALL (1822 – 1904) – The Favourite Melody – signed and dated 1863 – watercolour – 15¹/₂ x 26in.
(W.H. Lane & Son) £2,300 $3,887

JOHN STRICKLAND GOODALL (b. 1908) – Young girls reading in an orchard – signed – pencil and watercolour with touches of white heightening – 156 x 184mm.
(Christie's) £770 $1,247

ALBERT GOODWIN (1845–1932) – Clovelly – signed and inscribed – pencil, pen and ink and watercolour heightened with bodycolour – 228 x 301mm.
(Christie's) £2,420 $4,404

JOHN STRICKLAND GOODALL (b. 1908) – On the way to the beach – signed – pencil and watercolour with touches of white heightening – 184 x 207mm.
(Christie's) £770 $1,247

ALBERT GOODWIN (1845–1932) – Woolacombe Sands, North Devon – signed and inscribed – watercolour and bodycolour – 190 x 247mm.
(Christie's) £1,650 $2,673

ALBERT GOODWIN (1845–1932) – The Lady of Shalott – inscribed on the mount – pencil and watercolour with scratching out – 350 x 502mm.
(Christie's) £3,300 $6,006

ALBERT GOODWIN (1845–1932) – A baptism of flowers; Youth is full of sport; Age's breath is short – signed and dated 77 – oil on canvas – 92.7 x 141.6cm.
(Christie's) £19,800 $33,660

ALBERT GOODWIN, R.W.S. – The lady of Shalot – watercolour – 14 x 20in.
(Bearne's) £2,300 $3,990

HARRY GOODWIN – Old houses on the Reuss, Lucerne – signed with monogram and dated *1907?* – pencil and watercolour heightened with white – 9½ x 13¾in.
(Christie's) £385 $682

ALBERT GOODWIN, R.W.S. (1845–1932) – The Gardens, Pallanza, Lago Maggiore – signed – pencil, pen and black ink and watercolour – 282 x 390mm.
(Christie's) £2,640 $4,462

ALBERT GOODWIN (1845–1932) – Sun rising at Clovelly – signed and dated *1924* and inscribed – pen and black ink, black chalk and watercolour – 387 x 568mm.
(Christie's) £3,520 $6,406

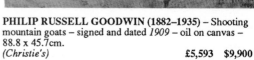

HARRY GOODWIN (circa 1840–1925) – Fribourg, Switzerland – signed with monogram and dated *1892–4* – pencil and watercolour – 337 x 502mm.
(Christie's) £1,870 $3,029

PHILIP RUSSELL GOODWIN (1882–1935) – Shooting mountain goats – signed and dated *1909* – oil on canvas – 88.8 x 45.7cm.
(Christie's) £5,593 $9,900

GEORGE TURLAND GOOSEY – Fishing Boats, St Ives
Harbour – signed – oil on board – 11^{1}/$_{2}$ x 15^{1}/$_{2}$in.
(W.H. Lane & Son) **£380 $642**

THOMAS COOPER GOTCH (1854–1931) – The sailor's
farewell – signed and dated *1887* – oil on canvas –
40^{1}/$_{4}$ x 27^{1}/$_{4}$in.
(W.H. Lane & Son) **£5,000 $8,075**

ROBERT JAMES GORDON (fl. 1871–1893) – Portrait
of Peggy, bust length, wearing a white bonnet – oil on
canvas – 45.8 x 35.5cm.
(Christie's) **£1,540 $2,726**

FREDERICK GORE, R.A. (b. 1913) – The roofs of
Forne Lutx, Majorca – signed – oil on canvas –
81 x 102cm.
(Christie's) **£4,400 $7,304**

JEAN RICHARD GOUBIE (French, 1842–99) – Lady
on horseback with artist, easel and dog – signed and dated
1890 – oil on canvas – 14 x 10^{3}/$_{4}$in.
(Du Mouchelles) **£8,681 $15,000**

COLIN GRAEME – The head of a bay mare with an
English setter and a hound in an open landscape – signed
and dated *1900* – oil on canvas – 40.5 x 35.5cm.
(*Christie's*)   **£990 $1,599**

MARY GOW (1851–1929) – Portrait of a young girl – oil
on canvas – 75.5 x 53.5cm.
(*Christie's*)   **£1,705 $2,933**

COLIN GRAEME (late 19th century) – Deer hounds –
signed and dated *93* – oil on canvas – 51 x 40.5cm.
(*Christie's*)   **£990 $1,752**

GERALD GRACE (b. 1918) – Interlude – signed – oil on
canvas – 66 x 55.9cm.
(*Butterfield & Butterfield*)   **£378 $660**

COLIN GRAEME – The end of the day – signed – oil on
canvas – 61 x 51cm.
(*Christie's*)   **£2,090 $3,375**

PETER GRAHAM, R.A. (1836–1921) – The seabird's resting place – signed and dated *1879* – oil on canvas – 108.6 x 166.4cm.
(Christie's) **£8,800 $14,256**

FRANÇOIS-MARIUS GRANET (1775–1849) – A monastery near Rome – signed – oil on panel – 35.5 x 44.5cm.
(Christie's) **£1,650 $2,871**

FREDERIC M. GRANT (b. 1886) – Venice – signed and dated *1913* – oil on canvas – unframed – 91.4 x 64.8cm.
(Sotheby's) **£481 $880**

GOTTHARD GRAUBNER (b. 1930) – Untitled – signed and dated *88* – acrylic on foam-filled canvas – unframed – 192 x 178cm.
(Christie's) **£26,400 $46,728**

CLEMENT ROLLINS GRANT (American, 1849–1893) – Reverie, profile of a seated woman – inscribed – oil on panel – 10³/₄ x 5⁷/₈in.
(Skinner Inc.) **£295 $522**

ABBOTT FULLER GRAVES (1859–1936) – Kingsbury House, Kennebunk, Maine – signed – oil on canvas – 63.5 x 76.2cm.
(Sotheby's) **£6,111 $11,000**

MORRIS GRAVES (b. 1910) – Pansy in pitcher – signed
– gouache and marker on paper – 26 x 26.7cm.
(Sotheby's) **£1,262 $2,310**

MORRIS GRAVES (b. 1910) – Winter bouquet – signed
and dated *73* – tempera on paper – 34.3 x 22.5cm.
(Christie's) **£5,423 $9,350**

H. BARNARD GRAY (fl. 1844–1871) – A woodpigeon
with a robin standing by – signed and dated *1856* – oil on
canvas – 30.5 x 46.5cm.
(Christie's) **£935 $1,515**

JACK. L. GRAY (American, 20th century) -- Fishing
schooner and dorymen – signed – oil on canvas – 30 x 40in.
(Eldred's) **£1,909 $3,300**

ULF GREDER (b. 1949) – East Battery, palm lined
residential street – signed – oil on canvas – 74 x 119cm.
(AB Stockholms Auktionsverk) **£716 $1,227**

CHARLES GREEN (1840–1898) – A game of chess –
signed with initials and dated *1874* – pencil and
watercolour heightened with white – 180 x 257mm.
(Christie's) **£1,705 $2,762**

ROLAND GREEN (1892–1972) – Snipe over the marshes; and Teal in flight – signed – pencil and watercolour heightened with white – 267 x 375mm.
(Christie's)   **£1,430 $2,317**

FRANCES GREENMAN (American, b. 1890) – Portrait of a seated girl – oil on canvas – 25 x 20in.
(Du Mouchelles)   **£1,013 $1,750**

ROBERT GREENHAM (1906–1975) – Dancers resting – signed with initials – oil on board – 18 x 23cm.
(Christie's)   **£2,090 $3,469**

C.F. GREGORY (Australian, 1815–1885) – The American ship Rutland – signed – watercolour - 18 x 24in.
(Eldred's)   **£2,228 $3,850**

ROBERT GREENHAM (1906–1975) – Henley Regatta – signed with initials – oil on board – 21.5 x 29cm.
(Christie's)   **£1,210 $2,009**

EDWARD JOHN GREGORY (1850–1909) – A study for 'Boulter's Lock' – signed – oil on paper laid down on panel – 31.1 x 51.4cm.
(Christie's)   **£2,420 $4,404**

GEORGE GREGORY (1849–1938) – Off the Needles,
Isle of Wight – signed and dated *1899* – oil on canvas –
71.2 x 51.4cm.
(Christie's) £3,520 $6,266

JAN GRIFFIER (Dutch 1645–1718) – Extensive
landscape with view of the Rhine and village scene – oil on
canvas – 50 x 63cm.
(Hôtel de Ventes Horta) £14,655 $25,500

SIR ROGER DE GREY (b. 1918) – Girl with a fan –
signed with initials – oil on canvas – 76 x 107cm.
(Christie's) £935 $1,552

KENNETH A. GRIFFIN (20th century) – The iron ship
Invercargill passing Start Point – signed – oil on canvas –
66 x 91.4cm.
(Christie's) £2,420 $4,308

BERNARD FINEGAN GRIBBLE (1873–1962) – A
cargo ship weighing anchor – signed and dated *94* – oil on
canvas – 71.1 x 91.4cm.
(Christie's) £1,210 $2,154

Circle of ABEL GRIMMER – The interior of a gothic
cathedral – bears signature and date on the gravestone *PN/
A: 1615* – oil on canvas – 36 x 47.5cm.
(Sotheby's) £8,580 $15,444

JOHN ATKINSON GRIMSHAW (1836–1893) – The lady of Shalott – signed and dated *1878XX* – oil on canvas – 82.5 x 122cm.
(Christie's) **£33,000** **$56,100**

JOHN ATKINSON GRIMSHAW (1836–1893) – Iris – signed – oil on canvas – 71 x 91.5cm.
(Christie's) **£25,300** **$43,010**

JOHN ATKINSON GRIMSHAW (1836–1893) – A shepherd with his flock in a mountainous lake landscape – signed and dated *1865* – oil on canvas – 44.5 x 59.7cm.
(Christie's) **£35,200** **$59,840**

CHARLES JOSEPH GRIPS (1852–1920) – Maternal love – signed and dated *1875* – oil on panel – 38.5 x 30.5cm.
(Christie's) **£5,500** **$9,625**

JOHN ATKINSON GRIMSHAW (1836–1893) – The trysting gate – signed and dated *1877* – oil on board – 28.5 x 44cm.
(Christie's) **£4,950** **$8,019**

FERDINAND E. GRONE, R.B.A. (Exh. 1888–1919) – Fishing weather – signed – oil on panel – 6¹/2 x 9¹/2in.
(David Lay) **£460** **$827**

GRONE

FERDINAND E. GRONE (Exh. 1888–1919) – On the Alder – signed – oil on board – 5¹/2 x 9¹/2in.
(David Lay) £320 $575

WILLIAM GROPPER (1897–1977) – Senate Series #100 – signed – oil on canvas – 24.2 x 19cm.
(Christie's) £1,367 $2,420

WILLIAM GROPPER (1897–1977) – The pedlars - signed – oil on canvas – 40.6 x 51.4cm.
(Christie's) £2,486 $4,400

FLORIAN GROSPIETSCH (German, 1789–1830) – Orpheus charming the animals – signed with monogram and dated *1821* – oil on canvas – 46 x 57cm.
(Sotheby's) £6,600 $11,682

WILLIAM GROPPER (1897–1977) – The preview – signed – gouache and brush and black ink on paper – 48.5 x 68.9cm.
(Christie's) £1,404 $2,420

CHAIM GROSS (1904–91) – The lute player – signed and dated *1963* – watercolour and ink on paper laid down on board – 18.4 x 56.5cm.
(Sotheby's) £1,262 $2,310

Follower of HENRI-JULES-CHARLES CORNEILLE DE GROUX (1867–1930) – Neptune – oil on canvas – 90 x 200cm.
(Christie's) £3,850 $6,699

ADELCHI DE GROSSI – An Italian beauty in festive costume – signed – pencil and watercolour heightened with white – 21 x 14in.
(Christie's) £638 $1,102

CHARLES PAUL GRUPPE (American, 1860–1940) – After a shower, the water tub – signed – oil on canvasboard – 12 x 16in.
(Skinner Inc.) £560 $990

EMILE ALBERT GRUPPE (1896–1978) – Street scene – signed and dated *1931* – oil on masonite – unframed – 61 x 76.2cm.
(Sotheby's) £1,503 $2,750

GEORGE GROSZ (1893–1959) – Fight between palettes & brushes – signed – watercolour on paper – 66.5 x 48.2cm.
(Christie's) £4,785 $8,250

EMILE ALBERT GRUPPE (American, 1896–1978) – Smith's Cove, Gloucester Harbour – signed – oil on canvasboard – 10 x 12in.
(Skinner Inc.) £886 $1,540

GIACOMO DE GUARDI (1764–1835) – In Venice; a
view of Sta Maria della Salute – signed on reverse –
gouache – 12.2 x 23.5cm.
(Lempertz) **£4,965 $8,440**

EMILE A. GRUPPE (1896–1978) – The boathouse –
signed – oil on canvasboard – 40 x 50.7cm.
(Christie's) **£1,491 $2,640**

**Attributed to PIERRE NARCISSE GUERIN (French,
1774–1833)** – Achilles' quarrel with Agamemnon – oil on
canvas – 112 x 146cm.
(Sotheby's) **£15,950 $28,231**

EMILE ALBERT GRUPPE (1896–1978) – Fishing boats
at dock – signed – oil on canvas – 45.7 x 50.8cm.
(Sotheby's) **£1,262 $2,310**

Follower of GIACOMO GUARDI – The Dogana and the
entrance to the Grand Canal, Venice – oil on canvas laid
down on panel – 26.6 x 30.5cm.
(Bonhams) **£2,000 $3,180**

R GUIETTE (1893–1976) – Composition with guitar –
signed – heightening with watercolour and gouache –
47 x 36cm.
(Hôtel de Ventes Horta) **£2,931 $5,100**

GUSTAVE GUILLAUMET (French, 1840–1887) – A
Moorish woman, seated – signed – sanguine on paper laid
down on board – 23.7 x 27.1cm.
(Butterfield & Butterfield) £630 **$1,100**

ARMAND GUILLAUMIN (1841–1927) – The Seine
Embankment at Paris, view of Notre-Dame – signed – oil
on canvas – 54.3 x 65cm.
(Christie's) £20,000 **$35,200**

ARMAND GUILLAUMIN (1841–1927) – House in a
landscape - signed – oil on canvas – 36.9 x 44.9cm.
(Christie's) £17,600 **$28,512**

ARMAND GUILLAUMIN (1841–1927) – The Seine at
Alfortville – signed – oil on canvas – 53 x 72cm.
(Christie's) £66,000 **$106,920**

ARMAND GUILLAUMIN (1841–1927) – On the Sedelle
heights – signed – oil on canvas – 60 x 80.8cm.
(Christie's) £13,200 **$21,384**

E.T. GUILLERMOT (late 19th century) – La Quai de la
Tournelle, Paris – signed – oil on canvas – 38.4 x 61.2cm.
(Christie's) £1,375 **$2,392**

RENATO GUTTUSO (1912–1987) – Autumnal still life –
signed and dated *1982* – oil and acrylic on canvas –
60 x 58cm.
(Finarte) £15,936 $27,171

SIR HERBERT JAMES GUNN, R.A. (1893–1964) – La
Belle – signed and dated *1912* – oil on canvas-board –
33 x 23cm.
(Christie's) £4,400 $7,304

**Attributed to CONSTANTIN GUYS (French, 1802–
1892)** – The turn-out – watercolour on paper – 25 x 38cm.
(Butterfield & Butterfield) £630 $1,100

HERBERT JACOB GUTE (1908–1977) – The
blacksmith– signed and dated *1939* - oil on board –
61 x 50.8cm.
(Butterfield & Butterfield) £1,261 $2,200

GIUSEPPE GUZZARDI (d. 1914) – Waiting for the
showers; and Off to market – both signed – oil on canvas –
31.1 x 21.9cm. – a pair
(Christie's) £2,200 $3,828

ROBERT GWATHMEY (b. 1903) – Study for Muse,
1967 – signed – oil on canvas – 25.4 x 40.6cm.
(Christie's)   £4,972 $8,800

ROBERT GWATHMEY (b. 1903) – Girl with a guitar --
signed – oil on canvas – 40.6 x 50.7cm.
(Christie's)   £2,983 $5,280

REMIGIUS VAN HAANEN (Dutch, 1812–94) – Figures
by a channel – oil on canvas – 50 x 63cm.
(Sotheby's)   £6,600 $11,682

ADRIANA-JOHANNA HAANEN (Dutch, 1814–95) – A
still life of flowers and peaches – signed with initials and
dated 1850 – oil on panel – 30 x 25cm.
(Sotheby's)   £9,900 $17,523

MAURITZ FREDERIK HENDRIK DE HAAS (1832–
1895) – Shipping off the coast – signed and dated 1875 –
oil on canvas – 61 x 101.6cm.
(Christie's)   £17,864 $30,800

HACKER

ARTHUR HACKER (1858–1919) – A morning walk –
signed and dated *1902* – oil on panel – 43.1 x 43.1cm.
(Christie's) **£5,400 $9,180**

KEELEY HALSWELLE, A.R.S.A. (1832–1891) –
Waiting for the blessing of Pius IX at St John Lateran,
Rome, 1869 – signed and dated *1869–78* –
145.5 x 233.8cm.
(Christie's) **£16,500 $26,730**

M. HAGEMANS (Belgian, 1852–1917) – The turkeys –
signed – watercolour on paper – 50 x 80cm.
(Hôtel de Ventes Horta) **£2,096 $3,565**

**HAMILTON HAMILTON (Anglo-American, 1847–
1928)** – Woman feeding sheep – signed – oil on canvas –
30 x 36in.
(Du Mouchelles) **£2,043 $3,500**

ERIC HALLSTRÖM (1893–1946) – Playground, winter
scene – signed – oil on canvas – 57 x 66cm.
(AB Stockholms Auktionsverk) **£1,814 $3,102**

**Attributed to JOHANN GEORGE DE HAMILTON
(1672–1737)** – A piebald stallion in a landscape –
indistinctly inscribed by a later hand on reverse and dated
1730 – oil on canvas – 42 x 57cm.
(Sotheby's) **£1,980 $3,564**

ARTHUR HENRY KNIGHTON HAMMOND – A
sunlit street – signed – watercolour – 16¼ x 12¼in.
(Bearne's) £620 $1,076

WILLIAM LEE HANKEY, R.A. (1869–1952) – The stile
– signed – watercolour and bodycolour – 37 x 26.5cm.
(Christie's) £1,012 $1,741

SIGMUND WALTER HAMPEL (1868–1949) –
Mortality and Vice – stamped on reverse – pencil and oil on
panel – 40 x 34cm.
(Christie's) £3,850 $6,699

HERMAN WENDELBORG HANSEN (1854–1924) -
Short cut – signed – watercolour on paper laid down on
paper – 75.5 x 51cm.
(Christie's) £4,466 $7,700

HANSEN

NIELS CHRISTIAN HANSEN (Danish, b. 1834) – A walk in the forest – signed and dated *1897* – oil on canvas – 50 x 66cm.
(Sotheby's) £3,960 $7,009

LEON WILLIAM HANSON (b. 1918) – Overlooking the Garrison Church, the Rocks, Sydney – signed – oil on board – 38.1 x 45.7cm.
(Christie's) £2,420 $4,259

HEYWOOD HARDY (1843–1933) – Picking up the scent – signed and dated *1903* – oil on canvas – 91.5 x 70.5cm.
(Christie's) £13,200 $21,384

GEORGE HARCOURT (English, 1869–1947) – A tangled skein – signed and dated *1917* – oil on canvas – unframed – 193 x 254cm.
(Sotheby's) £41,800 $73,986

HEYWOOD HARDY (1843–1933) – A wayside conversation – signed – oil on canvas – 63.5 x 94cm.
(Christie's) £13,200 $24,024

JAMES HARDY, Jun. (1832–1889) – Gillie on the look out – signed and dated *71* – pencil and watercolour with touches of white heightening and scratching out – 558 x 756mm.
(Christie's) £5,500 $9,295

THOMAS BUSH HARDY (1842–1897) – Entrance to the Giudecca, Venice – signed, inscribed and dated *1893* – pencil and watercolour – 45.7 x 71.2cm.
(Christie's) £1,980 $3,524

HEYWOOD HARDY (1843–1933) – The passing coach – signed – oil on canvas – 50.8 x 76.2cm.
(Christie's) £8,800 $14,960

THOMAS BUSH HARDY (English, 1842–1897) – Low tide, French coast – signed and dated *96* – watercolour – 11.4 x 33.7cm.
(Bonhams) £1,250 $2,063

HEYWOOD HARDY (1843–1933) – The meet – signed – oil on canvas – 50.8 x 76.2cm.
(Christie's) £14,300 $24,310

THOMAS BUSH HARDY – Entrance to Dartmouth Harbour – signed and dated *1893* – watercolour and scratching out – 15.8 x 43.2cm.
(Bonhams) £900 $1,485

KEITH HARING (1958–1990) – Untitled – signed and
stamped with date on reverse *Jul, 18, 1980* – acrylic spray
paint and ink on irregular paper – 141 x 122cm.
(Christie's)   **£11,000 $18,260**

WILLIAM M. HARNETT (1848–1892) – Still life with
lobster, fruit, champagne and newspaper – signed with
monogram and dated *1882* – oil on canvas – unframed –
24.8 x 20.3cm.
(Sotheby's)   **£61,111 $110,000**

ALEXIS HARLAMOFF (b. 1842) – A moment's rest – signed and dated *1886* – oil on canvas –
38.5 x 55.5cm.
(Christie's)   **£12,100 $19,723**

JOHN CYRIL HARRISON (1898–1985) – Sheldrake in flight – signed – pencil and watercolour –340 x 483mm.
(Christie's) **£2,090 $3,386**

HENRI JOSEPH HARPIGNIES (French, 1819–1916) – Village in Provence – signed – watercolour – 24 x 16cm.
(Sotheby's) **£1,980 $3,505**

JOHN CYRIL HARRISON (1898–1985) – Red grouse in flight over moorland – signed – pencil and watercolour heightened with white – 343 x 483mm.
(Christie's) **£3,850 $6,237**

JOHN CYRIL HARRISON – White fronted geese at Holkham – signed – watercolour – 13 x 18in.
(G.A. Key) **£1,500 $2,925**

JOHN CYRIL HARRISON – A fish eagle – signed – watercolour – 15 x 22in.
(G.A. Key) **£2,900 $5,133**

MARSDEN HARTLEY (1878–1943) – Flowers – signed – oil on canvas – 61 x 49.5cm.
(Sotheby's) **£22,611 $40,700**

CHILDE HASSAM (1859-1935) – The fishermen, Cos Cob – signed and dated *1907* – oil on canvas – 57.2 x 51.4cm.
(Sotheby's) **£110,000 $198,000**

CARL HARTMANN (German, b. 1861) – Autumn day -- signed and dated *1903* – oil on canvas – 93 x 54cm.
(Sotheby's) **£2,750 $4,867**

HAROLD HARVEY (1874–1941) – Boys bathing – signed – oil on canvas – 51 x 46.5cm.
(Christie's) **£6,380 $10,591**

JOHN HAUSER (American, 1859–1913) – A Sioux hunter – signed and dated *1912* – oil on board – 21 x 14¹/₂in.
(Du Mouchelles) **£4,805 $8,000**

G. HAUSTRAETE (Belgian, 1878–1949) – Barge at the
quayside in winter – signed – oil on canvas – 80 x 102cm.
(Hôtel de Ventes Horta)   £967 $1,644

ROBERT HAVELL, Jun. (1793–1878) – Partridge
shooting near Windsor; Snipe shooting near Cowley; and
Pheasant shooting, Black Park, near Uxbridge – pencil, pen
and ink and watercolour – 203 x 305mm. – a set of three
(Christie's)   £4,950 $8,712

LOUIS WELDEN HAWKINS (1849–1910) – Innocence
– signed – oil on canvas – 73 x 50.2cm.
(Christie's)   £15,400 $26,180

JOHN HAYES (1786–1866) – He who pays the piper
plays the tune - signed – oil on canvas – 64.2 x 76.7cm.
(Christie's)   £7,150 $11,726

JAMES HAYLLAR (1829–1920) – The rose tree – signed
and dated 1870 – pencil and watercolour with touches of
white heightening – 365 x 254mm.
(Christie's)   £4,400 $7,128

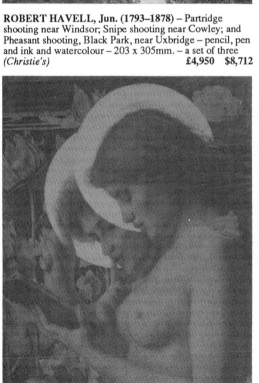

LOUIS WELDEN HAWKINS (English/French, 1849–
1910) – Les aureoles – signed – oil on canvas – 61 x 50cm.
(Sotheby's)   £13,200 $23,364

JESSICA HAYLLAR (1858–1940) – A lady making posies from primroses – signed and dated *1887* – oil on panel – 29 x 21.5cm.
(Christie's)   **£4,180 $6,772**

JESSICA HAYLLAR (1858–1940) – An azalea in a Japanese bowl, with Chinese vases on either side on an oriental rug – signed and dated *1887* – oil on panel – 28 x 22.5cm.
(Christie's)   **£5,500 $8,910**

MARTIN JOHNSON HEADE (1819–1904) – A glass of roses on gold cloth – signed – oil on canvas – 55.9 x 35.6cm.
(Sotheby's)   **£24,444 $44,000**

MARTIN JOHNSON HEADE (1819–1904) – Flatlands and haystacks – signed – oil on paper laid down on canvas laid down on aluminium – 23 x 55.5cm.
(Christie's)   **£7,018 $12,100**

JOSEPH HEARD (fl. 1839–1856) – An English brig off Table Bay with Cape Town beyond – signed with initials – oil on canvas – 53.3 x 76.2cm.
(Christie's)   **£12,100 $21,538**

ERICH HECKEL (1883–1970) – Still life with flowers –
signed and dated *56* – watercolour and charcoal on
embossed watercolour paper – 43 x 30.6cm.
(Lempertz)   **£8,304 $13,245**

RALPH HEDLEY (1851–1913) – The News-boy – signed
and dated *78* – oil on canvas – 76 x 51cm.
(Christie's)   **£3,850 $6,237**

FRANZ HECKENDORF (1888-1962) – Still life with
flowers and fruit – signed – 70 x 49.5cm.
(Lempertz)   **£6,228 $9,934**

PAUL-CESAR HELLEU (1859–1927) – Portrait of
Peggy Gillespie, bust length, holding a parasol – signed and
inscribed – pastel on canvas – 80 x 64.8cm.
(Christie's)   **£41,800 $68,134**

257

PAUL CESAR HELLEU (French, 1859–1927) – A portrait of Madame Rejane – signed – coloured chalk – 56 x 42cm.
(Sotheby's) **£11,000 $19,470**

PAUL CESAR HELLEU (French, 1859–1927) – Madame Letellier reading – signed – coloured chalk – 74 x 53cm.
(Sotheby's) **£16,500 $29,205**

PIET VAN DER HEM – Katjes – signed and dated *10* – pastel – 54 x 70cm.
(Glerum) **£1,060 $1,844**

PIET VAN DER HEM – Volendams picture – signed – oil
on canvas – 76 x 88.5cm.
(Glerum)   £5,924 $10,308

PIET VAN DER HEM – Bullfight – signed – oil on canvas
– 59 x 78cm.
(Glerum)   £3,055 $5,316

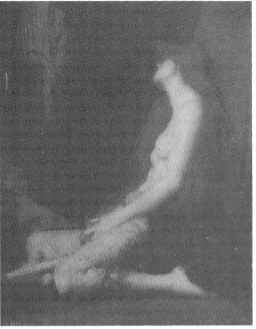

JEAN-JACQUES HENNER (French, 1829–1905) – The
Magdalene – signed – oil on panel – 33 x 21.5cm.
(Sotheby's)   £3,520 $6,230

LOUIS HENDRICKS (1827–1888) – Countryfolk in
extensive wooded landscapes – both signed with initials –
oil on panel – 21.7 x 26.3cm. – a pair
(Christie's)   £4,620 $8,039

ANNIE L. HENNIKER (fl. from 1897) – Sweet Hopes
that come with Spring – signed and dated *1898* – oil on
canvas – 97.2 x 57.1cm.
(Christie's)   £4,180 $7,608

JOSEF HERMAN (b. 1911) – The drinkers – oil on canvas – 51 x 66cm.
(Christie's) £3,850 $6,391

ROBERT HENRI (1865-1929) – Spanish girl – signed and dated *1912* – oil on canvas – 81.3 x 66cm.
(Sotheby's) £58,056 $104,500

ROBERT HENRI (1865–1929) – Au Champs de Mars Paris – signed and inscribed – panel laid down on composition board – 10.2 x 15.5cm.
(Christie's) £7,018 $12,100

JOHANN HERMANN – Jacob's sons presenting him with Joseph's robe – oil on canvas – 80 x 107cm.
(Christie's) £1,650 $2,838

WILHELM HENSEL (1794–1861) – The well – signed and dated *1844* – oil on canvas – 99 x 130.2cm.
(Christie's) £20,900 $34,067

LUDWIG HERMANN (1812–1881) – A riverside town in winter, possibly Danzig – signed and dated *1859* – oil on canvas – 70.1 x 97.8cm.
(Christie's) £7,920 $13,781

PATRICK HERON (b. 1920) – December V – gouache –
60 x 80cm.
(Christie's)   £3,960 $6,930

EUGENIO HERMOSO (1883–1963) – Dedi – signed and
dated *1910* – oil on canvas – 60 x 45cm.
(Duran)   £6,723 $11,832

PATRICK HERON (1920–?) – Abstract – Blue Circle –
oil on board – 18$^{1}/_{2}$ x 40in.
(W.H. Lane & Son)   £17,000 $28,730

PATRICK HERON (b. 1920) – Still life – signed on
canvas overlap – oil on canvas – 51 x 40.5cm.
(Christie's)   £3,850 $6,737

PATRICK HERON (b. 1920) – Lemon disc in sea green
with zig-zags – signed and dated *1982* – oil on canvas –
unframed – 152.5 x 213.5cm.
(Christie's)   £27,500 $48,125

JOSE CRUZ HERRERA (1890–1972) – Arab arcade –
signed – oil on board – 44 x 53cm.
(Duran) £1,114 $2,000

Attributed to JOHN FREDERICK HERRING, Sr. and
JAMES POLLARD (British, 1795–1865; 1792–1867) –
Horses and poultry in a farmyard – signed *J.F. Herring* –
oil on canvas – 76.2 x 127cm.
(Butterfield & Butterfield) £5,358 $9,350

HERMANN HERZOG (German/American, 1832–1932)
– Swiss mountain landscape – signed – oil on canvas –
41 x 32in.
(Du Mouchelles) £4,789 $8,500

JULES R. HERVE – In the park – signed – oil on canvas
– 52.2 x 62.8cm.
(Christie's) £2,310 $3,973

Attributed to JOHN HESSELIUS (1728–1778) – Portrait
of a young lady, circa 1765 – oil on canvas – 17 x 13³/₄in.
(Christie's) £7,656 $13,200

GUSTAV AUGUSTE HESSL (Austrian, b. 1849) – Preparing the meal – signed – oil on panel –
33 x 42.3cm.
(Bonhams) £4,500 $7,155

THEODORE BERNARD DE HEUVEL (1817–1906) –
The bird's nest – signed and dated *1872* – oil on canvas –
30.5 x 61cm.
(Christie's) £3,080 $5,359

ARTHUR HEYER (1872-1931) – White angora kittens
with a beetle – signed and dated *1929* – oil on canvas –
55.3 x 67.9cm.
(Christie's) £3,520 $5,773

ARTHUR HEYER (1872–1931) – Study of a bulldog – signed and dated *14* – oil on canvas – 79 x 99.5cm.
(Christie's) £2,200 $3,608

ARTHUR HEYER (1872–1931) – Two white Persian cats with a ladybird by a deckchair – signed – oil on canvas – 76.2 x 101.6cm.
(Christie's) £3,300 $5,412

ENRIQUE MARIN HIGUERO (b. 1876) – An Andalucian house and garden in summer – signed and inscribed – pencil and watercolour on paper – 52.8 x 36.5cm.
(Christie's) £1,650 $2,871

SIR HANS HEYSEN (1877–1968) – Sheep grazing by eucalyptus trees – signed – pencil and watercolour – 32.4 x 25.4cm.
(Christie's) £3,300 $5,808

JAMES JOHN HILL (1811–1882) – The harvesters – signed – oil on canvas – 48 x 38cm.
(Christie's) £3,300 $5,346

THOMAS HILL (1829–1908) – A hunter and his pointers
– signed and dated *1861* – oil on canvas – 51 x 76.2cm.
(Christie's)   **£10,846 $18,700**

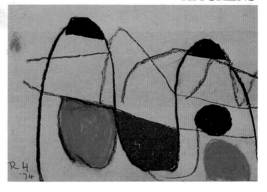

ROGER HILTON (1911–1975) – Untitled – signed with
initials and dated *74* – gouache and crayon – 28 x 43cm.
(Christie's)   **£1,430 $2,502**

TRISTRAM HILLIER, R.A. (b. 1905) – Portuguese
fishing boats – signed and dated *74* – oil on canvas –
51 x 76cm.
(Christie's)   **£4,400 $7,700**

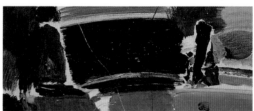

IVON HITCHENS (1893–1979) – Black wood – signed –
oil on canvas – 53 x 132cm.
(Christie's)   **£11,000 $19,250**

TRISTRAM HILLIER (b. 1905) – The Binegar road – signed and dated *44* – oil on panel – 15 x 21.5cm.
(Christie's)   **£4,620 $8,085**

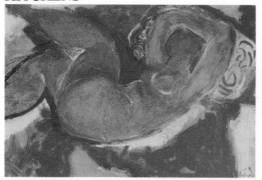

IVON HITCHENS (1893–1979) – Figure on red – signed
– oil on canvas – 51 x 76cm.
(Christie's)   **£10,450 $18,287**

WILLIAM HOARE (1706–1799) – Portrait of a lady, half
length, wearing a blue dress trimmed with ermine – pastel
on paper laid down on linen – 584 x 445mm.
(Christie's)   **£1,430 $2,517**

IVON HITCHENS (1893–1979) – Fir and silver birch –
signed and dated *34* – oil on canvas – 53 x 61cm.
(Christie's)   **£12,650 $22,138**

JONIEL HOCHMANN (Austrian, 19th century) –
Emperor Franz Josef at Gödölo – signed – oil on canvas –
74 x 103cm.
(Sotheby's)   **£1,760 $3,115**

IVON HITCHENS (1893–1979) – Spring mood – stamped
with studio stamp on reverse – oil on canvas – 71 x 102cm.
(Christie's)   **£26,400 $46,200**

DAVID HOCKNEY (b. 1937) – A male dancer – signed
with initials and dated *64* – pencil and coloured crayon –
26 x 34.5cm.
(Christie's)   **£2,750 $4,812**

GERHARD HOEHME (b. 1920) – Rote Zeichen – signed and dated *52* – oil on canvas – 73.5 x 101cm.
(Christie's) £19,800 $32,868

DAVID HOCKNEY (b. 1937) – Portrait of a seated man – signed with initials and dated *62* – pencil and coloured crayons – 30.5 x 25cm.
(Christie's) £5,500 $9,625

FRANZ HOEPFNER (late 19th century) – A mountainous wooded landscape with countryfolk by a river – signed and dated *1883* – oil on canvas – 132.7 x 224.5cm.
(Christie's) £4,400 $7,656

FRANCES HODGKINS (1869–1947) – Red earth – signed – watercolour – 45.7 x 57.2cm.
(Christie's) £4,510 $7,938

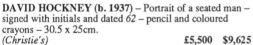

GERHARD HOEHME (1920–1989) – Berlin letter – signed and dated *Januar 1966* – acrylic, pencil and canvas collage on canvas – diptych, overall 200 x 360cm.
(Christie's) £154,000 $272,580

HEINRICH HOFER (German, 1825–1878) – Travellers on a mountainous path by the Staubbachfall near Lauterbrunnen – signed and dated *1876* – oil on canvas – 61 x 83cm.
(Sotheby's) £18,700 $33,099

KARL HOFER (1878–1955) – A view of a village in
Tessin – signed with monogram – oil on canvas –
60 x 80cm.
(Christie's)   **£65,321 $115,619**

JAMES HOLLAND (1799–1870) – The Chapel of St.
John the Baptist, San Roque, Lisbon – signed, inscribed and
dated *1837* – pencil and watercolour heightened with
bodycolour – 394 x 285mm.
(Christie's)   **£5,280 $9,293**

FRANCIS HOLMAN (fl. 1774–1784) – Merchant sailing
vessels off Yarmouth – signed – oil on canvas –
65.3 x 148.6cm.
(Christie's)   **£14,300 $25,454**

FRANCES MABEL HOLLAMS (fl. 1897–1929) –
Turning the waggon – signed and dated *01* – oil on canvas
– 125.7 x 185.4cm.
(Christie's)   **£7,700 $14,014**

BERNARD DE HOOG (Dutch, b. 1867) – The doll's
toilet – signed – oil on canvas – 20 x 16in.
(Du Mouchelles) £2,402 $4,000

Follower of MELCHIOR DE HONDECOETER –
Cockerels, chicks and pigeons by a wall, a dove-cot beyond
– oil on canvas – 124.5 x 94cm.
(Christie's) £7,480 $11,669

BERNARD DE HOOG (1867–1943) – A wee bit fractious
– signed – oil on canvas – 68.6 x 57.1cm.
(Christie's) £6,820 $11,867

ARTHUR HOPKINS (1848–1930) – The torn gown –
signed and dated *1909* – pencil, watercolour and gum
arabic with scratching out – 540 x 349mm.
(Christie's) £7,150 $13,013

HOPPER

EDWARD HOPPER (1882–1967) – The yellow house –
signed – dated and inscribed – watercolour on paper –
30 x 45.7cm.
(Christie's) **£127,600 $220,000**

WILLIAM B. HOUGH (fl. 1857–1894) – Still life with a
bird's nest and primroses on a mossy bank – signed –
watercolour and bodycolour – 229 x 307mm.
(Christie's) **£3,520 $6,406**

HUBERTUS VAN HOVE (Dutch, 1814–65) – A view of
Amsterdam market – signed and indistinctly dated *1860* –
oil on panel – 41 x 62cm.
(Sotheby's) **£13,200 $23,364**

LEON CHARLES HUBER (1858–1928) – Waiting for
more – signed – oil on canvas – 38.1 x 54.5cm.
(Christie's) **£2,860 $4,690**

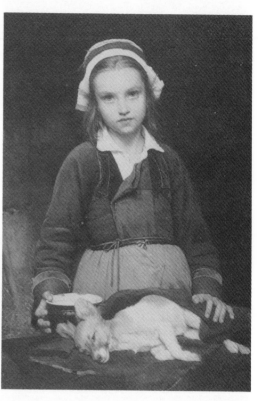

EMILE AUGUST HUBLIN (b. 1830) – A friend in need
– signed and dated *1872* – oil on canvas – 84.5 x 61cm.
(Christie's) **£14,300 $25,025**

HEINRICH HUBNER (German, b. 1869) – An interior
with flowers – signed – oil on canvas – 70 x 80cm.
(Sotheby's) **£3,300 $5,841**

ARTHUR HUGHES (1832–1915) – Silver and gold –
signed – oil on canvas – 99 x 67.3cm.
(Christie's) £220,000 $374,000

ARTHUR HUGHES (1832–1915) – The rescue – signed –
oil on canvas – 109.3 x 53.4cm.
(Christie's) £18,700 $31,790

ARTHUR HUGHES (1832–1915) – Audrey's toilet –
signed – oil on canvas – 76.2 x 108cm.
(Christie's) £16,500 $28,050

EDWARD ROBERT HUGHES, R.W.S. (1851–1914) –
Bertuccio's bride – signed and dated *1895* – pencil and
watercolour with scratching out – 1003 x 761mm.
(Christie's) £88,000 $148,720

FREDERICK WILLIAM HULME (1816–1884) – Sunny day, Woking Common, Surrey – signed, inscribed and dated *1856* – oil on canvas – 34.3 x 62.2cm.
(Christie's)   £2,860 $4,862

ABRAHAM HULK (1813–1897) – Shipping in an estuary; and Shipping offshore in a light breeze – both signed – oil on panel – 16 x 25cm. – a pair
(Christie's)   £7,150 $12,512

FRIEDENSREICH HUNDERTWASSER (b. 1928) – Zwolle – signed, inscribed and dated *13 Juli 1967* – egg tempera and gold paint on metal sheet – 44 x 62.5cm.
(Christie's)   £49,500 $87,615

ABRAHAM HULK Snr. (Dutch, 1813–97) – Fisherfolk and ships by the coast – signed – oil on panel – 33 x 50cm.
(Sotheby's)   £12,100 $21,417

CHARLES HUNT (1803–1877) – The Police Court – signed and dated *1867* – oil on canvas – unframed – 25.4 x 35.5cm.
(Christie's) £3,300 $6,006

CHARLES HUNT (1829–1900) – The trial – signed and dated *1866* – oil on canvas – 16.5 x 24.2cm.
(Christie's) £1,760 $2,851

EDGAR HUNT (1876–1953) – Chicks by a basket – signed and dated *1908* – oil on canvas – 25.4 x 30.5cm.
(Christie's) £6,600 $10,692

EDGAR HUNT – Domestic poultry by and on a wooden garden barrow with rabbit in a hutch – signed and dated *1919* – oil on canvas – 10 x 14in.
(G.A. Key) £7,200 $12,744

WILLIAM HOLMAN HUNT (English, 1827–1910) – The Walls of Jerusalem – signed with initials and dated *1869* – watercolour – 25.5 x 49.5cm.
(Sotheby's) £20,900 $36,993

273

HUNT

ALFRED WILLIAM HUNT, R.W.S. (1830–1896) –
Cochem on the Moselle – signed and dated *1860* – pencil
and watercolour – 305 x 250mm.
(Christie's)   **£1,980 $3,346**

LESLIE HURRY (1909–1978) – The Cenci (Percy Bysshe
Shelley), 1959, Old Vic Preliminary set design for the
Cenci Palace – signed – pen, black ink and watercolour –
29 x 39cm.
(Christie's)   **£902 $1,497**

**ROBERT GEMMELL HUTCHISON (Scottish, 1855–
1936)** – Before bedtime – signed – oil on canvas –
58.4 x 45.7cm.
(Bonhams)   **£6,200 $9,858**

LOUIS ICART (French, 1888–1950) – La Tete/Au
Cirque – signed – oil on canvas – 13 x 16in.
(Du Mouchelles) **£12,259 $21,000**

JORG IMMENDORF (b. 1945) – Show what you've got
– signed, inscribed and dated *83* – oil on canvas –
76 x 106cm.
(Christie's) **£11,000 $17,820**

FILIPPO INDONI (19th century) – Harvest flirtation –
signed – watercolour – 53 x 36cm.
(Duran) **£669 $1,201**

FILIPPO INDONI (late 19th century) – A Neapolitan
beauty – signed – oil on canvas – 100.3 x 75cm.
(Christie's) **£5,500 $9,625**

JEAN-AUGUSTE-DOMINIQUE INGRES (French, 1780–1867) – Portrait of Elizabeth Keating with a guitar – signed and dated *1816* – pencil - the signature and date strengthened by another hand in pen and ink at a later date – 26.5 x 20.5cm.
(Sotheby's)   **£121,000 $214,170**

VINCENZO IROLLI (1860–1942) – A dear companion – signed – oil on canvas – 35.5 x 25.4cm.
(Christie's)   **£41,800 $73,150**

GEORGES INNESS (1825–1894) – Montclair evening – signed and dated *1876* – oil on panel – 41.3 x 66cm.
(Sotheby's)   **£55,000 $99,000**

LOUIS-GABRIEL-EUGENE ISABEY (1803–1886) –
After the storm – signed – oil on canvas – 38.8 x 28.5cm.
(Christie's) £5,500 $9,625

LOUIS-GABRIEL-EUGENE ISABEY (1803–1886) –
Portrait of a lady, bust length – stamped with vente mark –
oil on canvas – 54.5 x 43.2cm.
(Christie's) £4,400 $7,172

ITALIAN SCHOOL (circa 1700) – Dish of black and green grapes – bears inscription on reverse – oil on
panel – 27 x 40cm.
(Christie's) £17,867 $29,659

JAMES RANALPH JACKSON (1886–1975) – The rowing boat – signed and dated *17* – 40 x 79.5cm.
(Christie's) **£10,120 $17,811**

SAMUEL JACKSON (1794–1869) – Cadir Idris from across the lake, a figure in the foreground – watercolour and bodycolour – 21 x 29cm.
(Allen & Harris) **£620 $1,091**

ANTONIO NICOLO GASPARO JACOBSEN (1850–1921) – The American screw steamer S.S. City of Birmingham – signed, inscribed and dated *1897* – oil on canvas – 55.8 x 91.4cm.
(Christie's) **£4,950 $8,811**

AR. JAMAR (1870–1946) – Vlissingen – signed and dated 1928 – mixed media on paper – 60 x 50cm.
(Hôtel de Ventes Horta) **£1,552 $2,700**

AR. JAMAR (1870–1946) – La Rochelle – signed and dated 1923 – oil on canvas – 68 x 48cm.
(Hôtel de Ventes Horta) **£2,586 $4,500**

LAJOS JAMBOR – Summer flowers – signed – oil on canvas – 101.7 x 76.2cm.
(Christie's) **£2,750 $4,730**

DAVID JAMES (fl. 1881–1898) – The breaking wave – signed and dated *93* – oil on canvas – 63.5 x 127cm.
(Christie's) **£6,050 $9,801**

LAJOS JAMBOR – A Summer afternoon – signed and dated *Jambor L 1915* – oil on canvas – 100.2 x 74.8cm.
(Christie's) **£16,500 $28,512**

JEAN JANSEM (French, b. 1920) – Masques a Venise – signed – oil on canvas – 59.1 x 80cm.
(Butterfield & Butterfield) **£7,564 $13,200**

279

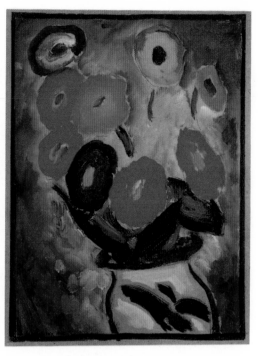

ALEXEJ VON JAWLENSKY (1864–1941) – Meditation
– signed with initials – oil on paper laid down on board –
20 x 14cm.
(Christie's)   **£18,700 $30,294**

ALEXEJ VON JAWLENSKY (1864–1941) – Still life
with flowers – signed and dated *1915* – oil on linen-
finished paper laid down on board – 35.3 x 26cm.
(Christie's)   **£55,000 $96,800**

ALEXEJ VON JAWLENSKY (1864–1941) – At the
Baltic – signed and dated *1911* – oil on board – 61 x 61cm.
(Christie's)   **£231,000 $378,840**

CARL MILTON JENSEN (Danish, 1855–1928) – Cattle watering in an extensive landscape – signed and dated *1909* – oil on canvas – 100 x 120cm.
(Sotheby's) £2,090 $3,699

CARLO CHRISTOFFER HORNUNG JENSEN (1882–1960) – On the Beach, Hornback – signed and dated *1925* – oil on canvas – 61 x 94cm.
(Christie's) £3,080 $5,544

Studio of JOHAN LAURENTZ JENSEN (1800–1856) –
A bouquet of roses – oil on canvas – 26 x 37.5cm.
(Christie's)   £2,420 $4,210

JOHAN LAURENTZ JENSEN (Danish, 1800–56) – A
still life with flowers in an earthenware vase – signed and
dated *1836* – oil on canvas – 35 x 27cm.
(Sotheby's)   £11,000 $19,470

JOHAN LAURENTZ JENSEN (1800–1856) – Pink roses
– signed – oil on panel – 23 x 32.3cm.
(Christie's)   £9,350 $16,362

JOHAN LAURENTZ JENSEN (Danish, 1800–1856) – Still life with roses in a basket – signed – oil on panel
– 28.6 x 38.1cm.
(Butterfield & Butterfield)   £4,413 $7,700

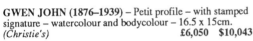

RICHARD JERZY – Louise – signed and dated 76 – oil on board – 12 x 9in.
(Du Mouchelles) **£524 $900**

GWEN JOHN (1876–1939) – Petit profile – with stamped signature – watercolour and bodycolour – 16.5 x 15cm.
(Christie's) **£6,050 $10,043**

JONATHAN EASTMAN JOHNSON (1824–1906) – Warming her hands – signed and dated 62 – oil on canvas – 31.5 x 24.3cm.
(Christie's) **£31,900 $55,000**

ANTONIO JOLI (Italian, circa 1700–1777) – A view of the Forum, Rome, with the Campo Vaccino, S. Francesca Romana, the Arch of Titus and the Colosseum – oil on canvas – 91.5 x 113cm.
(Sotheby's) **£34,100 $61,380**

PHILIPPE JOLYET (French, 1832–1908) – Mignon –
signed and dated *1892* – oil on board – 41 x 33cm.
(Butterfield & Butterfield) £4,097 $7,150

HUGH BOLTON JONES (1848–1927) – The country
lane – signed – oil on canvas – 56 x 81.5cm.
(Christie's) £6,380 $11,000

ALLEN JONES (b. 1937) – L.A. Sheer – signed and dated
1969 – oil on canvas and plastic steps – 229 x 152cm.
(Christie's) £13,200 $23,100

HUGH BOLTON JONES (1848–1927) – Cumberland Valley – signed and dated *1873* – oil on canvas – 77 x 137cm.
(Christie's) **£16,588** **$28,600**

GERM DE JONG – Heavy traffic on a Paris square – signed and dated *1927* – oil on panel – 36 x 45cm.
(Glerum) **£12,471** **$21,700**

JACOB JORDAENS (Flemish, 1593–1678) – The artist's model – oil on canvas – 116.8 x 96.5cm.
(Butterfield & Butterfield) **£6,304** **$11,000**

RUDOLF JORDAN (1810–1887) – Betrothal in Heligoland – signed with monogram – oil on canvas –
92 x 140cm.
(Lempertz)   **£14,184 $25,106**

PIO JORIS (Italian, 1843–1921) – The first communion – signed and inscribed – oil on canvas laid down on
board – 88.9 x 116.8cm.
(Butterfield & Butterfield)   **£8,195 $14,300**

ASGER JORN (1914–1973) – Untitled – signed and dated *45* – oil on canvas – 77.5 x 100cm.
(Christie's) £27,500 $48,675

ASGER JORN (1914–1973) – Brand – signed – oil on canvas – 48 x 38cm.
(Christie's) £24,066 $42,597

ASGER JORN (1914–1973) – Pixilated garden – signed and dated *66/69* – oil on canvas – 65 x 81.2cm.
(Christie's) £37,400 $60,588

AMEDEE-MARIE-ANTOINE JULLIEN (d. 1887) –
The woodland pool – signed and dated *1854* – oil on canvas
– 89 x 117cm.
(Christie's) £4,400 $7,656

BELA KADAR – Woman and child – signed – mixed
media on paper – 49 x 33cm.
(Hôtel de Ventes Horta) £2,414 $4,200

BELA KADAR (Hungarian, 1877–1955) – Seated nude –
signed – oil on canvas – 78 x 54cm.
(Germann) £8,064 $12,822

CHARLES SALIS KAELIN (American, 1858–1929) –
Sunday, a harbour view – signed – pastel on grey paper –
13¹/₄ x 15³/₈in.
(Skinner Inc.) **£1,058 $1,870**

WOLF KAHN (b. 1927) – Down to the valley II – oil on
canvas – 134.5 x 134.5cm.
(Christie's) **£6,061 $10,450**

WOLF KAHN (b. 1927) – Late afternoon – signed – oil on
canvas – 127 x 105.5cm.
(Christie's) **£7,658 $13,200**

ALOIS KALVODA (Czech, 1875–1934) – An autumn landscape with a lake – signed – oil on canvas – 149 x 150cm.
(Sotheby's) £4,400 $7,788

HUGO KAUFFMANN (1844–1915) – Young girl in traditional costume – signed and dated *91* – oil on wood – 15 x 11.8cm.
(Lempertz) £6,738 $11,455

WASSILY KANDINSKY (1886–1944) – Rapallo – signed and dated *1906* on reverse – oil on canvas – 23.5 x 33cm.
(Finarte) £107,570 $183,407

HUGO KAUFFMAN (German, 1844–1915) – Collecting wood in a winter storm – signed – oil on canvas laid down on masonite – 45.1 x 64.1cm.
(Butterfield & Butterfield) £3,782 $6,600

BERTALAN DE KARLOVSZKY (Austrian, 1858–1938) – Taking a prisoner – signed and inscribed – oil on panel – 77 x 100cm.
(Sotheby's) £2,420 $4,283

HUGO KAUFFMAN – A tavern scene – signed and dated *1877* – oil on panel – 6 x 7in.
(Michael J. Bowman) £7,500 $12,847

**MARIA ANNA ANGELICA CATHERINA
KAUFFMAN, R.A. (1741–1807)** – The mystic marriage of
St. Catherine (?) – with inscription on the mount – pen and
grey ink, grey wash – unframed – 265 x 320mm.
(Christie's) £715 $1,151

FRANTISEK KAVAN (Czech, 1866–1941) – The dream
of a good heart – signed and dated '97 – oil on canvas –
131 x 100cm.
(Sotheby's) £4,950 $8,761

FRIEDRICH AUGUST VON KAULBACH (1850–1920)
– Portrait of a Master Eckstein, standing full length, leaning
on a draped chest – signed and dated *1902* – oil on canvas –
162.5 x 99.7cm.
(Christie's) £9,900 $17,325

OTIS KAYE (1885–1974) – Three bills posted – signed –
oil on canvas laid down on panel – 32.9 x 24.7cm.
(Christie's) £7,656 $13,200

A.D. KAYGORDOV (1878–1929) – Springtime – signed
– oil on board – 60 x 80cm.
(Hôtel de Ventes Horta) **£1,694 $2,880**

CHARLES SAMUEL KEENE (1823–1891) – A good
night out! – signed with monogram – pen and ink –
unframed – 130 x 215mm.
(Christie's) **£715 $1,158**

TOM KEATING – Figures in a punt and cattle at the
water's edge before a farmhouse (painted in the manner of
Constable) – signed and dated 1972 – oil on canvas –
16½ x 20in.
(W.H. Lane & Son) **£720 $1,217**

**PAUL WILHELM KELLER-REUTLINGEN (German,
1854–1920)** – Day-dreaming – signed – oil on canvas –
29.2 x 40cm.
(Butterfield & Butterfield) **£4,097 $7,150**

C.J. KEATS – The Hague; and Paris – both signed and
inscribed – pencil and watercolour heightened with white –
19¾ x 12¾in. – a pair
(Christie's) **£264 $456**

FELIX KELLY (b. 1916) – A pleasure steamer
approaching a jetty – signed – oil on board – 42.6 x 57.2cm.
(Christie's) **£825 $1,468**

FELIX KELLY (b. 1916) – Tidal reaches – signed and dated *45* – gouache – 28.6 x 38.7cm.
(Christie's) £990 $1,742

CECIL KENNEDY (b. 1905) – Pink roses – signed – oil on canvas – 48 x 38.5cm.
(Christie's) £4,180 $6,938

PHILIP KELLY (b. 1953) – Plaza de Sa Cibelles, Mexico – signed and dated *90* – oil on board – 71 x 56.5cm.
(Christie's) £1,100 $1,826

LUCY ELIZABETH KEMP-WELCH (1869–1958) – Mare and foal – signed and dated *1903* – oil on canvas – 40.5 x 57cm.
(Christie's) £3,850 $6,622

CECIL KENNEDY (b. 1905) – Still life – Vase of hydrangeas and delphiniums – signed – oil on canvas – 30 x 25^{1}/2in.
(W.H. Lane & Son) £210 $355

CECIL KENNEDY (b. 1905) – Still life with flowers –
signed – oil on canvas – 64 x 77cm.
(Christie's) £4,180 $7,190

THOMAS BENJAMIN KENNINGTON (1856–1916) –
The letter - signed and dated *12* – oil on canvas –
94.6 x 132.1cm.
(Christie's) £3,250 $5,753

HERMANN KERN (Hungarian, 1839–1912) – The
caged mouse – signed – oil on panel – 68.6 x 47cm.
(Butterfield & Butterfield) £5,043 $8,800

THOMAS BENJAMIN KENNINGTON – Half length
portrait of a lady magician holding a wand and a sphere,
wreathed in smoke – signed and dated *(19)08* – 74 x 62cm.
(Spencer's) £3,800 $6,745

DICK KET (1902–1940) – Still life with violin and self
portraits of Schuhmacher and Hynckes – signed – oil on
canvas – 66 x 54cm.
(Christie's) £32,661 $57,809

FERNAND KHNOPFF (Belgian, 1858–1921) – A young girl with outstretched arms – signed – pencil – 24 x 14cm.
(Sotheby's)   **£6,820 $12,071**

FERNAND KHNOPFF (1858–1921) – H.R.H. Prince Leopold of Belgium, Duke of Brabant – signed – soft pencil, charcoal and sanguine on paper – 64.2 x 40cm.
(Christie's)   **£12,100 $21,296**

FERNAND KHNOPFF (1858–1921) – Portrait of Jeanne de Bauer – signed and dated *1890* – oil on panel – 53 x 35cm.
(Christie's)   **£231,000 $404,250**

FREDERIK CHRISTIAN KIAERSKOU (1805–1891) – Figures in a park by a statue of Adam Molthe – signed and dated *1862* – oil on canvas – 95.2 x 142.3cm.
(Christie's)   **£2,200 $3,828**

GEORGE GOODWIN KILBURNE (1839–1924) –
Afternoon tea – signed and dated 76 – pencil and
watercolour – 257 x 357mm.
(Christie's)   **£3,520 $5,702**

ANSELM KIEFER (b. 1945) – Deep water – two black
and white photographs with dispersion and grass on lead
mounted on a wood panel with steel artist's frame –
242 x 131.7cm.
(Christie's)   **£27,500 $48,675**

GEORGE GOODWIN KILBURNE (1839–1924) – A
little family history – signed – pencil and watercolour –
368 x 510mm.
(Christie's)   **£4,180 $6,772**

GEORGE GOODWIN KILBURNE (1839–1924) – The
pigeons of St. Mark's, Venice – signed and dated 76 –
pencil and watercolour with touches of white heightening –
370 x 635mm.
(Christie's)   **£3,850 $6,506**

GEORGE GOODWIN KILBURNE (1839–1924) – I
wish you luck – signed – pencil and watercolour with
touches of white heightening – 368 x 527mm.
(Christie's)   **£4,180 $6,772**

GEORGE GOODWIN KILBURNE – A letter of introduction – signed – pencil and watercolour – 14¹/2 x 20¹/2in.
(Christie's) £748 $1,326

GEORGE GOODWIN KILBURNE (1839–1924) – A faithful friend at tea time – signed – pencil and watercolour – 346 x 498mm.
(Christie's) £3,850 $6,237

GEORGE GOODWIN KILBURNE (1839–1924) – The music master – signed – pencil and watercolour – 248 x 177mm.
(Christie's) £3,520 $5,949

GEORGE GOODWIN KILBURNE (1839–1924) – The music room – signed – oil on panel – 30.4 x 40.6cm.
(Christie's) £7,480 $13,614

SARAH LOUISE KILPACK (fl. 1880–1909) – A harbour
at sunset; and Fisherfolk with beached fishing boats at dusk
– signed – oil on card – 31.7 x 25.4cm. – a pair
(Christie's)   **£1,210 $2,154**

RAYMOND KIMPE (b. 1885) – Composition with four
girls – signed – oil on canvas – 75 x 50cm.
(Christie's)   **£2,235 $3,956**

ALBERT F. KING (1854–1945) - A pail of apples –
signed – oil on canvas – 30.5 x 45.5cm.
(Christie's)   **£2,233 $3,850**

ALBERT F. KING (1854–1945) – Still life with
watermelon and fruit – signed – oil on canvas laid down on
board – 10.2 x 14.9cm.
(Sotheby's)   **£1,503 $2,750**

R. KIMPE (Belgian) – Dutch seaman – signed and dated
46 – oil on canvas – 70 x 52cm.
(Hôtel de Ventes Horta)   **£1,962 $3,356**

HAYNES KING (1831–1904) – Country girl carrying a brass pitcher in a meadow before a farmstead – signed – oil on canvas – 24 x 20in.
(W.H. Lane & Son)   **£2,000 $3,685**

HENRY JOHN YEEND KING (English, 1855–1924) – A gipsy encampment – signed – oil on canvas – 38.1 x 27.9cm.
(Bonhams)   **£750 $1,192**

HENRY JOHN YEEND KING (1855–1924) – Children on a bridge by a thatched cottage – signed – oil on canvas – 54.2 x 37.5cm.
(Christie's)   **£1,320 $2,138**

HENRY JOHN YEEND KING (English, 1855–1924) – Market morning – signed – oil on canvas – 36.3 x 33cm.
(Bonhams)   **£1,300 $2,067**

HENRY JOHN YEEND KING (1855–1924) – Crossing the lake – signed – oil on canvas – 92 x 152.5cm.
(Christie's) £4,400 $7,788

DONG KINGMAN (b. 1911) – San Francisco – signed and dated *Jan. 72* – mixed-media collage on paper laid down on board – 41.3 x 29.2cm.
(Sotheby's) £2,104 $3,850

PAUL KING (1867–1940) – A wooded winter landscape – signed – oil on canvas – 127 x 152.5cm.
(Christie's) £2,610 $4,620

PAUL KING (1867–1940) – A harbour scene – signed – oil on canvas – 101.6 x127cm.
(Christie's) £5,904 $10,450

FRANÇOIS KINSON (French, 1771–1839) – A portrait of Duchess Macmahon and her son – signed and dated *1827* – oil on canvas – unframed – 242 x 165cm.
(Sotheby's) £19,800 $35,046

ERNST LUDWIG KIRCHNER (1880–1938) – Mary Wigman's Dance of Death – signed – black and coloured chalks on paper – 33 x 48cm.
(Lempertz) £11,419 $18,213

OTTO KIRCHNER – A Bavarian smoking a pipe – signed and inscribed – oil on board – 22.8 x 16.5cm.
(Christie's) £605 $1,045

ERNST LUDWIG KIRCHNER (1880–1938) – Portrait of a young man – signed – watercolour and pencil on paper – 50 x 35cm.
(Christie's) £7,700 $12,474

ERNST LUDWIG KIRCHNER (1880–1938) – Peasants before a hut – signed – watercolour and pencil on paper – 38.4 x 50cm.
(Lempertz) £38,062 $60,709

OTTO KIRCHNER – A new vintage – signed – oil on panel – unframed – 17.8 x 13.9cm.
(Christie's) £495 $851

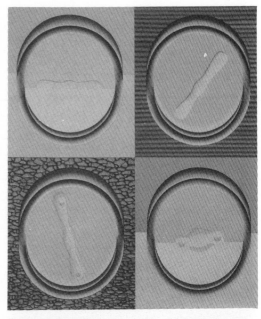

MOISE KISLING (1891–1953) – Still life with bottles and books – signed and dated *1917* – watercolour and pencil on paper – 48.5 x 35.5cm.
(Christie's) £7,150 $11,583

KONRAD KLAPHECK (b. 1938) – Four lifestyles – signed on the reverse – oil on canvas – 80 x 70cm.
(Christie's) £27,500 $48,675

MOISE KISLING (1891–1953) – Bouquet of flowers: dahlias, tulips and lilies – signed – oil on canvas – 81 x 54.5cm.
(Christie's) £79,200 $139,392

PAUL KLEE (1879–1940) – Duettino des Passanten – signed and dated on mount *1938* – gouache on paper – 34 x 21.6cm.
(Christie's) £23,100 $40,656

YVES KLEIN (1928–1962) – IKB – signed on reverse – pigment and synthetic resin on paper – 21.4 x 17.9cm.
(Christie's) £17,600 $29,216

GEORGE KNAPTON (1698–1778) – Portrait of the Hon. William Napier, 1735, aged eight, three-quarter length, wearing a green coat – pastel on paper laid down on linen – 558 x 407mm.
(Christie's) £1,650 $2,904

WILLIAM ADOLPHUS KNELL (1805–1875) – Fishing boats and other vessels approaching the mouth of a harbour, possibly in the Thames Estuary –signed – oil on canvas – 63.5 x 91.5cm.
(Christie's) £7,700 $13,706

Circle of GEORGE KNAPTON – Portrait of a huntsman, three-quarter length, wearing a red coat embroidered with gold – oil on canvas – 116.8 x 94.5cm.
(Bonhams) £1,800 $2,862

WILLIAM ADOLPHUS KNELL (English, 1805–1875) – Outward bound, entering Funchal Roads, Madeira – signed – oil on canvas – 61 x 106.7cm.
(Bonhams) £10,000 $16,500

WILLIAM CALLCOTT KNELL (fl. 1848–1871) – All in the Downs the Fleet was moored – signed and dated *1876* – oil on canvas – 30.4 x 60.9cm.
(Christie's)   £3,080 $5,482

Follower of KNELLER – Portrait of a gentleman in armour – oil on canvas – 40 x 32in.
(David Lay)   £500 $795

School of SIR GODFREY KNELLER (British, 1646–1743) – Portrait of King William III of Orange – oil on canvas – 77.5 x 64.1cm.
(Butterfield & Butterfield)   £630 $1,100

Studio of SIR GODFREY KNELLER – Portrait of a nobleman, thought to be George I as Kurprinz of Hanover, in an armour breastplate – oil on canvas – 81.9 x 64.8cm.
(Christie's)   £1,430 $2,309

DAME LAURA KNIGHT, R.A. (1877–1970) – A Clown and a member of the orchestra – signed – black crayon – 33.5 x 25.5cm.
(Christie's)   £825 $1,419

DAME LAURA KNIGHT – Conversation on the beach –
signed and dated *Aug 10 1920* – pencil – 20 x 26.5cm.
(Christie's) £1,100 $1,749

DAME LAURA KNIGHT, R.A. (1877–1970) – Herbert
the acrobat – signed – black crayon, watercolour and
bodycolour – 35.5 x 26cm.
(Christie's) £3,850 $6,622

DAME LAURA KNIGHT, R.A. (1877–1970) – Cellist –
signed – black crayon – 33.5 x 25cm.
(Christie's) £935 $1,608

HAROLD KNIGHT (1874–1961) – A meal by the fireside
– signed – oil on board – 10 x 13¹/₂in.
(W.H. Lane & Son)   **£2,300 $4,238**

DANIEL RIDGWAY KNIGHT (1839–1924) – The
potato harvester – signed and inscribed – watercolour and
gouache on paper laid down on board – 36.8 x 26.7cm.
(Sotheby's)   **£1,443 $2,640**

A. KNIP – Ducks at a pond with deer beyond in an
ornamental garden – signed – oil on canvas – painted
arched top – 73.7 x 57.7cm.
(Christie's)   **£1,870 $3,231**

DANIEL RIDGWAY KNIGHT – A trip to market – signed
and inscribed – oil on canvas – 63.5 x 76.2cm.
(Christie's)   **£5,423 $9,350**

H. KNIP (circa 1840) – The poacher; a larder still life with
a tortoise-shell cat with a blackbird, and other birds –
signed – oil on canvas – 71.1 x 90.8cm.
(Christie's)   **£8,250 $13,530**

GEORGE SHERIDAN KNOWLES (1863–1931) –
Portrait of Miss Agnes A. Marshall, seated half length –
signed and dated *1891* – oil on canvas – 61 x 51.5cm.
(Christie's)   **£1,430 $2,317**

JOSEPH ANTON KOCH (1768–1839) – Heroic
landscape with rainbow – signed and dated *1824* – oil on
canvas – 108 x 96cm.
(Christie's)   **£836,000 $1,362,680**

JOSEF ANTON KOCH (German, 1768–1839) –
Landscape with Ruth and Boaz – signed – oil on canvas –
84.5 x 110cm.
(Sotheby's)   **£247,500 $438,075**

GEORGE SHERIDAN KNOWLES (1863–1931) – The
saga of King Olaf – signed and dated *1892* – oil on canvas
– 91.5 x 71.5cm.
(Christie's)   **£2,420 $4,283**

PAUL R. KOEHLER (1875–1909) – The bird estuary –
signed – pastel on paper – 49.5 x 74.9cm.
(Butterfield & Butterfield)   **£536 $935**

BAREND CORNELIS KOEKKOEK (Dutch, 1803–62)
– Figures in a winter landscape – signed and dated *1842* –
oil on panel – 74 x 95cm.
(Sotheby's)   £187,000 $330,990

WILLEM KOEKKOEK (Dutch, 1839–95) –
Washerwomen by a canal – signed – oil on canvas –
46 x 61cm.
(Sotheby's)   £17,050 $30,178

BAREND CORNELIS KOEKKOEK (1803–1862) – A
winter landscape with a skater and faggot-gatherers on a
frozen river and travellers on a road – signed and dated
1842 – oil on canvas – 59 x 71.2cm.
(Christie's)   £48,400 $84,700

WILLEM KOEKKOEK (1839–1895) – A street scene,
Amsterdam – signed – oil on canvas – 70 x 90cm.
(Christie's)   £46,200 $75,306

JAN HERMANUS KOEKKOEK – The storm – signed
– oil on panel – 13.8 x 17.8cm.
(Christie's)   £1,760 $3,027

WILLEM KOEKKOEK (1839–1895) – A street scene
with townsfolk, Woudrichem – signed and dated *83* – oil on
canvas – 85.7 x 124.5cm.
(Christie's)   £19,800 $34,650

WILLEM KOEKKOEK (1839–1895) – A Dutch street
scene – signed – oil on panel – 46.7 x 35.5cm. unframed.
(Christie's) **£7,150 $12,512**

WILLIAM H.D. KOERNER (1878–1938) – Repartee –
signed and dated *1917* – oil on board en grisaille –
90.2 x 64.8cm.

WILLIAM H.D. KOERNER (1878–1938) – Down by the
wharf – signed with initials – oil on board – 48.3 x 74.9cm.
(Sotheby's) **£1,082 $1,980**

(Sotheby's) **£1,443 $2,640**

WILLIAM H.D. KOERNER (1878–1938) – Her first
view of the wilderness – signed with initials – oil on board
– 61 x 91.4cm.
(Sotheby's)   **£1,082 $1,980**

**WILLIAM HENRY DETHLEF D. KOERNER (1878–
1938)** – Tall in the saddle – signed – oil on canvas –
56 x 102.3cm.
(Christie's)   **£6,061 $10,450**

ALEXANDER KOESTER (1864–1932) – Ducks on a
river bank – signed – oil on canvas – 45.7 x 75.5cm.
(Christie's)   **£37,400 $65,450**

OSKAR KOKOSCHKA (1886–1980) – Girl with yellow
hairband – signed with initials – watercolour and soft pencil
on paper – 44.5 x 31.1cm.
(Christie's)   **£60,500 $98,010**

OSKAR KOKOSCHKA (1886–1980) – Richmond
Terrace – signed with initials – oil on canvas –
89 x 124.5cm.
(Christie's) **£660,000 $1,082,400**

OSKAR KOKOSCHKA (1886–1980) – Harbour view,
Polperro – signed with initials – oil on board –
50.5 x 60.5cm.
(Christie's) **£77,000 $124,740**

KATHE KOLLWITZ (1867–1945) – Working class
woman (with earring) – original etching on copperplate
paper – 32.8 x 24.5cm.
(Lempertz) **£1,747 $2,786**

J. KOLITH –Duck shooting in the marshes – signed – oil
on panel – unframed – 31.2 x 40cm.
(Christie's) **£770 $1,324**

KATHE KOLLWITZ (1867–1945) – Self portrait at the
table II – original etching and aquatint on vellum –
18 x 12.8cm.
(Lempertz) **£1,384 $2,207**

JOSEPH KOLSCHBACH (b. 1892) – St Francis with the
animals – oil on canvas – 54 x 64cm.
(Lempertz)   **£13,841 $22,076**

ENDRE KOMAROMI-KACZ – Arranging the flowers --
signed – oil on canvas – 101 x 75.6cm.
(Christie's)   **£1,320 $2,281**

CARL KRAFFT (1884–1938) – In from the fields –
signed – oil on canvas – 40.6 x 50.8cm.
(Butterfield & Butterfield)   **£756 $1,320**

JOHANN KONIG (1586–1642) – The Adoration of the
Shepherds – oil on copper – 75 x 52cm.
(Sotheby's)   **£18,700 $33,660**

Manner of CHARLES LOUIS KRATKE – Tempting
fate – oil on canvas – 45.7 x 67.3cm.
(Christie's) **£418 $722**

GEORG-MELCHIOR KRAUS (1737–1806) – The
money lender – signed – oil on panel – 64.5 x 55cm.
(Christie's) **£8,375 $13,902**

RUDOLF KRATKY (Austrian, 1824–1901) – Lady with
a dog – signed – oil on canvas – 43 x 22.5cm.
(Sotheby's) **£1,100 $1,947**

JOHANN-HERMANN KRETZSCHMER – The House
of Cards – signed – oil on canvas – 40.7 x 35.6cm.
(Christie's) **£2,200 $3,784**

HERMAN KRIKHAAR (b. 1930) – Woman with water melon – signed and dated *5'90* – pen and black ink and gouache on paper – 90 x 63cm.
(Christie's)   **£2,063 $3,651**

LOUIS KRONBERG (American, 1872–1965) – Ballerina – signed – pastel and graphite on tan paper/board – 21³/₈ x 14³/₈in.
(Skinner Inc.)   **£405 $715**

HERMAN KRIKHAAR (b. 1930) – My garden – signed with initials and dated *'84* – oil on canvas – 120 x 60cm.
(Christie's)   **£6,876 $12,170**

LOUIS KRONBERG (American, 1872–1965) – Beach scene, Etretat – signed and dated *1932* – watercolour on paper – 9³/₄ x 13¹/₂in.
(Skinner Inc.)   **£139 $247**

LOUIS KRONBERG (American, 1872–1965) – At the opera, The Ballet in Green – signed – pastel on paper/board – 23 x 28in.
(Skinner Inc.)   **£405 $715**

PEDER SEVERIN KRØYER (1851–1909) – The
departure of the fishing fleet – signed and dated *94* – oil on
canvas – 135.9 x 224.8cm.
(Christie's)   **£154,000 $269,500**

ALFRED KUBIN (1877–1959) – The will – signed – pen
and black ink and watercolour on paper – 18.5 x 27.5cm.
(Christie's)   **£7,700 $12,474**

MAX KUEHNE (1880–circa 1968) – Still life with vase
of anemones and fruit – bears artist's estate stamp – oil on
panel – 61 x 41cm.
(Christie's)   **£3,190 $5,500**

MAX KUEHNE (1880–1968) – The open window –
signed – oil on masonite – 62.3 x 83.8cm.
(Christie's)   **£8,294 $14,300**

KUEHNE

MAX KUEHNE (1880–1968) – A corner of the city –
signed – oil on canvas – 76.2 x 63cm.
(Christie's) **£1,914 $3,300**

WILHELM KUHNERT (1865–1926) – A tigress
watching for prey; and Tigers resting – both signed and
dated *1913* – oil on panel – 40.6 x 83.1cm. – two
(Christie's) **£121,000 $211,750**

WILHELM KUHNERT (1865–1926) – A lion and lioness
at a stream – signed – oil on panel – 40 x 80cm.
(Christie's) **£71,500 $116,545**

WALT KUHN (American, 1877–1949) – Seated nude
with robe – signed – ink on paper – 12³/₄ x 8³/₄in.
(Skinner Inc.) **£264 $467**

FRANK KUPKA (1871–1957) – Chromatic concentration
– signed – gouache on paper – 27.3 x 18.1cm.
(Christie's) **£20,350 $32,967**

Follower of MADAME ADELAIDE LABILLE-GUIARD – Portrait of a young lady, seated three-quarter length, in a grey silk dress, at a table holding a sprig of flowers – oil on canvas – oval – 99.1 x 73.7cm.
(Christie's) **£2,420 $3,775**

GASTON LACHAISE (1882–1935) – An Egyptian dancer – signed – pencil on paper – 58.4 x 46.5cm.
(Christie's) **£2,424 $4,180**

A. LACH – A bird's nest and roses on a bank – signed – oil on canvas – 33 x 43.3cm.
(Christie's) **£3,740 $6,433**

LADBROOKE

Attributed to JOHN BERNEY LADBROOKE (1803–1879) – A wayside chat – with indistinct signature – oil on canvas – 76.2 x 63.5cm.
(Christie's) £1,210 $2,202

JOHN BERNEY LADBROOKE – Travelling fish monger – monogrammed – oil – 23 x 28in.
(G.A. Key) £3,200 $5,664

JEAN BAPTISTE ADOLPHE LAFOSSE (1814–1879) – Portrait of a child resting on a draped high back chair – signed and dated *1847* – oval – oil on panel – 31.5 x 22.7cm.
(Christie's) £5,500 $8,965

EDWARD LADELL (1821–1886) – Grapes, plums, whitecurrants, strawberries, raspberries, a peach and hazelnuts with a glass of wine on a wooden ledge – signed with monogram – oil on canvas – 43 x 35.5cm.
(Christie's) £20,900 $35,530

Attributed to JEAN-FRANÇOIS LAGRENEE (1725–1805) – The death of the Dauphin – oil on canvas – 118 x 97cm.
(Christie's) £12,284 $20,391

LOUIS-JEAN-FRANÇOIS LAGRENEE (1725–1805) –
The embassy of Popilius to Antioch Epiphanus seeking a
halt to his depredations in Egypt – signed and dated *1778* –
black chalk, pen and grey and black ink, brown wash –
410 x 536mm.
(Christie's) £7,817 $12,976

CARLOS LAHARRAGUE – A corner in Madrid – signed
and dated *1982* – oil on canvas – 50 x 65cm.
(Duran) £836 $1,501

CARLOS LAHARRAGUE – Córdoba – signed – oil on
canvas laid down on panel – 28 x 36cm.
(Duran) £279 $501

HENRI-ADOLPHE LAISSEMENT (d. 1921) – Word
from on High – signed – oil on panel – 62.2 x 55.7cm.
(Christie's) £7,700 $13,398

HENRY LAMB, R.A. (1883–1960) – Family group – oil
on canvas-board – 48 x 59.5cm.
(Christie's)   £2,420 $4,017

HENRY LAMB (1883–1960) - The stable – pencil and
watercolour – 21.5 x 25cm.
(Christie's)   £418 $694

ALPHONSE LALAUZE – Murat and his Generals –
signed and dated 1913 – pastel and watercolour on paper –
80 x 60cm.
(Hôtel de Ventes Horta)   £2,241 $3,900

HENRY LAMB – Head study of a Gola girl – inscribed –
soft pencil – 29.7 x 22.7cm.
(Christie's)   £825 $1,312

EUGENE LOUIS LAMBERT (1852–1900) – The
occupied kennel – signed – oil on panel – 35 x 27.3cm.
(Christie's)   £3,300 $5,412

JAN BAPTIST LAMBRECHTS – Figures taking
refreshment outside a house – oil on canvas – 82 x 87.5cm.
(Sotheby's)   **£4,840 $8,712**

EUGENE LAMI (French, 1800–90) – A cavalry officer –
signed and dated *1820* – pen and ink and watercolour –
12.5 x 16cm.
(Sotheby's)   **£880 $1,558**

CHET HARMON LAMORE (American, b. 1908) – The
Necromancer, 1943 – signed – oil on canvas – 40 x 30in.
(Skinner Inc.)   **£1,182 $2,090**

GEORGE LANCE (1802–1864) – The village coquette –
signed – oil on canvas – 110.5 x 86cm.
(Christie's)   **£33,000 $56,100**

ALFRED DOBREE LANCASTER – At the helm –
inscribed on reverse – oil on canvas – 124.5 x 81.3cm.
(Christie's)   **£2,860 $5,069**

GEORGE LANCE – Interior with girl and fruit – signed
and dated *1851* – oil on board – 7³/₄ x 6³/₄in.
(Bearne's)   **£700 $1,214**

JOHN ST HELIER LANDER (1869–1944) – Portrait of
Mrs Arthur Wood, seated three-quarter length, wearing a
black dress and a broad-rimmed black hat – signed and
dated *1909* – oil on canvas – unframed – 127 x 102cm.
(Christie's)   **£4,400 $7,128**

FITZ HUGH LANE (1804-1865) – Camden mountains from the south entrance to the harbour – signed and dated *1859* – oil on canvas – 55.9 x 91.4cm. *(Sotheby's)* £412,500 $742,500

RICARDO VERDUGO LANDI (1871–1930) – Demonstration in St Petersburg – signed – oil on canvas – 55 x 38cm. *(Duran)* £1,400 $2,465

SIR EDWIN HENRY LANDSEER, R.A. (1802–1873) – A King Charles spaniel – black, red and white chalk and touches of white bodycolour – 16.5 x 24.5cm. *(Christie's)* £4,400 $7,216

O. LANDUYT – Don't fence me in – signed – oil on canvas – 120 x 140cm. *(Hôtel de Ventes Horta)* £8,191 $14,007

FRANCOIS-LOUIS LANFANT DE METZ (1814–1892) – The slide – signed – oil on panel – 36 x 17.8cm. *(Christie's)* £3,300 $5,742

323

WALTER LANGLEY (1852–1922) – Figures on the
quayside before cottages, Polperro Harbour, Cornwall –
signed – watercolour – 14 x 10in.
(W.H. Lane & Son)   £2,000 $3,685

WALTER LANGLEY (1852–1922) – Head and shoulder
portraits of a fisherman and fisherwoman – pair of
watercolours – 7½ x 5¼in.
(W.H. Lane & Son)   £580 $980

WALTER LANGLEY (1852–1922) – Head and shoulder
portrait of a young woman in flower decorated hat – signed
– pastel – 9 x 7in.
(W.H. Lane & Son)   £600 $1,106

WALTER LANGLEY (1852–1922) – The telegram – signed and dated *1880* – watercolour – 6¹/₄ x 9¹/₄in.
(W.H. Lane & Son)   £2,300 $3,715

MARK W. LANGLOIS (British, 19th century) –
Curiosity – signed – oil on panel – 8¹/₂ x 6¹/₄in.
(Skinner Inc.)   £443 $770

MARK W. LANGLOIS (British, 19th century) – The toy
seller/A genre scene – signed – oil on panel – 8¹/₂ x 6¹/₄in.
(Skinner Inc.)   £570 $990

MARK W. LANGLOIS (fl. 1862–1873) – The village fair – signed with initials – oil on canvas – 71.5 x 91.3cm.
(Christie's)   £5,060 $8,956

GIOVANNI LANZA (b. 1827) – The Bay of Naples – signed – watercolour on paper – 44 x 75.5cm.
(Christie's)   £2,640 $4,594

VICENZO LANZA (mid 19th century) – The Temple of Zeus with the Acropolis beyond, Athens; and The Parthenon, Athens – signed – pencil and watercolour, one heightened with white, on paper – 24.1 x 36.2cm. – a pair
(Christie's)   £3,300 $5,742

Follower of NICOLAS DE LARGILLIERE – Portrait of a lady, said to be the Duchesse de Valier, in masquerade costume – oil on canvas – 137.5 x 105cm.
(Sotheby's)   £7,700 $13,860

OLE LARSEN – Going to cover – signed – oil on canvas –
22 x 28in.
(Du Mouchelles) £195 $325

GASPARD LATOIX (19th–20th century) – Apache
indian on horseback – signed – oil on canvas –
61 x 50.8cm.
(Sotheby's) £4,889 $8,800

GASPARD LATOIX (19th/20th century) – Cowboy on
horseback – signed – watercolour on paper laid down on
board – unframed – 50.8 x 38.1cm.
(Sotheby's) £962 $1,760

G. LATOUCHE (1854–1913) – Naiads – signed –
charcoal and pastel on paper – 45.5 x 32.5cm.
(Hôtel de Ventes Horta)　　　　£2,218　$3,793

MARIE YVONNE LAUR (1879–1943) – The bottom
drawer – signed – oil on canvas – 55.2 x 46.3cm.
(Christie's)　　　　£2,860　$4,690

GASTON DE LATOUCHE (1854–1913) – A sale –
signed – oil on panel – 47.5 x 55cm.
(Christie's)　　　　£7,480　$12,192

MARIE YVONNE LAUR (1879–1943) – A watchful eye
– signed – oil on panel – 37.5 x 45.7cm.
(Christie's)　　　　£2,640　$4,329

SYDNEY LAURENCE (1865–1940) – Venice – signed –
watercolour on paper – 43.2 x 29.2cm.
(Butterfield & Butterfield)　　　　£756　$1,320

MARIE LAURENCIN (1885–1956) – Young girl with guitar –signed – oil on canvas – 61 x 50.2cm.
(Christie's)   **£143,000**   **$234,520**

MARIE LAURENCIN (1885–1956) – Self portrait – pencil and coloured crayon on paper – 20 x 15.5cm.
(Christie's)   **£8,800**   **$15,488**

MARIE LAURENCIN (1885–1956) – Vase of flowers – signed and dated *1939* – oil on canvas – 54.8 x 46.1cm.
(Christie's)   **£41,800**   **$73,568**

MARIE LAURENCIN (1885–1956) – Marguerite or the Girl with the pink bow – signed and dated *1923* – oil on canvas – 42.5 x 33cm.
(Christie's)   **£33,000**   **$53,460**

LAURENCIN

MARIE LAURENCIN (1885–1956) – Head of a young
girl – signed – watercolour and pencil on paper laid on
board – 32 x 26cm.
(Christie's) £8,800 $15,488

AUGUST LAUX (1847–1921) – Gooseberries – signed -
oil on canvas – 25.5 x 35.5cm.
(Christie's) £3,509 $6,050

MARIE LAURENCIN (1885–1956) – Young women –
signed – watercolour on paper – 31 x 23cm.
(Christie's) £9,350 $15,147

GEORGE LAWRENCE – The orchard – signed and dated *47* – oil on board – 31 x 38cm.
(Australian Art Auctions) **£835 $1,486**

JOHN LAVALLE (American, b. 1896) – Miss Laetitia Orlandini – signed and dated *1928* – oil on canvas – 40 x 30in.
(Skinner Inc.) **£1,245 $2,200**

DENYS LAW – Lamorna valley in spring – signed – oil on board – 24 x 30in.
(David Lay) **£820 $1,304**

CARL LAWLESS (American, 1896–1934) – Batik, a still life – signed – oil on canvas – 15 x 15in.
(Skinner Inc.) **£560 $990**

HENRY LAWRENCE (fl. 1871–1884) – The duellist – signed and inscribed – oil on canvas – 76.5 x 50.5cm.
(Christie's) **£1,650 $2,673**

JACOB LAWRENCE (b. 1917) – Underground railroad: fording a stream – signed twice and dated *1948* – India ink and pencil on paper – 41.9 x 58.4cm.
(Sotheby's)   **£2,855 $5,225**

ERNEST LAWSON (1873-1939) – River scene in winter – signed – oil on canvas – 76.2 x 76.2cm.
(Sotheby's)   **£51,944 $93,500**

SIR THOMAS LAWRENCE (British, 1769–1830) – Portrait of the artist's wife – pencil on paper – 26 x 21.6cm.
(Butterfield & Butterfield)   **£2,049 $3,575**

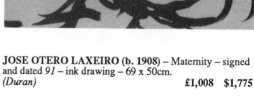

ERNEST LAWSON (1873–1939) – The Biltmore Hotel, Palm Beach – signed – oil on canvas – 52 x 62.2cm.
(Christie's)   **£11,484 $19,800**

JOSE OTERO LAXEIRO (b. 1908) – Maternity – signed and dated *91* – ink drawing – 69 x 50cm.
(Duran)   **£1,008 $1,775**

BENJAMIN WILLIAMS LEADER, R.A. (1831–1923) –
Evening light - signed and dated *1902* – oil on canvas –
152.4 x 121.9cm.
(Christie's) £7,700 $13,629

JEAN-RAYMOND-HIPPOLYTE LAZERGUES (1817–
1887) – The Descent from the Cross – signed and dated
1885 – oil on canvas – 348 x 238cm.
(Christie's) £22,334 $37,074

BENJAMIN WILLIAMS LEADER, R.A. (1831–1923) –
A croquet party – signed and dated *1871* – oil on board –
23 x 30.5cm.
(Christie's) £9,350 $15,147

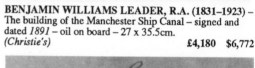

BENJAMIN WILLIAMS LEADER, R.A. (1831–1923) –
The building of the Manchester Ship Canal – signed and
dated *1891* – oil on board – 27 x 35.5cm.
(Christie's) £4,180 $6,772

NOEL HARRY LEAVER (British, 1889–1951) – A
mosque in Cairo – signed – watercolour on paper –
36.2 x 26cm.
(Butterfield & Butterfield) £1,198 $2,090

EDWARD CHALMERS LEAVITT (1842–1904) – A
still life with dead game – signed and dated *1872* – oil on
canvas – 50.8 x 42cm.
(Christie's) £1,243 $2,200

EDWARD CHALMERS LEAVITT (1842–1904) – Still life with pink and yellow roses – signed and dated *1895* – oil on canvas – 61 x 73.7cm.
(Sotheby's) **£2,404 $4,400**

HENRI LEBASQUE (1865–1937) – Girl in the garden, le Pradet – signed – oil on canvas – 59.5 x 45.7cm.
(Christie's) **£37,400 $60,588**

HENRI LEBASQUE (1865–1937) – The banks of the Marne – signed – oil on canvas – 54.3 x 64.7cm.
(Christie's) **£41,800 $73,568**

HENRI LEBASQUE (1865–1937) – Women on the terrace at Préfailles – oil on canvas – 65 x 73cm.
(Christie's) **£49,500 $80,190**

HENRI LEBASQUE (1865–1937) – Port of Saint Tropez – signed and dated *1906* – oil on canvas – 73 x 92cm.
(Christie's) **£68,200 $120,032**

LAWRENCE LEBDUSKA (b. 1894) – The Garden of Eden – signed and dated *2–62* – oil on canvas – 138.5 x 213.4cm.
(Christie's) **£3,107 $5,500**

LEBENSTEIN

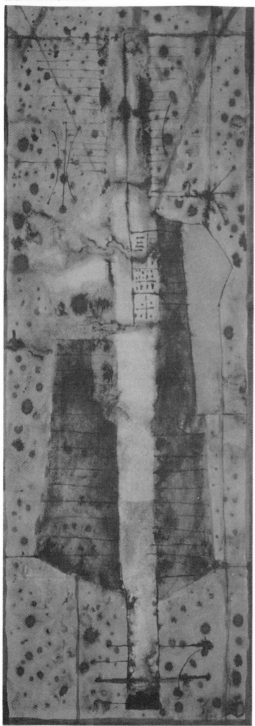

LOUISE ELISABETH VIGEE LEBRUN (1755–1842) –
Portrait of Countess Catherine Vladimirowna Apraxina –
signed and dated *1796* – oil on canvas, unlined –
112 x 94cm.
(Sotheby's)   £330,000 $594,000

JAN LEBENSTEIN (b. 1930) – Untitled – watercolour,
pen and ink – 80 x 29cm.
(Christie's)   £1,210 $1,924

A. LEBOURG – The pond in the Tuileries – bears
signature – oil on panel – 27.5 x 35cm.
(Hôtel de Ventes Horta)   £1,379 $2,400

LOUISE ELISABETH VIGEE LEBRUN (1755–1842) –
Portrait of Aglaé de Polignac, Duchesse de Guiche – signed
and dated *1784* – pastel, oval – 80.5 x 64cm.
(Sotheby's)   £77,000 $138,600

PAUL EMILE LECOMTE (1877–1950) – Spanish street
scene with distant mountains – signed – oil on canvas –
23¹/₂ x 29¹/₂in.
(W.H. Lane & Son)   **£4,000 $6,460**

WILLIAM LEE (1810–1865) – Hide and seek – pencil
and watercolour – 533 x 610mm.
(Christie's)   **£1,045 $1,766**

PAUL LEDUC (Belgian, 1876–1943) – Evening at
Dordrecht – signed – oil on canvas – 60.5 x 80.5cm.
(Hôtel de Ventes Horta)   **£5,484 $9,323**

WILLIAM LEE-HANKEY (1869–1952) – The River
Conway, North Wales – signed – oil on canvas –
61 x 76cm.
(Christie's)   **£4,400 $7,304**

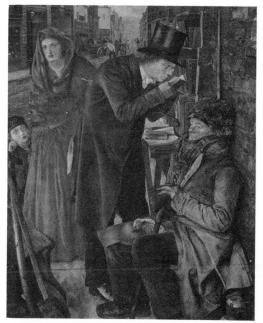

JOHN J. LEE (fl 1850–1867) – The bookstall – signed and
dated *1863* – oil on canvas – 101.6 x 81.2cm.
(Christie's)   **£101,200 $172,040**

WILLIAM LEE-HANKEY (1869–1952) – Girl with a
staff – signed – watercolour – 9¹/₄ x 13in.
(W.H. Lane & Son)   **£1,200 $2,211**

337

CORNELIS VAN LEEMPUTTEN (1841–1902) –
Chickens, ducks and rabbits by a pond – signed and dated
1867 – oil on canvas – 25.4 x 35.5cm.
(Christie's) £2,420 $4,211

CHARLES LEFEVRE – A drover with cattle, sheep and a
goat on a track – signed – oil on canvas – 52 x 89cm.
(Christie's) £1,210 $2,091

FERNAND LEGER (1881–1955) – Sketch for
polychrome sculpture – signed with initials and dated *54* –
gouache, brush and black ink on paper laid down on canvas
– 51.5 x 36cm.
(Christie's) £14,300 $23,166

FERNAND LEGER (1881–1955) – Composition with
vase – signed with initials - pencil on buff paper –
62.2 x 47.6cm.
(Christie's) £7,700 $12,474

FERNAND LEGER (1881–1955) – Composition –
gouache and black ink on paper – 34 x 26cm.
(Christie's) £6,050 $10,648

FERNAND LEGER (1881–1955) – Deauville – signed with initials and dated *50* – gouache and pencil on paper – 22 x 27cm.
(Christie's) £9,350 $15,147

WILLIAM ROBINSON LEIGH (1866–1955) – Seated Navajo – signed and dated *1951* – pencil on paper – 43.2 x 49.5cm.
(Butterfield & Butterfield) £7,564 $13,200

Circle of CHARLES LEICKERT – A winter townscape with figures – with signature – oil on canvas – 45.7 x 35.6cm.
(Christie's) £990 $1,711

FREDERIC, LORD LEIGHTON(1830–1896) – Study of the young girl who posed for 'Wide Wondering Eyes' – signed and dated *1874* – black and white chalk on brown paper – 215 x 152mm.
(Christie's) £2,420 $4,404

KATHRYN WOODMAN LEIGHTON (1876–1952) –
Old Indian deep in thought – signed – oil on canvas –
111.8 x 91.4cm.
(Butterfield & Butterfield) £1,261 $2,200

FREDERIC, LORD LEIGHTON (1830–1896) – Sketch
for 'The Death of Brunelleschi' – with inscription – oil on
canvas, unframed – 36.5 x 30.5cm.
(Christie's) £5,280 $8,554

WILLIAM LEIGHTON LEITCH – Fishing vessels on
an Italian lake – signed with initials and dated *1870?* –
pencil and watercolour – unframed – 4³/₄ x 7¹/₂in.
(Christie's) £385 $682

FREDERIC, LORD LEIGHTON (1830–1896) –
Portrait of a woman, quarter length – oil on canvas –
25.3 x 18.3cm.
(Christie's) £7,150 $11,583

After SIR PETER LELY (British, 1618–1680) – George
Villiers (1628–1687), second Duke of Buckingham –
inscribed on reverse – oil on canvas – 69.2 x 63.5cm.
(Butterfield & Butterfield) £347 $605

Follower of SIR PETER LELY – Portrait of a young girl, half length in a gold dress with a blue wrap holding a posy of flowers – oil on canvas – in a painted cartouche – 73.6 x 62.8cm.
(Christie's) £1,320 $2,132

Follower of SIR PETER LELY – A young lady, head and shoulders, her curling brown hair adorned with flowers and wearing a brown dress – on panel – 15 x 11³/₄in.
(Bearne's) £520 $902

LUCY BROWN L'ENGLE (b. 1889) – Turtle Dance, Taos – signed and dated *1941* – oil on canvas – 77 x 101.8cm.
(Christie's) £2,233 $3,850

LENKIEWICZ

Attributed to BERNARD LENS III (1682–1740) – A prospect of Woburn Farm, Surrey – signed with initials – watercolour and bodycolour – unframed – 158 x 210mm.
(Christie's) £1,045 $1,839

IGNACIO LEON Y ESCOSURA (1834–1901) – A quiet read – signed and dated *1881* – oil on panel – 32 x 40cm.
(Duran) £11,142 $20,000

ROBERT O LENKIEWICZ – Painter with Joanne – signed to verso – 16 x 12½in.
(W.H. Lane & Son) £800 $1,352

ROBERT O LENKIEWICZ –Painter with Gemma – signed to verso – unframed – oil on canvas – 24 x 18in.
(W.H. Lane & Son) £400 $676

LOUIS HECTOR LEROUX – Maidens at the Shrine of Asclepius – signed – oil on panel – 66 x 44.5cm.
(Christie's) £1,210 $2,081

342

JULES LEROY (French, 1833–1865) – Kittens making mischief – signed – oil on canvas – 43.2 x 48.9cm.
(Butterfield & Butterfield) £1,891 $3,300

THERESE LESSORE (1884–1945) – Girl resting on a chaise longue – signed and dated *1922* – oil on canvas – 49.5 x 59.5cm.
(Christie's) £1,980 $3,406

THERESE LESSORE –Bruges market – signed and dated *1921* – watercolour – 10³/₄ x 8³/₄in.
(Bearne's) £440 $763

ANDRE LEVEILLE (French, 1880–1963) – Landscape
by the river bank – signed – oil on panel – 40.6 x 49.5cm.
(Butterfield & Butterfield) **£1,891 $3,300**

EMILE AUBERT LESSURE (French, 1805–1876) –
Breakfast – signed and dated *1852* – oil on panel –
50.8 x 40cm.
(Bonhams) **£1,900 $3,021**

ANTONIO LETO (1844–1913) – A summer afternoon –
signed – oil on canvas – 38.7 x 64.2cm.
(Christie's) **£39,600 $69,300**

RICHARD HAYLEY LEVER (1876–1955) – St. Ives,
Cornwall, England – signed – oil on board – 33 x 41.2cm.
(Christie's) **£2,486 $4,400**

CHARLES LEVIER (French, 20th century) – Moored sailing boats – signed – oil on board –
52.1 x 152.4cm.
(Butterfield & Butterfield) **£1,261 $2,200**

DAVID LEVINE (b. 1926) – Portrait of Walter Fillin – signed, dated and inscribed – oil on panel – 30.5 x 25.5cm.
(Christie's) **£415 $715**

LUCIEN LEVY-DHURMER (1865–1953) – Head of a girl – signed, inscribed and dated *79* – pastel on light brown paper laid down on board – 41.3 x 33cm.
(Christie's) **£1,980 $3,445**

DAVID LEVINE (b. 1926) – Boardwalk at Coney Island – signed and dated – watercolour and pencil on paper – 36.8 x 55cm.
(Christie's) **£829 $1,430**

STEPHEN LEWIN (fl. 1890–1910) – The stag – signed
and dated *1903* – oil on canvas – 61 x 81.2cm.
(Christie's) £2,200 $4,004

JOHN FREDERICK LEWIS (1805–1876) – Study of an
Arab Sheikh – signed – coloured chalks, watercolour and
bodycolour heightened with gum arabic – 279 x 203mm.
(Christie's) £9,350 $16,456

CHARLES JAMES LEWIS (1830–1892) – Going to
church –signed – oil on card – 38 x 54.5cm.
(Christie's) £5,280 $8,554

EDMUND DARCH LEWIS (American, 1837–1910) –
Lehervale – signed and dated – oil on canvas – 30 x 50in.
(Du Mouchelles) £4,051 $7,000

PERCY WYNDHAM LEWIS (1882–1957) – Crouching
nude – signed and dated *1919* – pencil and watercolour –
28.5 x 25.5cm.
(Christie's) £3,850 $6,391

LEON LHERMITTE (French, 1844–1925) – A portrait of an old woman – signed – charcoal – 59 x 43cm.
(Sotheby's) **£1,980 $3,505**

MATHIAS LEYENDECKER (1822–1871) – Thrush hanging from a hook – signed and dated *1869* – oil on canvas – 35.5 x 22.2cm.
(Christie's) **£1,430 $2,488**

LEON AUGUSTIN LHERMITTE (1844–1925) – Itinerants at evening – signed – oil on canvas – 55.2 x 77.5cm.
(Christie's) **£20,900 $34,067**

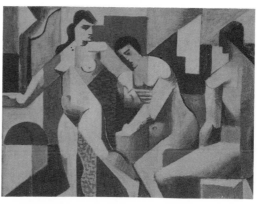

GYSBRECHT LEYTENS (1586–1643/56) - A wooded landscape in winter with wood gatherers – oil on panel – 55.5 x 77cm.
(Sotheby's) **£63,800 $114,840**

ANDRE LHOTE (1885–1962) – Three bathers – signed and dated *18* – oil on paper laid down on canvas – 40.5 x 56cm.
(Christie's) **£9,900 $16,038**

MAX LIEBERMANN (1847–1935) – The net mender – signed – charcoal drawing heightened with white on paper – 24.5 x 31.5cm.
(Lempertz) £3,460 $5,519

LUDOLF LIBERTS (Latvian, 1895–1945) – Paris street at night – signed – oil on canvas – 88.9 x 59.7cm.
(Butterfield & Butterfield) £3,152 $5,500

Follower of JACQUES LINARD – Still life of plums in a bowl, a book, a knife and a pitcher on a partly draped table – oil on canvas – 38 x 44cm.
(Sotheby's) £3,300 $5,940

CHARLES SILLEM LIDDERDALE (1831–1895) – Una Senorita – signed with initials and dated *70* – oil on canvas – 47 x 39.3cm.
(Christie's) £990 $1,753

TOD LINDENMUTH (American, 1885–1976) – Setting out lobster traps – signed – oil on board – $17^3/_4$ x $23^1/_2$in.
(Skinner Inc.) £498 $880

Circle of JOHANNES LINGELBACH – A market scene with a fruitseller and a shepherd, Oriental traders conversing – oil on canvas – 86.3 x 106.8cm.
(Bonhams) £5,500 $8,745

NORMAN ALFRED WILLIAMS LINDSAY (1879–1969) – Young lovers – signed – pencil and watercolour heightened with white – 21.6 x 22.8cm.
(Christie's) £1,650 $2,904

JOHANNES LINGELBACH (1622–1674) – An Italianate harbour with figures loading livestock onto a small vessel moored by a quay – oil on canvas – 51 x 68.5cm.
(Sotheby's) £13,200 $23,760

JOHN LINNELL (1792–1882) – A Welsh dairy farm – signed and dated *1847* – oil on panel – 27.2 x 40.6cm.
(Christie's) £7,150 $12,155

PERCIVAL CHARLES LINDSAY (1870–1952) – Fossacking for gold – 40.7 x 30.5cm.
(Christie's) £11,550 $20,328

WILLIAM LINNELL (1826–1906) – A shepherd and his flock in a sunlit wooded landscape; and Under the beech tree – one signed and dated *1875* and the other signed – oil on canvas – 51 x 66.5cm and 46 x 63.5cm. – a pair
(Christie's) £5,280 $8,554

LINSON

CORWIN KNAPP LINSON (1864–1934) – Autumn glow
– signed – oil on canvas laid down on board –
55.9 x 45.7cm.
(Sotheby's) **£1,082 $1,980**

CORWIN KNAPP LINSON (1864–1934) – Views of
Jordan, Jerusalem, and Bethany: five paintings – each
signed, and dated *1898*, one dated *1899* – each oil on board
– average size: 16.5 x 22.9cm.
(Sotheby's) **£3,607 $6,600**

SIR JAMES DROMGOLE LINTON (1840–1916) – A
seated woman holding a fan – signed with initials and dated
89 – pencil and watercolour – 253 x 355mm.
(Christie's) **£825 $1,394**

EDWARD BARNARD LINTOTT (American, 1875–
1951) – Tuberose Begonia – signed – oil on canvas –
24 x 20in.
(Skinner Inc.) **£506 $880**

RICHARD LIPPS (German, 1857–1926) – Marketplace,
Venice – signed – oil on canvas – 44 x 32in.
(Skinner Inc.) **£8,230 $14,300**

350

JOHN GEOFFREY CARRUTHERS LITTLE (b. 1928)
– Farmhouse in the city – signed and dated *51* – oil on
canvas – 50.8 x 61cm.
(Fraser–Pinneys) £3,007 $5,217

JOHN GEOFFREY CARRUTHERS LITTLE (b. 1928)
– Bonsecours Church – signed and dated *54* – oil on board
– 61 x 76.2cm.
(Fraser–Pinneys) £4,010 $6,957

DOROTHEA M. LITZINGER (American, 1889–1925) –
Still life with laurel, foxglove and daisies – unsigned – oil
on canvas (unstretched) – $21^1/_4$ x $13^1/_2$in.
(Skinner Inc.) £158 $275

PHILIP LITTLE (American, 1857–1942) – Tropical
lagoon – signed and dated *25* – watercolour on paper –
19 x 13in.
(Skinner Inc.) £222 $385

GASPER MIRO LLEO (1859–1930) – L'Ile de la Cité,
Paris – signed – oil on panel – 21.2 x 27cm.
(Christie's) £1,870 $3,254

LLOPIS

WALTER STUART LLOYD (fl. 1875–1929) – Waiting for the ferry – signed and dated *1902* – pencil and watercolour with touches of white heightening – 293 x 653mm.
(Christie's) £880 $1,602

CARLOS RUANO LLOPIS – Picador – signed– oil on canvas – 154 x 106cm.
(Duran) £1,400 $2,465

W. STUART LLOYD (English, fl. 1875–1929) – Feeding the ducks – signed – oil on canvas – 50.8 x 76.2cm.
(Bonhams) £1,800 $2,862

CLYDE LO-A-NJOE (b. 1937) – Alice in Lop-Lop land – signed and dated *1990* – acrylics on canvas – 120 x 99cm.
(Christie's) £1,031 $1,825

WALTER STUART LLOYD – Lincoln Cathedral – signed and dated *1911* – pencil and watercolour heightened with white – 14¼ x 28in.
(Christie's) £550 $975

GEORGE EDWARD LODGE (1860–1954) – A pair of mute swans – signed – bodycolour – 235 x 298mm.
(Christie's) £1,320 $2,138

LUIGI LOIR (1845–1916) – Les Champs Elysées, Paris –
signed and dated *1894* – oil on card laid down on panel –
15.5 x 30.8cm.
(Christie's)   **£11,550 $18,826**

GUSTAVE LOISEAU (1865–1935) – Normandy cliffs –
signed and dated *1901* – oil on canvas – 60.3 x 73cm.
(Christie's)   **£66,000 $116,160**

EDWIN LONG, R.A. (1829–1891) – Listening to the
anthem – signed with monogram and dated *1879* – oil on
panel – 76 x 53cm.
(Christie's)   **£2,200 $4,633**

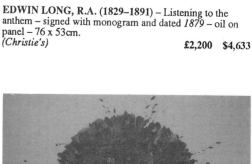

EDWIN LONG (1829–1891) – The new dress – signed
and dated *1872* – oil on canvas – 61 x 45.7cm.
(Christie's)   **£3,850 $7,007**

RICHARD LONG (b. 1945) – River Avon mud – signed,
titled and dated *1983* – mud on paper – 84 x 105cm.
(Christie's)   **£17,600 $28,512**

AMEDEE VAN LOO (1719–1795) – Portrait of King
Frederick II of Prussia, bust length – oil on canvas –
80 x 65.5cm.
(Lempertz) **£5,319 $9,042**

A.H. LONGMAID (late 19th century) – A young woman
standing by a tiger skin in a classical building with rose
doves entering by a window – signed and dated *85* – oil on
canvas – 128.2 x 69.2cm.
(Christie's) **£6,600 $10,692**

HENRY LOOS (circa 1893) – The three-masted
Norwegian barque Victoria off the Eddystone Lighthouse –
signed and dated *1893* – oil on canvas – 66.1 x 96.6cm.
(Christie's) **£4,950 $8,811**

JOHN HENRY LORIMER (1856–1936) – A dog and a mirror – signed and dated *1896* – oil on canvas – 127 x 96.5cm.
(Christie's) £15,400 $25,256

ALBERT LOUDEN – The fat and the thin – pastel – 53.5 x 79cm.
(Christie's) £1,100 $1,749

TOM LOVELL (b. 1909) – Saratoga trunk – signed and dated *41* – oil on canvas – 58.5 x 79cm.
(Butterfield & Butterfield) £1,891 $3,300

LAURENCE STEPHEN LOWRY (1887–1976) – Ferry boats – signed and dated *1960* – oil on canvas – 30.5 x 40.5cm.
(Christie's) £44,000 $73,040

LAURENCE STEPHEN LOWRY (1887–1976) – Northern river scene – signed and dated *1959* – oil on canvas – 50.8 x 76.2cm.
(Christie's) £51,700 $85,822

JOHN SEYMOUR LUCAS, R.A. (1849–1923) – The call to arms – signed and dated *1894* – oil on canvas – 65.1 x 99cm.
(Christie's) £9,900 $17,523

LUCCHESI

MAXIMILIEN LUCE (1858–1941) – Vase of dahlias – signed – oil on paper laid on canvas – 45.5 x 38cm.
(Christie's) **£11,000 $19,360**

MAXIMILIEN LUCE (1858–1941) – The Bievre tanneries – signed and dated *87* – oil on canvas – 59 x 72cm.
(Christie's) **£46,200 $81,312**

GIORGIO LUCCHESI (Italian, 1855–1941) – The Passing of Autumn – signed and dated *1904* – oil on canvas – 39¹/₂ x 28in.
(Skinner Inc.) **£11,825 $20,900**

MAXIMILIEN LUCE (1858–1941) – Portrait de Georges Seurat – signed and dated *1888* – charcoal and watercolour on paper – 29.5 x 23cm.
(Christie's) **£13,200 $21,384**

LUCEBERT – The violinist – signed and dated *76* – oil on canvas – 56 x 46cm.
(Glerum) **£1,612 $2,761**

CHARLES LUCY – Portrait of a young Italian peasant girl – signed with monogram and dated *1856* – oil on panel – 27.3 x 19.7cm.
(Christie's) £935 $1,657

LUCEBERT (b. 1924) – Nieuwe bruiloftsdans – signed and dated '67 – oil on canvas – 130 x 100cm.
(Christie's) £13,064 $23,124

ALBERT LUDOVICI, Jnr. (1852–1932) – The proposal; and An unwanted suitor – both signed – oil on canvas – 31.1 x 41.3cm. – a pair
(Christie's) £2,200 $4,004

School of BERNARDINO LUINI (Italian, 1475–1532) –
Holy Family with John the Baptist in a landscape – oil on
canvas – 39¹/₂ x 28¹/₄in.
(Skinner Inc.)   **£3,423 $6,050**

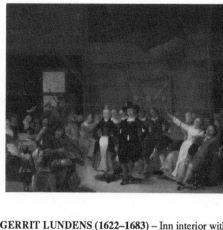

GERRIT LUNDENS (1622–1683) – Inn interior with a
village wedding – signed and dated *1658* – oil on wood –
60 x 83cm.
(Hôtel de Ventes Horta)   **£11,945 $20,426**

THOMAS LUNY (1759–1837) – The Battle of Toulon, 11
February 1744 – signed and dated *1780* – oil on canvas –
43.2 x 60.4cm.
(Christie's)   **£6,600 $11,748**

GEORGE LUKS (1867–1933) – Giraffes – signed – red
chalk on paper – 25.7 x 20.3cm. and 25.7 x 19.7cm. – two
(Christie's)   **£746 $1,320**

THOMAS LUNY (English, 1759–1837) – Unloading the
catch – signed and dated *1807* – oil on canvas –
44.8 x 65.2cm.
(Bonhams)   **£6,800 $11,220**

THOMAS LUNY – A coaster beached at Teignmouth –
signed and dated *1834* – 19 x 26³/₄in.
(Bearne's) **£5,200 $9,022**

JUAN RAMON LUZURIAGA (b. 1938) – Portugalete –
signed and dated *1976* on reverse – oil on canvas –
41 x 33cm.
(Duran) **£501 $899**

THOMAS LUNY (English, 1759–1837) – St. Michael's
Mount – signed and dated *1831* – oil on canvas –
57 x 69cm.
(Bonhams) **£6,000 $9,900**

THOMAS LUNY (1759–1837) – A harbour in the
Bosphorous with Turkish traders – signed and dated *1822* –
oil on canvas – 38.1 x 50.8cm.
(Christie's) **£2,640 $4,699**

JUAN RAMON LUZURIAGA (b. 1938) – Buoy and
barge – signed and dated *77* – oil on canvas – 41 x 33cm.
(Duran) **£560 $986**

JOHN ABERNETHY LYNAS-GREY (b. 1869) – A girl seated under climbing roses by a cottage door – signed and dated 1909 – watercolour – 24 x 34cm.
(Allen & Harris)   **£160 $282**

MARGEL LYON – A harbour scene near Valletta, Malta – signed and dated *84* – oil on canvas – 10¹/₂ x 18in.
(Geering & Colyer)   **£950 $1,572**

MICHAEL LYNE – Pony mares and foals – signed – 71 x 91.5cm.
(Christie's)   **£880 $1,399**

ANDREW MACARA (b. 1944) – Late afternoon, Woollacombe – signed and dated *1989* – oil on canvas – 39.5 x 49.5cm.
(Christie's)   **£550 $913**

MICHAEL LYNE (1912–1990) – The Heythrop – signed and dated *1956* – pencil, watercolour and bodycolour – 42.5 x 59.5cm.
(Christie's)   **£4,400 $7,568**

ANDREW MACARA (b. 1944) – Ilfracombe, Devon – signed and dated *1990* – oil on canvas – 51 x 102cm.
(Christie's)   **£550 $913**

ANDREW MACARA (b. 1944) – Mundy Pool, Marketon Park, Derby – signed and dated *1990* – oil on canvas – 42 x 76cm.
(Christie's) £660 $1,096

J. MACDONALD (fl. 1907) – Mary-le-Bow on the Strand – signed and dated *Macdonald/07* – pencil, watercolour and bodycolour – 230 x 330mm.
(Christie's) **£1,320 $2,138**

THOMAS MACKAY (fl. 1893–1912) – A girl with ducks by a stream – signed – pencil and watercolour with scratching out – 197 x 324mm.
(Christie's) **£1,540 $2,803**

AUGUST MACKE (1887–1914) – Young woman in fashionable hat – signed and dated *1905* – charcoal and pastel on paper – 34.4 x 23.4cm.
(Lempertz) **£8,997 $14,350**

WILL MACLEAN (b. 1941) – Death fish study – signed and dated *83* – mixed media, relief – 26.5 x 41cm. *(Christie's)* **£1,430 $2,502**

AUGUST MACKE (1887–1914) – Still life with Barlach group and dish with apples – oil on canvas on board – 44.3 x 48cm.
(Lempertz) **£51,903 $82,785**

ADOLF MACKERPRANG – Deer by ferns in an extensive landscape, an estuary beyond – signed – oil on canvas – 53.3 x 76.2cm.
(Christie's) **£1,760 $3,041**

JESSIE MACLEOD (fl. 1845–1875) – Visiting an old friend in prison – signed and dated *1856* – oil on panel – 41 x 33cm.
(Christie's) **£6,050 $9,801**

DODGE MACKNIGHT (American, 1860–1950) – A quiet stroll through the village – signed – watercolour on paper – 15½ x 19½in.
(Skinner Inc.) **£498 $880**

DANIEL MACLISE (1806–1870) – The mock duenna – signed and dated 1853 – watercolour and bodycolour – 317 x 495mm.
(Christie's) **£1,980 $3,346**

DANIEL MACLISE, R.A. (1806–1870) – Three children playing with a pug – signed with monogram – pencil with touches of watercolour – 279 x 223mm.
(Christie's)   £770 $1,355

EMMA FORDYCE MACRAE (b. 1887) – Four of a kind – signed – oil on masonite – 66 x 45.7cm.
(Sotheby's)   £962 $1,760

JOHN THOMAS HAMILTON MACULLUM (1841–1896) – The Shrimpers – signed and dated 1885 – oil on canvas – 22¹/₂ x 42in.
(W.H. Lane & Son)   £3,600 $6,084

EMMA FORDYCE MACRAE (1887–1974) – A Belgian girl – signed – oil and pencil on canvas stretched over panel – 77.5 x 64cm.
(Christie's)   £2,424 $4,180

ANDREAS PETER MADSEN – Geese and chickens in a farmyard – signed and dated *1873* – pencil, pen and black ink and watercolour – 8¹/₄ x 11in.
(Christie's)   £132 $228

JEAN-BAPTISTE MAES (1794–1850) – The young
Roman girl's toilet – signed and dated *1855* – oil on canvas
– 97 x 134cm.
(Hôtel de Ventes Horta)   **£7,508 $12,839**

MICHELANGELO MAESTRI (Italian, d. circa 1812) –
Amor volubile – signed and inscribed – bodycolour over
engraved base on paper – 23.5 x 32.4cm.
(Butterfield & Butterfield)   **£441 $770**

NICOLAS MAES (1634–1693) – Portrait of a lady
wearing a red dress – signed – oil on canvas –
63.3 x 50.2cm.
(Sotheby's)   **£6,600 $11,880**

JOHN CHARLES MAGGS – Winter coaching scenes –
signed and dated *1898* – pair of oils – 14 x 25in.
(G.A. Key)   **£5,000 $8,850**

**Attributed to MICHELANGELO MAESTRI (early
19th century)** – Mythological scenes – pen and brown ink
and bodycolour on paper – 52 x 83cm. and smaller – four
(Christie's)   **£6,820 $11,867**

**School of ALESSANDRO MAGNASCO called Il
Lissandro (Italian, 1667–1749)** – The day's labours – oil
on panel – 5¹/₄ x 8³/₄in.
(Skinner Inc.)   **£2,645 $4,675**

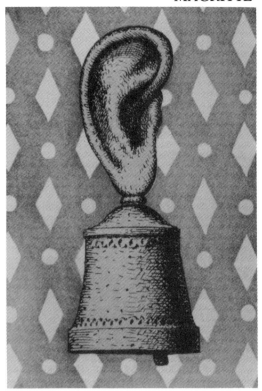

ALESSANDRO MAGNASCO (1667–1749) – The
temptation of Christ – oil on canvas, in a carved frame –
35 x 27cm.
(Sotheby's) £28,600 $51,480

RENE MAGRITTE (1898–1967) – The music lesson –
colour etching – 27.5 x 22cm.
(Germann) £443 $705

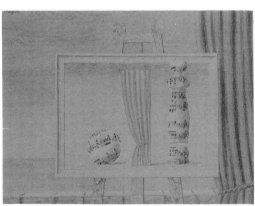

RENE MAGRITTE (1898–1967) – The invisible world –
signed – gouache on paper – 37.7 x 27cm.
(Christie's) £93,500 $164,560

RENE MAGRITTE (1898–1967) – La Partition – signed
– pencil, watercolour, pen, black ink and collage on paper –
30.5 x 40.6cm.
(Christie's) £110,000 $193,600

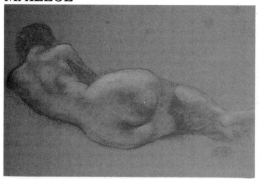

ARISTIDE MAILLOL (1861–1944) – Reclining nude
from behind – signed with monogram – sanguine
heightened with white on buff card laid on board –
33.3 x 42.8cm.
(Christie's)   £8,800 $15,488

HENRY MALFROY (b. 1895) – Martigues – signed – oil
on canvas – 59.6 x 92cm.
(Fraser–Pinneys)   £2,632 $4,566

LEROY LEVESON LAURENT JOSEPH DE
MAISTRE (1894–1968) – Deposition – signed – oil on
board – 47 x 40.6cm.
(Christie's)   £3,080 $5,421

ROBERT MALLETT – Sheep grazing in parkland setting
with cottages in background – signed – oil on canvas –
15 x 18in.
(G.A Key)   £150 $268

FELIX MALARD (b. 1840) – Elegant figures
promenading by the sea – signed – oil on canvas –
60.3 x 76.2cm.
(Christie's)   £5,500 $9,570

Follower of JAN MANDYN – The Temptation of Saint
Anthony – oil on panel – 54 x 69.5cm.
(Sotheby's)   £20,900 $37,620

MANE-KATZ (1894–1962) – Bunch of poppies – signed – oil on canvas laid down on board – 73 x 54cm.
(Christie's) **£13,200 $23,232**

JAN MANKES – Portrait of the painter's father – pastel – 26 x 21cm.
(Glerum) **£2,806 $4,882**

HENRI MANGUIN (1874–1949) – Nude reclining on one elbow – signed – oil on canvas – 50 x 61cm.
(Christie's) **£94,600 $166,496**

HARRINGTON MANN (1865–1937) – Portrait of Lord
Duveen – signed and dated *1921* – oil on canvas –
101.6 x 76.2cm.
(Sotheby's)   **£1,202 $2,200**

WILLIAM MANNERS – Figures before a cottage on a
river bank – signed and dated *1892* – 12¹/₂ x 7¹/₂in.
(John Maxwell of Wilmslow)   **£670 $1,179**

**JOSHUA HARGRAVE SAMS MANN (English, fl.
1849–1884)** – Girl reading – signed – oil on board –
30.5 x 25.4cm.
(Bonhams)   **£650 $1,033**

GIACOMO MANTEGAZZA (Italian, 1853–1920) – The
entertainer – signed and dated *1884* – oil on canvas –
83 x 120cm.
(Sotheby's)   **£11,000 $19,470**

Follower of MICHELE MARIESCHI – The Grand Canal at the Rialto Bridge, Venice – oil on canvas – 62.2 x 92cm. *(Christie's)* £4,620 $7,208

Circle of MICHELE MARIESCHI (1710–1744) – A village harbour on the Adriatic coast – oil on canvas - 72 x 96cm. *(Christie's)* £17,867 $29,659

School of MANTUA (circa 1587) – Portrait of Vincenzo I Gonzaga, Duke of Mantua (1562-1612), three-quarter length, in armour – oil on canvas – 137.6 x 107.7cm. *(Sotheby's)* £11,000 $19,800

JEAN MARCHAND (1882–1941) – Landscape with poplars – signed – oil on canvas – 59.6 x 72.4cm. *(Christie's)* £8,250 $13,365

MARIN

ENRIQUE MARIN (1876–1900) – Toledo – signed –
watercolour – 14 x 9cm.
(Duran) £501 $899

ENRIQUE MARIN (Spanish, 19th/20th century) – A
laden donkey – signed and inscribed – watercolour –
44 x 32cm.
(Sotheby's) £1,100 $1,947

JOHN MARIN (1870–1953) – Sunset – signed –
watercolour and pencil on paper – 21 x 28cm.
(Christie's) £4,466 $7,700

MARINE SCHOOL – Three-masted sailing vessel with
two figures in rowing boat in foreground – oil on canvas –
9³/₄ x 8¹/₂in.
(Hobbs & Chambers) £350 $581

MARINO MARINI (1901–1980) – Horse – signed and
dated *938* – tempera on paper – 23 x 30cm.
(Finarte) £11,155 $19,019

MARINO MARINI (b. 1901) – The roundabout – signed
and dated *1934* – oil on panel – 39 x 59.5cm.
(Christie's) £16,500 $26,730

LAJOS MARK – The artist's model – signed – oil on canvas – 119.4 x 99cm.
(Christie's) £550 $950

JOSE MARIA MARQUES (1862–1936) – On the river – signed and dated *881* – oil on canvas – 83 x 51cm.
(Duran) £1,400 $2,465

ALBERT ERNEST MARKES (1865–1901) – Shipping docked in the Thames at moonlight; and A barque in a squall – both signed – pencil and watercolour heightened with white – 26.1 x 36.8cm. – a pair
(Christie's) £1,100 $1,958

ANDREAS MARKO (Austrian, 1824–1895) – Goatherders in the Roman Campagna – signed and dated *1872* – oil on canvas – 102.9 x 135.9cm.
(Butterfield & Butterfield) £10,716 $18,700

ALBERT MARQUET (1875–1947) – Algiers, the Consular Palace and Government Square – signed – oil on canvas – 50.5 x 61cm.
(Christie's) £66,000 $116,160

ALBERT MARQUET (1875–1947) – The port of Algiers
– signed – oil on canvas – 50.2 x 61cm.
(Christie's)   £55,000 $96,800

ALBERT MARQUET (1875–1947) – The harbour at
Saint-Jean de Luz – signed – oil on canvas – 49 x 60cm.
(Christie's)   £93,500 $151,470

REGINALD MARSH (1898–1954) – Seated nude –
initialled – oil on canvas – 61 x 35.6cm.
(Butterfield & Butterfield)   £1,261 $2,200

G. MARRIAN – Harvesters in a cornfield; and a
Fisherman by a footbridge at sunset – one signed – oil on
canvas – 23 x 33cm. – a pair
(Christie's)   £1,045 $1,735

REGINALD MARSH (1898–1954) – Skyscrapers –
signed and dated – watercolour on paper – 35.5 x 50.9cm.
(Christie's)   £8,932 $15,400

REGINALD MARSH (1898–1954) – In the surf – signed and dated *1947* – ink wash on paper –
68.6 x 101.6cm.
(Butterfield & Butterfield) £4,227 $8,250

REGINALD MARSH (1898-1954) – 14th Street shopper
– signed and dated *1950* – tempera on board –
40.6 x 30.5cm.
(Sotheby's) £5,194 $9,350

REGINALD MARSH (1898–1954) – On the boardwalk –
signed and dated *1050–3* – oil on masonite –
25.4 x 20.3cm.
(Sotheby's) £2,254 $4,125

(1849–circa 1923) – An extensive landscape with sheep grazing by a stream – signed – pencil and watercolour – 356 x 533mm.
(Christie's) £2,420 $4,404

THOMAS FALCON MARSHALL (1818–1878) – The coming footstep – signed – oil on board – 48.3 x 48.3cm.
(Christie's) £1,210 $1,960

PETER PAUL MARSHALL (1830–1900) – Scenes of Clerical life; The Countess Czerlaski and her brother, and the Rev. Amos Barton and his family – both signed – oil on panel – 50.8 x 40cm. – a pair
(Christie's) £7,150 $12,155

WILLIS ELSTOB MARSHALL (fl. 1859–1881) – An English and a Gordon setter in the Highlands – signed and dated *1875* – unframed – oil on canvas – 125.7 x 99.1cm.
(Christie's) £3,080 $5,051

HENRI MARTIN (1860–1943) – Boy by the pond, Luxembourg Gardens – signed – oil on canvas – 65 x 54cm.
(Christie's) **£44,000** **$71,280**

FLETCHER MARTIN (1904–1979) – The poker players – signed – watercolour on paper – 48.3 x 35.6cm.
(Butterfield & Butterfield) **£945** **$1,650**

ANGELES MARTINI – Flowers – signed and dated *1896* – watercolour – 56 x 42cm.
(Duran) **£235** **$414**

FLETCHER MARTIN (1904–79) – Profile of a sailor – oil on canvas – unframed – 50.8 x 40.6cm.
(Sotheby's) **£721** **$1,320**

GIOVANNI MARTINO (b. 1908) – November snow – signed – oil on board – 28.3 x 41.3cm.
(Sotheby's) **£451** **$825**

FRANK HENRY MASON (1876–1965) – Clippers on the high seas – both signed – pencil, watercolour and bodycolour heightened with white – 36.2 x 49.5cm. – a pair
(Christie's)   £2,090 $3,720

FRANK HENRY MASON – A schooner yacht and a barque in a swell – pencil and watercolour – 29.9 x 42cm.
(Bonhams)   £500 $825

FRANK HENRY MASON (1876–1965) – Ships of the Mediterranean fleet lying in Valetta Harbour, Malta – signed – oil on canvas laid down on board – 87 x 102.9cm.
(Christie's)   £8,800 $15,664

FRANK HENRY MASON (English, 1876–1965) – Outward bound (down Channel off the Needles) – signed and dated 1947 – oil on canvas – 50.8 x 61cm.
(Bonhams)   £1,000 $1,650

POMPEO MASSANI (1850–1920) – The card players – signed – oil on canvas – 42.5 x 60cm.
(Christie's) £3,080 $5,359

POMPEO MASSANI (Italian, 1850–1920) – The old violinist – signed – oil on canvas laid down on board – 34.9 x 25.4cm.
(Butterfield & Butterfield) £1,261 $2,200

ANDRES MATEO – The antique dealer – signed – oil on canvas – 41 x 43cm.
(Duran) £235 $414

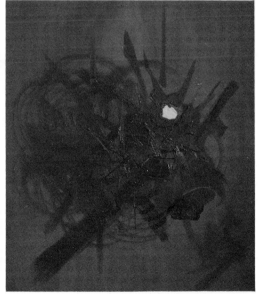

JOHANN HENDRIK MASTENBROEK (Dutch, 1875–1945) – Moored sailing boats; Along the canal – signed – oil on panel – 20.3 x 29.8cm. – a pair
(Butterfield & Butterfield) £1,261 $2,200

GEORGES MATHIEU (b. 1921) – O douleur O douleur Le temps mange la vie... – signed – oil on canvas – 143.5 x 111.7cm.
(Christie's) £33,000 $53,460

HENRI MATISSE (1869–1954) – The model resting (The great odalisque) – signed and dated 25 – charcoal and estompe on paper – 40.7 x 51.6cm.
(Christie's) £220,000 $360,800

HENRI MATISSE (1869–1954) – Female head – signed – pencil on paper – 26.9 x 20.5cm.
(Christie's) £11,000 $17,820

HENRI MATISSE (1869–1954) – Pont St. Michel, Paris – signed – oil on canvas – 45 x 55cm.
(Christie's) £396,000 $649,440

MATTA (b. 1911) – Untitled –signed – oil on canvas –
64 x 79cm.
(Christie's) **£19,800 $35,046**

MAXIME MAUFRA (1861–1918) – Les Pavilions, Paris
Exposition Internationale, 1900 or La Ville éphémère –
signed and dated *1900* – oil on canvas – 60 x 73cm.
(Christie's) **£24,200 $42,592**

MATTA (b. 1911) – Morning of Morning – oil on canvas –
118 x 180cm.
(Christie's) **£71,500 $126,555**

ALEXANDER JAMES MAVROGORDATO – Pull's
Ferry, Norwich – signed – watercolour – 33.7 x 53.4cm.
(Bonhams) **£280 $475**

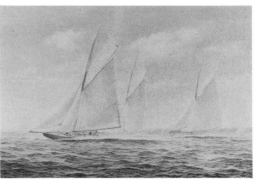

JAN MATULKA (1890–1972) – New York landscape –
oil on canvas – 35.6 x 50.8cm.
(Sotheby's) **£962 $1,760**

BRIAN MAY – 20 Raters' racing in 1896 – signed – oil on
canvas – 61 x 92cm.
(Bonhams) **£520 $858**

AUGUSTE-ETIENNE-FRANÇOIS MAYER (1805–1890) – Boats on the Bosphorous, off Constantinople – signed and dated *1846* – oil on canvas – 56 x 82cm.
(Christie's) £15,950 $25,998

FRIEDRICH MAYER (Swiss, 1792–1870) – A view of Rome – signed and dated *1841* – oil on canvas – 56 x 79.5cm.
(Sotheby's) £14,300 $25,311

FRIEDRICH MAYER (Swiss, 1792–1870) – A view of the Bay of Naples and Vesuvius – oil on canvas – 56 x 79.5cm.
(Sotheby's) £22,000 $38,940

GEORGE WILLOUGHBY MAYNARD (1843–1923) – The Fort, Marblehead, Mass. – signed and dated *19* – oil on board – 20.4 x 38.7cm.
(Christie's) £1,367 $2,420

E. MAYO – Portrait of F.J. Braghe, aged 3, standing full length, beside a toy cart – inscribed on reverse – oil on canvas – 55.8 x 45.7cm.
(Bonhams) £850 $1,352

SEBASTIANO MAZZONI (1611–1678) – Sophonisba – oil on canvas – 113.5 x 98.8cm.
(Sotheby's) £67,100 $120,780

ILA MCAFEE (b. 1897) – Indians on horseback – signed
– oil on board – 30.5 x 40.6cm.
(Butterfield & Butterfield)   £1,261 $2,200

CLARA MCCHESNEY (1860–1928) – Mother and child
– signed – watercolour and gouache on paper –
40.6 x 33cm.
(Butterfield & Butterfield)   £1,261 $2,200

CHARLES MCCALL (1907–1989) – Domestic interior –
signed and dated *57* – oil on board – 40.5 x 25.5cm.
(Christie's)   £935 $1,608

ARTHUR DAVID MCCORMICK (1860–1943) – A fine
ale; and A good smoke – signed with initials *A.D. McC* –
oil on canvas – 61 x 46cm. – a pair
(Christie's)   £2,860 $5,062

HOWARD MCCORMICK (American, 1875–1943) –
Hopi Katchina – signed – oil on gessoed and tooled panel –
14 x 14in.
(Skinner Inc.)   **£823**   **$1,430**

MARY MCCROSSAN (fl. 1864–1934) – Thames barges
– signed and dated *1928* – oil on board – 33 x 41cm.
(Christie's)   **£1,980**   **$3,406**

MARY MCCROSSAN (fl. 1864–1934) – Padstow,
Cornwall – signed – oil on panel – 39.5 x 32cm.
(Christie's)   **£770**   **$1,324**

GEORGE MCCULLOCH – The young harvester – signed and dated *1977* – watercolour – 40 x 29.8cm. *(Bonhams)* £450 $763

HENRY LEE MCFEE (1886–1953) – Still life with kitchen utensils – signed – oil on canvas – 61 x 50.8cm. *(Christie's)* £2,871 $4,950

NORAH MCGUINESS (b. 1903) – Ochre and heather – signed - oil on canvas – 51 x 61cm. *(Christie's)* £1,925 $3,195

MCGUINESS

ARTHUR JOSEPH MEADOWS (1843–1907) – Fishing boats in Dunkerque Harbour – signed and dated *1887* – oil on canvas – 30.5 x 40.6cm.
(Christie's) £3,080 $5,482

NORAH MCGUINESS (b. 1903) – The black gate – signed with initials and dated– oil on canvas – 29 x 38cm.
(Christie's) £1,320 $2,191

ARTHUR JOSEPH MEADOWS (1843–1907) – Dinant on the Meuse – signed and dated *96* – oil on canvas – 30.5 x 50.8cm.
(Christie's) £1,870 $3,310

WILLIAM KIMMINS MCMINN (1818–1898) – The ship Shepherdess passing Perch Rock Fort and Lighthouse as she arrives in the Mersey – signed and dated *1856* – oil on canvas – 60.9 x 91.4cm.
(Christie's) £9,350 $16,643

JAMES EDWIN MEADOWS (1828–1888) – Children on a path by a pond – signed and dated *1859(?)* – oil on canvas – 76.2 x 122cm.
(Christie's) £6,050 $11,011

ARTHUR JOSEPH MEADOWS (1843–1907) – A race for the derelict – with strengthened signature and the date *1873* – oil on canvas – 77.4 x 120.2cm.
(Christie's) £4,180 $7,440

JAMES EDWIN MEADOWS (1828–1888) – The harvesters' midday rest – signed and dated *1866* – oil on canvas – 76.2 x 122cm.
(Christie's) £13,200 $23,364

GARI MELCHERS (1860–1932) – Portrait of Mrs. Mackall – signed and dated *1909* – oil on canvas – 56.2 x 46.3cm.
(Christie's) £1,554 $2,750

JOSEPH R. MEEKER (1827–1889) – Bayou landscape – signed and dated *1877* – oil on canvas – 68.6 x 55.9cm.
(Sotheby's) £12,222 $22,000

FRANZ MEERTS (Belgian, 1836–1896) – Merry gossip – signed – oil on canvas – 101 x 80cm.
(Hôtel de Ventes Horta) £2,218 $3,793

JULIUS GARI MELCHERS (1860–1932) – Lady in plum – signed and dated *1927* – oil on canvas – 97.4 x 71cm.
(Christie's) £1,659 $2,860

CAMPBELL A. MELLON (1876–1955) – On the beach, Gorleston – signed – oil on canvas – 25.5 x 35.5cm. *(Christie's)* **£902 $1,497**

WILHELM JOHANN MELCHIOR (German, 1817–1860) – Intrigued – signed and dated *1851* – oil on canvas – unframed – 106.7 x 119.4cm.
(Bonhams) **£7,200 $11,448**

XAVIER MELLERY (1845–1921) – L'Amitié: Entrez et vous serez consolé – signed with monogram, shaped top – oil on canvas – 80 x 130cm.
(Christie's) **£1,980 $3,445**

CAMPBELL A. MELLON (1876–1955) – On the sands, Gorleston – signed – oil on panel – 23 x 30.5cm. *(Christie's)* **£1,045 $1,735**

CAMPBELL A. MELLON (1876–1955) - Haddiseoe Cut, St. Olaves, Nr. Oulton Broad, Norfolk – signed – oil on panel – 23 x 30.5cm.
(Christie's) **£418 $694**

WILLIAM MELLOR (English 1851–1931) – Elter Water & Langdale Pikes, Westmoreland – signed – oil on canvas – 61 x 91.4cm. – and companion-piece, a pair
(Bonhams) **£6,200 $9,858**

Manner of ANTON RAPHAEL MENGS – The Madonna, head and shoulders – in a painted oval – oil on canvas – 61.6 x 50.8cm.
(Christie's) **£880 $1,373**

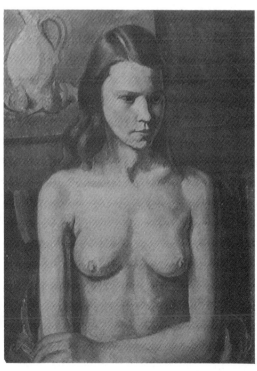

MORTIMER L. MEMPES – Arab street scenes with children – signed – a pair of oils on board – 11.4 x 7.6cm.
(Woolley & Wallis) **£1,100 $1,958**

BERNARD MENINSKY (1891–1950) – Seated nude girl – signed and dated *26* – oil on canvas – 71 x 56cm.
(Christie's) **£4,620 $7,669**

SIGMUND MENKES (Polish, b. 1896) – Portrait of a young girl – signed – oil on canvas – 79 x 61cm.
(Butterfield & Butterfield) £1,891 $3,300

HUGHES MERLE (French, 1823–81) – A portrait of a woman – oil on canvas – 45 x 37.5cm.
(Sotheby's) £2,860 $5,062

DANIEL MERLIN (1861–1933) – The accident – signed – oil on canvas – 38.1 x 55.3cm.
(Christie's) £6,050 $9,922

ADOLF FRIEDRICH ERDMANN MENZEL (1815–1905) – Costume study of Lieutenant-General Hans Karl von Winterfeldt – signed and dated *AM/50* – charcoal heightened with white on paper laid down on card – 30.2 x 24.8cm.
(Christie's) £16,500 $26,895

ANTONIO CRUZ MESA – The glass hall – signed – oil on canvas – 50 x 61cm.
(Duran) £280 $493

WILHELM ALEXANDER MEYERHEIM (1815–1882)
– Feeding the rabbits – signed – oil on canvas –
68.5 x 94cm.
(Christie's)   **£1,320 $2,297**

MICHELANGELO MEUCCI (late 19th century) –
Pomegranates and grapes – signed – oil on canvas – oval –
56 x 43.3cm.
(Christie's)   **£2,970 $5,168**

FRANS PIETER TER MEULEN (1843–1927) – Loading
sand – signed – watercolour – 38 x 61cm.
(Fraser-Pinneys)   **£776 $1,366**

THEOBALD MICHAU (1676–1765) – A village scene
with peasants going to market – indistinctly signed *C.P.
iqee F*.. – oil on panel – 35.5 x 48.5cm.
(Sotheby's)   **£27,500 $49,500**

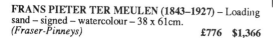

MICHAUX

JOHN MICHAUX – The way of happiness – signed -- oil on canvas – 100 x 95cm.
(Hôtel de Ventes Horta) £1,621 $2,772

J. MICHIE – A rustic beauty – signed and dated *1858* – oil on canvas – 38.2 x 33cm.
(Christie's) £715 $1,267

WILLIAM HENRY MIDWOOD (fl. 1866–1871) – Faraway thoughts – signed and dated *1866* – oil on panel – 20 x 15cm.
(Christie's) £2,200 $3,564

WILLIAM HENRY MIDWOOD (fl. 1867–1876) – The centre of attention - signed and dated *1876* – oil on canvas – 70.5 x 91.5cm.
(Christie's) £7,700 $13,629

After **WILLEM VAN MIERIS** –The market stall – oil on canvas – 38.7 x 33.7cm.
(Christie's) £990 $1,544

FRIEDRICH MIESS (German, b. 1854) – Children in the forest – signed – oil on canvas – 70 x 100cm.
(Sotheby's) £13,200 $23,364

THOMAS ROSE MILES (fl. 1869–1888) – Fishermen off
the Kent Coast – signed – oil on canvas – 61 x 106.7cm.
(Christie's) £2,200 $3,916

RAOUL MILLAIS (b. 1901) – Horses startled by fire –
signed – oil on canvas – 41 x 51cm.
(Christie's) £3,300 $5,478

RAOUL MILLAIS (b. 1901) – In the paddocks – signed –
pastel – 17.5 x 27cm.
(Christie's) £1,265 $2,100

**SIR JOHN EVERETT MILLAIS, Bt., P.R.A. (1829–
1896)** -- Portrait of Alice Sophia Caroline Wortley, the
artist's third daughter – signed with monogram and dated
1887 – oil on canvas – 110.5 x 85.1cm.
(Christie's) £24,200 $41,140

RAOUL MILLAIS (b. 1901) – Horses grazing, summer in
the Cotswolds – signed – oil on canvas – 30.5 x 41cm.
(Christie's) £770 $1,278

ADDISON THOMAS MILLAR (American, 1860–1913)
– Working at the hearth – signed and inscribed – oil on
canvas – 24 x 18in.
(Skinner Inc.) £373 $660

Attributed to FRED MILLARD (b. 1857) –Love knows
no bounds – oil on canvas – 36 x 28in.
(W.H. Lane & Son)   **£3,300 $5,577**

FRANCIS D. MILLET (1846–1912) – Portrait of a
woman – signed and dated *1881* – oil on canvas –
91.4 x 66cm.
(Sotheby's)   **£361 $660**

FRANÇOIS MILLET (1851–1917) – Before the meal –
signed and indistinctly dated – oil on canvas – 50 x 65.2cm.
(Christie's)   **£4,400 $7,656**

JEAN FRANÇOIS MILLET (French, 1814–1875) – A study for Le berger et la mer – stamped with the cachet de vente (Lugt 1460) – charcoal – unframed – 20.2 x 13.2cm. (Sotheby's) £2,200 $3,894

JEAN FRANÇOIS MILLET – The wild geese – signed – pastel and black crayon – 60 x 43cm. (Sotheby's) £572,000 $1,012,440

JEAN FRANÇOIS MILLET – The sick child – signed – black crayon and pastel – 38 x 31cm. (Sotheby's) £242,000 $428,340

WILLIAM MILLS – Regent Circus – signed and dated 1885 – oil on canvas – 38.7 x 31.2cm. (Christie's) £2,420 $4,289

JOHN MINTON (1917–1957) – Micheline to Bastia by train – pen, brush and black ink – 17 x 16.5cm.
(Christie's) £935 $1,608

VICTOR MARAIS MILTON (French, b. 1872) – The siesta – signed – watercolour – 34 x 26cm.
(Sotheby's) £1,540 $2,726

JOHN MINTON (1917–1957) – Barge and warehouses – signed and dated *1946* – brush, black ink, grey wash, watercolour and bodycolour – 25.5 x 38cm.
(Christie's) £4,180 $7,315

JOAN MIRO (1893–1983) – Personnage – dedicated and dated *48* – wax crayon, charcoal and pencil on paper – 26.9 x 20.5cm.
(Christie's) £10,450 $16,929

JOAN MIRO (1893–1983) – Personnage – signed – gouache, wax crayon and black ink on paper – 55 x 69cm.
(Christie's) £85,800 $151,008

FERDINAND MISTI-MIFLIEZ – Portrait of a young girl in a white party dress – signed and dated *1921* – pastel – 47¹/₂ x 22in.
(Christie's) £1,100 $1,892

JOAN MIRO (1893–1983) – Femme Etoile – signed – oil on canvas – 28 x 22cm.
(Christie's) £79,200 $139,392

WILLIAM FREDERICK MITCHELL – The Battle of Trafalgar – signed – watercolour heightened with white – unframed – 40.7 x 69.5cm.
(Bonhams) £800 $1,320

MITCHELL

WILLIAM FREDERICK MITCHELL – H.M.S. Agincourt – signed and dated *1894* – watercolour heightened with white – unframed – 16.2 x 24.2cm. – and three others
(Bonhams) £600 $990

WILLIAM FREDERICK MITCHELL (English, 1845–1914) – H.M.S. Bacchante with H.M. Yacht Osborne – signed and dated *1883* – watercolour heightened with white – 50.2 x 70.5cm.
(Bonhams) £950 $1,568

WILLIAM FREDERICK MITCHELL (English, 1845–1914) – H.M. Yacht Osborne – signed and dated *1896* – watercolour heightened with white – 50.2 x 72.4cm.
(Bonhams) £3,400 $5,610

JOSEPH MITTEY (b. 1853) – Studies of exotic birds, including Golden and Amherst Pheasants, and Hummingbirds – signed, indistinctly inscribed and dated *1877* – oil on canvas – 57 x 70cm.
(Christie's) £9,900 $17,226

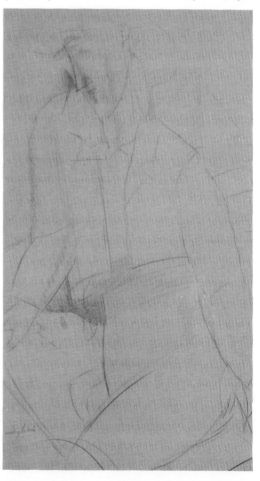

WILLIAM FREDERICK MITCHELL – Shipping in a choppy sea – signed and dated *1878* – watercolour over traces of pencil, heightened with white – 50.8 x 73.7cm.
(Woolley & Wallis) £580 $1,032

AMEDEO MODIGLIANI (1884–1920) – The Pilgrim, Charles Douglas (1916–1917) – signed – pencil on paper – 42.5 x 24.5cm.
(Finarte) £27,888 $47,549

ROSS E. MOFFETT – The West End, autumn – signed – oil on canvas – 36¼ x 46¼in.
(Du Mouchelles) £2,676 $4,750

JOHN HENRY MOLE (1814–1886) – At Peter Tavy, South Devon – signed and dated *1874* – pencil and watercolour with touches of white heightening – 172 x 248mm.
(Christie's) £1,430 $2,603

ROSS E. MOFFETT (American, 1888–1971) – The cod fisherman – signed – oil on canvas – unframed – 48 x 60in.
(Skinner Inc.) £2,801 $4,950

CARL MOLL (Austrian, 1861–1945) – A view of the gardens at Schonbrunn, Vienna – signed – oil on panel – 34.5 x 34.5cm.
(Sotheby's) £26,400 $46,728

JAMES D. MOHAN (American, d. 1987) – The train yard/A Boston scene – signed – gouache on paperboard – unframed – 20 x 30in.
(Skinner Inc.) £218 $385

Circle of PETER MONAMY (1689–1749) – An English two-decker with a Royal Yacht under her stern – oil on canvas – unframed – 72.3 x 121.8cm.
(Christie's) £2,860 $5,091

397

Circle of PETER MONAMY – British men-o'-war at sea –
bears signature – oil on canvas – 51.4 x 61.6cm.
(Bonhams) £1,400 $2,310

EMILIO MONCAYO (Ecuadorian, 20th century) –
Coastal landscape, Ecuador; Ecuadorian landscape with
volcano – signed – oil on board and oil on canvas –
40.6 x 50.8cm. and 52.7 x 87.6cm. – two
(Butterfield & Butterfield) £315 $550

PEDER MØNSTED (1859–1941) – A wooded river
landscape – signed and dated *1910* – oil on canvas –
110 x 110cm.
(Christie's) £11,000 $19,140

PEDER MØNSTED (Danish, 1859–1941) – In the
outskirts of Cairo – signed and dated *1893* – oil on canvas –
40 x 55cm.
(Sotheby's) £4,950 $8,761

ALFRED MONTAGUE (1832–1888) – Boats on a canal, Rotterdam – indistinctly signed – oil on canvas – 76 x 63cm.
(Christie's) **£2,860 $4,633**

W. HOWARD MONTGOMERY (American, 20th century) – Passing of Summer – signed – oil on board – 24¹/4 x 23¹/2in.
(Skinner Inc.) **£253 $440**

ALFRED MONTAGUE – View in Rheims – signed, inscribed and dated *1896* – oil on canvas – 30.4 x 45.7cm.
(Christie's) **£1,555 $2,753**

CLARA MONTALBA (1842–1929) – An orange seller by a road leading to a town – signed – oil on panel – 21 x 31.1cm.
(Christie's) **£1,430 $2,603**

A. MONTI – A welcome distraction – signed – oil on canvas – 58.4 x 38.2cm.
(Christie's) **£990 $1,703**

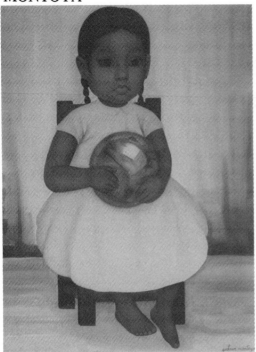

GUSTAVO MONTOYA (Mexican, b. 1905) – Girl in a
pink dress – signed – oil on canvas – 55.9 x 45.7cm.
(Butterfield & Butterfield) **£2,837 $4,950**

R. MONTREUX – Rue Bertier, Paris – signed –
watercolour – 28 x 21.5cm.
(Duran) **£168 $295**

FANNY MOODY (b. 1861) – Awaiting the master, a
black and tan Dachshund – signed and dated *1892* – oil on
canvas – 40.7 x 50.8cm.
(Christie's) **£2,420 $3,969**

ALBERT JOSEPH MOORE (1841–1893) – Roses –
signed with anthemion – pastel – 97.8 x 38cm.
(Christie's) **£44,000 $74,800**

BARLOW MOORE – A Yawl sailing to windward in a
squall – signed, inscribed and dated *1888* – pencil and
watercolour heightened with white – 22 x 24in.
(Christie's) **£550 $950**

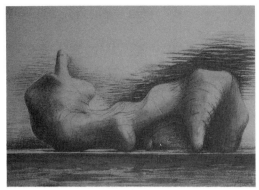

HENRY MOORE (1898–1986) – Reclining figure –
signed – charcoal, pencil and wash on paper –
17.5 x 25.4cm.
(Christie's) £13,200 $23,232

HENRY MOORE (1898–1986) – Figures in a landscape;
Stringed figures in lead – signed and dated *40* – pen, black
ink, watercolour, black crayon and coloured wax –
12.5 x 21cm.
(Christie's) £8,250 $14,437

EDWARD PERCY MORAN (1862–1935) – George
Washington and Benjamin Franklin – signed – oil on
canvas – 71.1 x 55.9cm.
(Sotheby's) £1,503 $2,750

EDWARD MORAN (1819–1878) – Fish Pond, Orient
Bay, Long Island – signed – oil on canvas – 76.8 x 57.8cm.
(Sotheby's) £11,000 $19,800

EDWARD PERCY MORAN (1862–1935) – In the garden
– signed – oil on canvas – 61 x 46.4cm.
(Sotheby's) £4,358 $7,975

MORAN

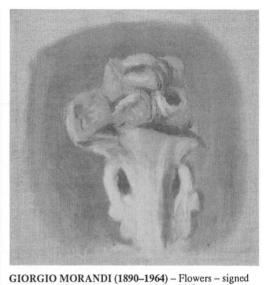

GIORGIO MORANDI (1890–1964) – Flowers – signed and dated *1947* – oil on canvas – 22.8 x 23.5cm. *(Christie's)* **£71,500 $125,840**

THOMAS MORAN (1837–1926) – Portrait of a man in a hat – signed – oil on board – 25.4 x 20.3cm. *(Butterfield & Butterfield)* **£1,733 $3,025**

GIORGIO MORANDI (1890–1964) – Still life – signed and dated *1939* – oil on canvas – 23 x 25cm. *(Christie's)* **£275,000 $451,000**

WALTER MORAS (German, 1856–1925) – Child with a gaggle of geese – signed – oil on canvas – 39.4 x 31.1cm.
(Butterfield & Butterfield) **£1,734 $3,025**

ANGELO MORBELLI (1853–1919) – Landscape of the Monferrato – signed and dated *1911* – oil on canvas – 83 x 73.5cm.
(Christie's) **£19,800 $32,274**

ADRIEN MOREAU (French, 1843–1906) – Receiving his affections – signed – oil on panel – 18 x 14³/₄in.
(Skinner Inc.) **£1,680 $2,970**

CASPARUS JOHANNES MOREL (Dutch, 1798–1861) – A Dutch merchantman at anchor – signed – oil on canvas – 40.7 x 50.8cm.
(Bonhams) **£1,500 $2,475**

J.E. MOREL – Landscape with two figures – signed – oil on wood panel – 13³/₄ x 20¹/₄in.
(Du Mouchelles) **£2,604 $4,500**

JAN EVERT MOREL, the Younger (Dutch, 1835–1905) – A wooded river landscape with figures and sheep on a path – signed – oil on panel – 35.6 x 51.4cm.
(Bonhams) **£6,200 $9,858**

MOREL

EVELYN DE MORGAN, née Pickering (1855–1919) –
The Crown of Glory – signed and dated *1896* – oil on
canvas – 104.7 x 53.9cm.
(Christie's)   £55,000 $93,500

JAN EVERT MOREL, the Younger (Dutch, 1835–1905)
– Figures in a river landscape – signed – oil on canvas –
63.5 x 92.7cm.
(Bonhams)   £2,400 $3,816

Attributed to GEORGE MORELAND (British, 1763–
1804) - Morning chores – initialled *G.M.* – oil on panel –
7³/₄ x 10³/₄in.
(Skinner Inc.)   £342 $605

HENRI MORET (1856–1913) – Le Moulin de Riec,
Finistère – signed and dated *09* – oil on canvas –
73 x 92cm.
(Christie's)   £49,500 $87,120

EVELYN DE MORGAN, née Pickering (1855–1919) –
Clytie – signed with initials and dated *EP 1886–7* – oil on
canvas – 104 x 44.5cm.
(Christie's)   £99,000 $168,300

FREDERICK MORGAN (1856–1927) – The Home of
the Swans – signed – oil on canvas – 118.7 x 84.5cm.
(Christie's) **£15,400 $26,180**

WILLIAM MORGAN (1826–1900) – The visit – signed –
oil on canvas – 61 x 87cm.
(Sotheby's) **£1,683 $3,080**

After GEORGE MORLAND – The Effects of
Extravagance and Idleness – stipple engraving by Dareis,
with hand colouring, trimmed – 59.1 x 46.9cm. – together
with three others – framed
(Bonhams) **£680 $1,152**

Follower of GEORGE MORLAND – A traveller taking
refreshment outside a cottage – oil on canvas – unframed –
30.5 x 38.2cm.
(Christie's) £495 $799

After GEORGE MORLAND – The barn door – mezzotint
by William Ward, with hand colouring, published by T.
Simpson, 1792, with margins – 45.1 x 55.3cm. – together
with Sailor's conversation, a mezzotint after the same artist
– framed
(Bonhams) £300 $508

ROBERT MORLEY – Toadstool and toads in a landscape
– signed – oil – 13 x 11in.
(G.A. Key) £1,000 $1,950

SIR CEDRIC MORRIS, Bt. (1889–1982) – Caldas –
signed and dated *50* – oil on canvas – 75 x 62cm.
(Christie's) £3,080 $5,113

GEORGE L.K. MORRIS (1905–1975) – Indians Hunting
#1 – signed and dated *1934* – oil on board – 40.6 x 51.1cm.
(Christie's) £7,656 $13,200

T. MORTIMER – A thatched cottage at Crockernwell –
indistinctly signed – pencil and watercolour heightened
with white – 12³/4 x 19¹/2in.
(Christie's) £154 $266

GEORGE MORTON (active 1879–1904) – The Veterans' church service – signed and dated *1884* – oil on canvas – 26.6 x 21cm.
(Fraser–Pinneys) £1,804 $3,129

LLOYD MOYLAN (American, b. 1893) – Road signs – signed – watercolour and gouache on paper – 18½ x 15in. *(Skinner Inc.)* £253 $440

TOM MOSTYN (1864–1930) – The garden – signed – oil on canvas – 62 x 75cm.
(Christie's) £440 $730

M.S. – St Levan Church and farmstead, St Levan, West
Penwith, Cornwall – signed with monogram and dated *1910*
– oil on canvas – 190¼ x 23in.
(W.H. Lane & Son)   **£500 $921**

ALPHONSE MUCHA (Czech, 1860–1939) – The life of
the old Slavs – oil on canvas – 148 x 114cm.
(Sotheby's)   **£33,000 $58,410**

ANGELO FAIRFAX MUCKLEY – The letter – signed
and dated *1880* – watercolour and bodycolour heightened
with gum arabic – unframed – 9 x 6½in.
(Christie's)   **£605 $1,056**

FREDERICK JOHN MULHAUPT (American, 1871–1938) – Gloucester Harbour – signed – oil on board – 7³/₄ x 9³/₄in.
(Skinner Inc.)   £4,115 $7,150

WILLIAM JAMES MULLER (1812–1845) – Two camels at Xanthus – signed with initials and dated *1843* – pencil and watercolour with touches of white heightening – 495 x 343mm.
(Christie's)   £935 $1,646

AUGUSTUS E. MULREADY – Left to herself – signed and titled – oil on panel – 17.1 x 20.8cm.
(Woolley & Wallis)   £640 $1,094

SIR ALFRED MUNNINGS, P.R.A. (1878–1959) – Reeds by a river bank, Mendlam, Harleston, Norfolk – oil on panel – 14 x 9³/₄in.
(Christie's)   £2,420 $4,162

SIR ALFRED MUNNINGS (1878–1959) – Suffolk horse fair – signed – pencil – 18 x 25cm.
(Christie's)   £715 $1,187

MURILLO

School of BARTOLOME ESTEBAN MURILLO
(Spanish, 1618–1682) – The game of morra – oil on canvas
– 95 x 135cm.
(Butterfield & Butterfield) £946 $1,650

BARTOLOME ESTEBAN MURILLO (1618–1682) –
Head of a boy – oil on canvas – 66.5 x 52cm.
(Sotheby's) £22,000 $39,600

J. FRANCIS MURPHY (American, 1853–1921) –
Landscape – signed and dated *89* – oil on canvas –
12 x 19in.
(Du Mouchelles) £1,736 $3,000

BARTOLOME ESTEBAN MURILLO and Studio
(Spanish, 1618–1682) – The vision of Saint Vincent of
Ferrara – oil on canvas – 64.1 x 44.5cm.
(Butterfield & Butterfield) £9,456 $16,500

HERMAN DUDLEY MURPHY (1867–1945) – Mount
Monadnock – signed – oil on canvas – 62.2 x 75.5cm.
(Christie's) £3,828 $6,600

CHARLES FAIRFAX MURRAY (1849–1919) – A classical maiden playing a lyre; and Studies of seated women – pencil – 260 x 172mm. – two
(Christie's) £308 $520

SIR DAVID MURRAY, R.A. (1849–1933) – The flower pickers – oil on canvas – 122 x 183cm.
(Christie's) £30,800 $49,896

SIR DAVID MURRAY, R.A. (1849–1933) – Hampstead's Happy Heath – signed and dated *97* – oil on canvas – 122 x 183cm.
(Christie's) £39,600 $64,152

EBEN H. MURRAY (late 19th century) – The Spirit of Christmas – signed and indistinctly dated *188(?)* – oil on canvas – 40.6 x 50.8cm.
(Christie's) £1,650 $3,003

F. SYDNEY MUSCHAMP (fl. 1870–1903) – A clumsy suitor – signed – oil on canvas laid down on board – 50.8 x 76.2cm.
(Christie's) £2,200 $3,894

AUGUSTE MUSIN (1852–1920) – Fishing barges in an estuary – signed – oil on panel – 40.6 x 36.2cm.
(Christie's) £1,650 $2,937

411

MUSIN

FRANÇOIS-ETIENNE MUSIN (1820–1888) –
Unloading the catch – signed – oil on canvas –
71 x 107.5cm.
(Christie's) £7,260 $11,834

Manner of JAN MYTENS – Portrait of a young
nobleman, seated small three-quarter length in classical
costume – oil on canvas – 58.4 x 54.7cm.
(Christie's) £858 $1,338

JEROME MYERS (1867–1940) – Woman of 1905 –
signed and dated – charcoal and pencil on paper –
22.5 x 15.9cm.
(Christie's) £702 $1,210

PAUL JACOB NAFTEL (1817–1891) – The landing
place at Havre Gosselin, Sark – signed and dated *1888* –
pencil and watercolour heightened with white and
scratching out – 635 x 489mm.
(Christie's) £2,860 $4,633

JOHN NASH (1889–1924) – The deserted beach, Audierne – signed and dated *1938* – pencil and watercolour – 40.5 x 56cm.
(Christie's) **£4,400 $7,304**

GEORGE NATTRESS (fl. 1866–1888) – Sport at the Mill Pool; and Cleve Mill near Goring on Thames – both signed, the first dated *1878*, the second dated on label *1876* – pencil and watercolour heightened with white – 337 x 587mm. and 295 x 500mm. – two
(Christie's) **£1,650 $2,788**

JOSEPH NASH (1809–1878) – A town house, Rouen – pencil and watercolour – 356 x 257mm.
(Christie's) **£990 $1,594**

HEINRICH NAUEN (1880–1940) – Madonna with the animals – signed – oil on canvas – 150 x 220cm.
(Lempertz) **£24,221 $38,632**

ERNST WILHELM NAY (1902–1968) – Dichotomies –
signed and dated *53* – oil on canvas – 100 x 120cm.
(Christie's)   **£115,500 $204,435**

JOHN NEAGLE (1796–1865) – Portrait of Joseph C. Neal
– signed with initials and dated *1867* – oil on canvas –
51 x 43cm.
(Christie's)   **£1,243 $2,200**

NAZARENE SCHOOL (German, 19th century) –
Bathsheba at the well – pencil, pen and brown wash on buff
paper – 29.2 x 41.3cm.
(Butterfield & Butterfield)   **£536 $935**

NEAPOLITAN SCHOOL (late 19th century) – Naples
from the Marinella; and Naples from Mergellina –
bodycolour on paper laid down on card – 30.5 x 44.5cm. –
a pair
(Christie's)   **£2,860 $4,976**

Attributed to JOHN NEAGLE (1799–1865) – A little girl
with a basket of flowers – oil on canvas – 55.9 x 68.5cm.
(Christie's)   **£684 $1,210**

NEAPOLITAN SCHOOL – Vesuvius erupting by night –
bodycolour – 10³/₄ x 16in.
(Christie's)   **£748 $1,293**

NEAPOLITAN SCHOOL (18th century) – Mary
Magdalen – oil on canvas – 38.1 x 49.5cm.
(Butterfield & Butterfield) £536 $935

NEAPOLITAN SCHOOL (19th century) – Eruzione
dell'anno 1813 – inscribed – gouache – 7.6 x 10.7cm. – and
companion – both framed
(Bonhams) £520 $827

NEAPOLITAN SCHOOL (mid 19th century) – View of
Naples from Capodimonte; and View of Naples from the
sea – inscribed as titled on the mounts – bodycolour on
paper – 47.5 x 69cm. – a pair
(Christie's) £6,820 $11,867

NEAPOLITAN SCHOOL (mid 19th century) – The
Island of Nisida, near Posilipo – oil on paper –
26 x 38.1cm.
(Christie's) £1,540 $2,679

NEAPOLITAN SCHOOL - Fishing vessels in the Bay of
Naples – pencil and bodycolour – 8¹/₂ x 11in.
(Christie's) £2,640 $4,541

VICTOR NEHLIG (French, 1830–1910) – House to let –
signed – oil on canvas – 10 x 8in.
(Skinner Inc.) £1,369 $2,420

ANTAL NEOGRADY – A peasant woman peeling vegetables in a farmyard – signed – oil on canvas – 50.8 x 60.5cm.
(Christie's) £880 $1,521

FRANCES E. NESBITT – The Punch and Judy Show – signed – watercolour – 12^1/$_4$ x 9^1/$_2$in.
(Bearne's) £860 $1,492

FRANCES E. NESBITT – A French street scene – signed – watercolour – 20^1/$_2$ x 14in.
(Bearne's) £540 $937

Follower of CASPAR NETSCHER – Portrait of a lady, small half length, in a blue dress with a gold wrap – oil on canvas – unframed – 30.5 x 25.4cm.
(Christie's) £682 $1,064

Attributed to CONSTANTINE NETSCHER – A marriage
proposal – oil on panel – 29 x 22cm.
(Spencer's) £950 $1,515

MAUD NEVILLE – Chrysanthemums in oriental vase –
signed and dated *1926* – 19 x 30in.
(John Maxwell of Wilmslow) £400 $704

**Attributed to CONSTANTINE NETSCHER (1668–
1723)** – Portrait of three children – oil on canvas –
47 x 38cm.
(Sotheby's) £3,300 $5,940

LUDWIG NEUBERT (German, 1846–1892) – The
Pontine Marshes – signed – oil on canvas – 15³/₄ x 31³/₄in.
(Bonhams) £2,100 $3,339

**CHRISTOPHER RICHARD WYNNE NEVINSON,
A.R.A.** – A French street scene – signed – 27¹/₄ x 119¹/₄in.
(Bearne's) £5,700 $9,889

HENRY C. NEWELL (active 1865–1885) – August day on the North Shore – signed and dated 75 – oil on canvas – 35.5 x 61cm.
(Christie's) **£2,042 $3,520**

CHRISTOPHER RICHARD WYNNE NEVINSON, A.R.A. (1889–1946) – Ludgate Circus, Fleet Street, London – signed – pencil, watercolour, bodycolour and black crayon – 35 x 24.5cm.
(Christie's) **£6,050 $10,043**

ALFRED PIZZEY NEWTON (English 1830–1883) – The Acropolis – signed – pastel on paper – 44 x 82cm.
(Hôtel de Ventes Horta) **£2,500 $4,350**

FREDERICK CLIVE NEWCOMBE (1847–1894) – A view across the valley – signed – oil on panel – 22 x 34cm.
(Christie's) **£1,650 $2,673**

BEN NICHOLSON (1894–1982) – Pistaccio, June 1961 – signed and dated *1961* – thinned oil on carved relief board, mounted on the artist's prepared board, in the artist's frame – 22.8 x 33cm.
(Christie's)   £27,500 $48,400

BURR NICHOLLS (1848–1915) – On the canal – signed – oil on canvas – 50.8 x 35.6cm.
(Butterfield & Butterfield)   £945 $1,650

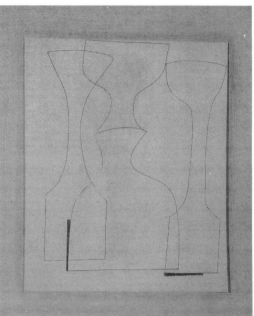

DALE NICHOLS (b. 1904) – Man on a Wyoming Island – signed and dated *1970* – oil on canvas – 61 x 76cm.
(Christie's)   £2,552 $4,400

BEN NICHOLSON (1894–1982) – Ronco 29 – signed and dated *58* – pencil and watercolour on paper laid down on artist's prepared board – 36.3 x 29.9cm.
(Christie's)   £6,050 $10,648

HOBART NICHOLS (1869–1962) – Across the valley – signed – oil on canvas – 64 x 76cm.
(Christie's)   £3,509 $6,050

BEN NICHOLSON, O.M. (1894–1982) – Agate – signed and dated *54 Agate* – oil, pencil and watercolour on textured board laid down on hardboard – 60.4 x 65.5cm.
(Christie's)   £165,000 $270,600

SIR WILLIAM NICHOLSON – Female nude standing –
signed – pencil and watercolour – 38 x 28cm.
(Christie's) £935 $1,486

GEORGE W. NICHOLSON (1832–1911) – Coastal
village – signed – oil on board – 58.4 x 40.6cm.
(Butterfield & Butterfield) £1,418 $2,475

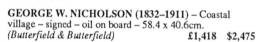

SIR WILLIAM NICHOLSON – A musketeer – signed
and dated *97* – pen and ink and watercolour – 10¹/₂ x 8in.
(Bearne's) £580 $1,006

ERSKINE NICOL, R.S.A., A.R.A. (1825–1904) – A
willing pupil – signed and dated *1878* – oil on canvas laid
down on board – 68 x 52cm.
(Christie's) £1,980 $3,505

NOEL LAURA NISBET (1887–1956) – The Seven
Deadly Sins – oil on canvas – 87.6 x 173.4cm.
(Christie's) **£5,280 $9,346**

NOEL LAURA NISBET (1887–1956) – 'A little sorrow, a
little pleasure, fate meets us from the dusty measure' –
signed and inscribed – watercolour – 660 x 980mm.
(Christie's) **£1,650 $2,673**

Circle of GUISEPPE DE NITTIS – Figures in a Parisian
street – with signature – oil on panel – unframed –
35.6 x 43.8cm.
(Christie's) **£1,210 $2,091**

NOEL LAURA NISBET (1887–1956) – An autumn
pastoral – signed and inscribed – watercolour –
660 x 1004mm.
(Christie's) **£1,980 $3,208**

JAMES GEORGE NOBLE – Daniel O'Rourke winning
the Derby 1852 – signed and dated on reverse *1852* –
watercolour – unframed
(Hobbs & Chambers) **£75 $125**

JOHN SARGENT NOBLE (1848–1896) – On the moors
– signed – oil on canvas – 53.3 x 43.2cm.
(Christie's) £1,870 $3,403

JULIUS NOERR (1827–1897) – The hawking party –
signed and dated *1875* – oil on canvas – 35.5 x 69.8cm.
(Christie's) £5,060 $8,804

EMIL NOLDE (1867–1956) – Red poppy – signed –
watercolour on Japan paper – 17 x 23.5cm.
(Lempertz) £44,983 $71,748

EMIL NOLDE (1867–1956) – Beach in autumn I – signed
– oil on canvas – 39 x 65cm.
(Christie's) £110,000 $178,200

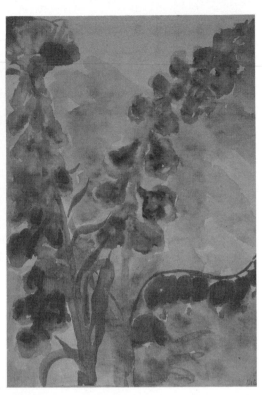

EMIL NOLDE (1867–1956) – Larkspur – signed –
watercolour on Japan paper – 47 x 35cm.
(Christie's) £33,000 $53,466

EMIL NOLDE (1867–1956) – Floral still life with dahlias
and poppies – signed – watercolour on Japan paper –
22.9 x 26.7cm.
(Christie's) £74,800 $121,176

CARL JOHN DAVID NORDELL (b. 1885) – Still life
with jug and teapot – signed – oil on canvas – 61 x 81.3cm.
(Butterfield & Butterfield) £2,206 $3,850

EMIL NOLDE (1867–1956) – Man and girl – signed –
original etching – 30.6 x 23.8cm.
(Lemperlz) £3,806 $6,071

OLLE NORDBERG (1905–1986) – Engagement presents
– signed and dated *60* – oil on panel – 37 x 45cm.
(AB Stockholms Auktionsverk) £1,146 $1,964

AUGUST HENRY NORDHAUSEN (b. 1901) –
Daydreaming – signed – oil on canvas – 50.8 x 40.6cm.
(Sotheby's) £511 $935

NORTH ITALIAN SCHOOL (circa 1690) – Portrait of a
nobleman, wearing the robe and insignia of the order of The
Golden Fleece – oil on canvas – 99.2 x 76.7cm.
(Sotheby's) £4,180 $7,524

ORLANDO NORRIE – A French cavalry troop on the
move – signed – watercolour – 29.3 x 47cm.
(Bonhams) £320 $529

JOHN WILLIAM NORTH (1842–1924) – The House of
Roses, Tripoli – signed with initials – pencil and
watercolour with touches of white heightening and
scratching out – 654 x 934mm.
(Christie's) £12,100 $22,022

DAVID EMIL JOSEPH DE NOTER (1825–1875) –
Fruits of the garden – signed – oil on panel –
81.5 x 26.5cm.
(Christie's) £13,200 $23,100

DAVID EMIL JOSEPH DE NOTER (1825–1875) –
Back from market – signed and dated *46* – oil on panel --
66 x 55.2cm.
(Christie's) £9,900 $17,325

PIERRE FRANCOIS DE NOTER – A wooded landscape
with a drover, sheep and a cow on a track by a watermill –
signed and dated *1834* – oil on panel – 30.5 x 25.4cm.
(Christie's) £2,200 $3,801

ERNST NOWAK (Austrian, 1853–1919) – A cardinal
with a glass of wine – signed – oil on canvas –
47 x 38.1cm.
(Butterfield & Butterfield) £2,206 $3,850

DAVID EMIL JOSEPH DE NOTER (1825–1875) –
Preparing the meal – signed and dated *1859(?)* – oil on
panel – 71.1 x 57.7cm.
(Christie's) £4,950 $8,662

ERNST NOWAK (Austrian, 1853–1919) – Selene visiting
the sleeping Endymion – signed – oil on canvas –
129 x 179cm.
(Sotheby's) £6,600 $11,682

JUSTIN MAURICE O'BRIEN (b. 1917) – Portrait –
signed and dated *1942* – oil on board – 55.2 x 37.7cm.
(Christie's) £3,520 $6,195

GEORGIA O'KEEFFE (1887–1986) – Blue morning
glory – titled and dated *1936* – oil on canvas –
30.5 x 25.4cm.
(Sotheby's) £61,111 $110,000

LUIS GARCIA OCHOA (b. 1920) – Man looking –
signed – drawing – 29 x 21cm.
(Duran) £251 $451

EUGENIO OLIVA (1857–1925) – Portrait of a lady –
signed and dated *1887* – oil on canvas – 121 x 84cm.
(Duran) £448 $788

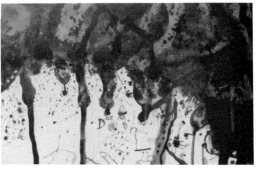

WILLIAM OLIVER – Learning to talk – signed and dated 1879 – oil on canvas – 35.6 x 27.9cm.
(Christie's)   £880 $1,560

JOHN OLSEN – Landscape – signed – mixed media – 62 x 97cm.
(Australian Art Auctions)   £1,768 $3,139

JULIAN ONDERDONK (1882-1922) – Spring blossoms – signed – oil on canvas – 40.5 x 61.3cm.
(Christie's)   £2,552 $4,400

MICHEL BARTHELEMY OLIVIER (1712–1784) – A young woman standing in profile to the right holding a fan – black, red and white chalk on blue paper – 233 x 166mm.
(Christie's)   £3,908 $6,487

DANIEL O'NEILL, R.H.A. (1920–1974) – Young man in a romantic costume – signed – oil on board – 58.5 x 49.5cm.
(Christie's)   £3,080 $5,298

O'NEILL

DANIEL O'NEILL, R.H.A. (1920–1974) – Orpheus –
signed – oil on canvas laid down on panel – 61 x 51cm.
(*Christie's*)   **£4,400 $7,568**

DANIEL O'NEILL, R.H.A. (1920–1974) – An old house
– signed – oil on board – 40.5 x 51cm.
(*Christie's*)   **£4,180 $7,190**

RAYMOND EDGAR O'NEILL (1893–1962) – On trial –
signed and dated *1935* – oil on masonite – 124.5 x 99cm.
(*Christie's*)   **£10,846 $18,700**

HONORIO ROMERO OROZCO (1867–1920) – Interior of a workroom – signed and dated *1897* – oil on canvas – 200 x 140cm.
(Duran) £6,685 $12,000

Manner of BERNARD VAN ORLEY – The return from the flight into Egypt with the Infant Saint John the Baptist greeting the Christ Child – oil on panel – 41.8 x 31.7cm.
(Christie's) £935 $1,459

ARTURO ORSELLI – The new doll – signed – pencil and watercolour – 14$^1/_2$ x 10in.
(Christie's) £495 $855

HANS ORLOWSKI (1894–1967) – A young girl seated – signed – oil on board – 110 x 66.5cm.
(Christie's) £1,444 $2,555

EDMUND H. OSTHAUS (1858–1928) – At the rendezvous – signed – oil on canvas – 48.9 x 125.7cm.
(Sotheby's) £18,333 $33,000

EDMUND OSTHAUS – Black and white spaniel –signed
– watercolour – 23 x 18in.
(Du Mouchelles)   **£2,102 $3,500**

EDMUND H. OSTHAUS (1858–1928) – Retrieving –
signed and dated *1891* – oil on canvas – 71.8 x 54.6cm.
(Sotheby's)   **£15,278 $27,500**

EDMUND OSTHAUS – Three hunting dogs – signed – oil
on canvas – 39 x 59in.
(Du Mouchelles)   **£18,018 $30,000**

JOSE M. OTEGUI – Head of an old man – signed – oil on
canvas – 23 x 15cm.
(Duran)   **£308 $542**

JEAN-BAPTISTE OUDRY (1686–1755) – The lion and
the spider – signed – black and white chalk on blue paper –
313 x 314mm.
(Christie's)   **£5,583 $9,268**

KEVIN OXLEY – Nude in the wildflowers – signed – oil
on board – 31 x 26cm.
(Australian Art Auctions)   **£66 $117**

Manner of PALAMEDESZ PALAMEDES – Cavalry taking a bridge – oil on canvas – 87.8 x 143.5cm.
(Christie's) £1,650 $2,574

ROBERT PAGE (fl. 1880–1890) – Which hand will you have? – signed, inscribed and dated – oil on canvas – 50.8 x 40.7cm.
(Christie's) £3,300 $5,841

FILIPPO PALIZZI (Italian, 1818–99) – A dog on a cliff – signed and dated *1849* – oil on canvas – 32 x 46cm.
(Sotheby's) £6,050 $10,708

MIMMO PALADINO (b. 1948) – The perfect room – signed and dated on the reverse *1987* – oil, gold leaf, wood and metal bowl on wood in the artist's painted frame – 198.2 x 149.8cm.
(Christie's) £38,500 $62,370

ALFRED PALMER – The caddie – signed – gouache on card – 46 x 39cm.
(Hôtel de Ventes Horta) £1,293 $2,250

SAMUEL PALMER (1805–1881) – Sheep in the shade –
signed – pencil and watercolour with touches of white
heightening – 375 x 530mm.
(Christie's) **£12,650 $22,264**

WALTER LAUNT PALMER (1854–1932) – Harvest
time – signed and dated *1881* – oil on board – 73 x 90.2cm.
(Butterfield & Butterfield) **£6,304 $11,000**

Attributed to RUGGERO PANERAI – A Shepherdess
and sheep on a country track – with signature – oil on
canvas – 49.5 x 63.5cm.
(Christie's) **£2,750 $4,730**

RUGGERO PANERAI (1862–1923) – In the paddock –
signed – oil on panel – 20.2 x 34.3cm.
(Christie's) **£17,600 $30,800**

ANTONIO PAOLETTI (Italian, 1834–1912) – The
young greengrocer – signed and inscribed – oil on panel –
33.5 x 53cm.
(Sotheby's) **£15,400 $27,258**

SYLVIUS D. PAOLETTI (1864–1921) – The fishergirl –
signed and inscribed – oil on canvas – 55.2 x 40.7cm.
(Christie's) **£2,530 $4,402**

JOHN ANTHONY PARK (1880–1962) – Fish Street, St. Ives – signed – oil on board – 40.5 x 30.5cm.
(Christie's) £1,045 $1,797

JOHN ANTHONY PARK, R.O.I., R.B.A. (1880–1962) – High tide, St. Ives harbour – signed – oil on board – 13 x 16in.
(David Lay) £900 $1,431

HENRY H. PARKER (1858–1930) – The Church Pool, Bettws-y-Coed, North Wales – signed – oil on canvas – 61 x 92cm.
(Christie's) £2,640 $4,277

JOHN ANTHONY PARK, R.O.I., R.B.A. (1880–1962) – Norway Lane, St. Ives harbour – signed, inscribed to reverse and with label dated *1921* – oil on board – 15$^1/_2$ x 11$^1/_2$in.
(David Lay) £900 $1,431

EDWARD PARKMAN – Figures on a rural track, possibly Cheddar valley – signed and dated *86* – watercolour – 34 x 50cm.
(Allen & Harris) £350 $616

Manner of **PARMIGIANINO** – The Madonna (?), head
and shoulders – oil on panel – 44 x 34.5cm.
(Christie's) **£825 $1,287**

GINES PARRA (1899–1961) – Fruit bowl – signed – oil
on canvas – 26 x 40cm.
(Duran) **£2,368 $4,250**

PARRA – Still life with lobster – signed – oil on canvas –
40 x 58cm.
(Duran) **£669 $1,201**

EDMUND THOMAS PARRIS – Study of a boy – pencil
and watercolour heightened with gum arabic –
11¹/₂ x 8³/₄in.
(Christie's) **£264 $456**

WILLIAM PARROTT (1813–1869) – Windsor Castle
from the Thames – signed – oil on canvas – 30.5 x 48.2cm.
(Christie's) **£4,620 $8,408**

ALFRED A. PARTRIDGE (British, 19th–20th century)
– Black hunter in a loose box; Bay hunter in a loose box –
one signed and dated *90* – oil on canvas – 46 x 61cm. – a
pair
(Butterfield & Butterfield) **£1,135 $1,980**

JULES PASCIN (1885–1930) – Nude (The brunette in the blue necklace) – signed – oil on canvas – 47 x 55cm.
(Christie's)   **£28,600 $46,332**

TOM PATERSON – A September day – signed – watercolour – 10 x 13in.
(G.A Key)   **£350 $623**

Attributed to JOSEPH PAUL – An extensive East Anglian river landscape with figures ploughing, a windmill beyond – oil on canvas – 76.2 x 127cm.
(Christie's)   **£3,300 $5,850**

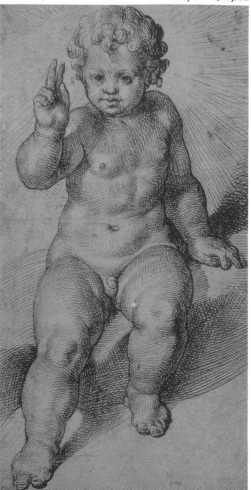

JOSEPH PAULMAN (English, 19th century) – Haymaking – signed – oil on canvas – 30.5 x 40.7cm. – and companion piece – a pair
(Bonhams)   **£1,600 $2,544**

BARTOLOMMEO PASSAROTTI (1529–1592) – The Christ child – bears inscription – pencil and brown ink – 33.5 x 18.4cm.
(Glerum)   **£2,826 $4,995**

N. CHR. PAULSEN (Danish, 19th century) – Naval gun battle involving two fleets – signed – oil on canvas – 28¹/₂ x 45in.
(Du Mouchelles)   **£2,676 $4,750**

HERMANN MAX PECHSTEIN (1881–1955) – Fruit trees in blossom – signed and dated *1928* – watercolour, gouache and wax crayon on paper – 50.2 x 61.6cm.
(Christie's)   **£13,200 $23,232**

CLEMENS VON PAUSINGER (Austrian, 1855–1936) – The tambourine girl – signed and dated *'91* – pastel on panel – 70 x 54cm.
(Sotheby's)   **£4,180 $7,399**

MAX PECHSTEIN (1881–1955) – Grey weather – signed and dated *1919* – oil on canvas – 80 x 70cm.
(Christie's)   **£88,000 $142,560**

HARRIET CARY PEALE (1800–1869) – Portrait of a girl with bonnet – signed and dated *1854* – oil on canvas (in a painted oval) – 76 x 63.5cm.
(Christie's)   **£2,042 $3,520**

Attributed to TITO PELLICCIOTTI (Italian, 1872–1943) – An interior genre scene – indistinctly signed on reverse – oil on panel – 6 x 11³/₄in.
(Skinner Inc.)   **£295 $522**

ALBERT PELS (b. 1910) – Waiting room, train station – signed – oil on canvas – 30.5 x 40.7cm.
(Christie's) £870 $1,540

GEORG PENCZ (1500–1550) – Lucretia – signed and dated *154* – oil on panel – 82 x 68.5cm.
(Sotheby's) £22,000 $39,600

AGNES PELTON (b. 1881) – Gladiolas – signed – watercolour on paper – 89.5 x 73.6cm.
(Christie's) £1,616 $2,860

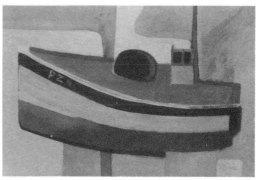

JACK PENDER (b. 1918) – High and dry – signed – oil on board – 51 x 76cm.
(Christie's) £880 $1,514

A.R. PENCK (b. 1939) – Important Meeting, number 1 – acrylic on canvas – 250 x 330cm.
(Christie's) £39,600 $70,092

E.A PENLEY – Cadir Idris from across the lake with mill and figures before – signed and dated *187...* – watercolour – 35.5 x 74cm.
(Allen & Harris) £440 $774

Attributed to JOHN RITTO PENNIMAN (1782–1841) –
Portrait of a family – watercolour on paper – 8 x 10¼in.
(Christie's)   **£6,380 $11,000**

CHARLES OLIVIER DE PENNE (French, 1831–1897)
– Beagles after the hunt – signed indistinctly – oil on
cradled panel – 45.7 x 37.5cm.
(Butterfield & Butterfield)   **£2,521 $4,400**

Attributed to EDWARD PENNY – The confession –
inscribed – oil on copper – 35.5 x 28cm.
(Christie's)   **£550 $975**

JOSEPH PENNELL (1860–1926) – The Canongate,
Edinburgh – indistinctly signed, titled and dated *1882* –
gouache, India ink and pencil on paper laid down on board
– 35.6 x 25.4cm.
(Sotheby's)   **£721 $1,320**

SIDNEY RICHARD PERCY (1821–1886) – Fishing on
the lake – signed – oil on canvas – 25 x 43cm.
(Christie's)   **£2,200 $3,564**

MADELAINE PERENY (b. 1896) – Escape – signed – oil
on canvas – 101.6 x 92.7cm.
(Butterfield & Butterfield)   £315 $550

RAFAEL SENET PEREZ (1856–1927) – Church of the
Jesuits, le Zattere, Venice – signed and inscribed – oil on
canvas – 35.5 x 57cm.
(Christie's)   **£11,550 $18,826**

BERNARD PERLIN (b. 1918) – Divorce – signed –
tempera on illustration board – 62.2 x 45.7cm.
(Sotheby's)   **£2,404 $4,400**

GEORG PERLBERG (1807–1884) – View from a
window in Nurnberg Castle – signed and dated *1861* – oil
on canvas – 40.8 x 33cm.
(Lempertz)   **£9,929 $16,879**

MATTHEW WILLIAM PETERS (British, 1742–1814)
– Portrait of a young lady holding a bouquet of flowers –
oil on canvas – 76.2 x 62.9cm.
(Butterfield & Butterfield)   **£1,891 $3,300**

439

JANE PETERSON (1876–1965) – The garden pool –
signed twice – gouache, watercolour and charcoal on grey-
green paper – 45.7 x 61cm.
(Christie's)   **£5,104 $8,800**

ROBERT PHILIPP (1895–1981) – Rochelle in red
kimono – signed – oil on canvas – 76.2 x 63.5cm.
(Sotheby's)   **£1,262 $2,310**

ROY PETLEY (b. 1951) – Sandy pier – signed – oil on
board – 23.5 x 33.5cm.
(Christie's)   **£990 $1,703**

**CHARLES R. PETTAFOR (fl. 1862–1900) and
CHARLES WALLER SHAYER (fl. 1870–1880)** – The
watering place – signed and dated *81* – oil on canvas –
76 x 127cm.
(Christie's)   **£3,300 $5,346**

ROBERT PHILIPP (1895–1981) – At the theatre – signed
– oil on canvas – 45.7 x 38.1cm.
(Christie's)   **£2,486 $4,400**

GORDON PHILLIPS (b. 1927) – A welcome sight –
signed and dated '66 – oil on board – 58.4 x 81.3cm.
(Sotheby's) **£10,389 $18,700**

HENRY WYNDHAM PHILLIPS (1820–1868) – The
leopard skin – signed – oil on canvas – 33 x 64.5cm.
(Christie's) **£3,850 $6,237**

FRANCIS PICABIA (1879–1953) – Spanish women –
gouache on board – 101 x 86cm.
(Christie's) **£63,800 $112,288**

LOUIS PICARD (French, b. 1861) – Evening by the sea
– signed – oil on canvas – 59 x 91cm.
(Sotheby's) **£4,400 $7,788**

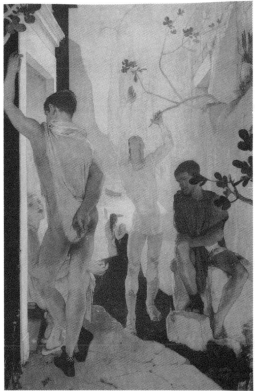

GLYN WARREN PHILPOT, R.A. (1884–1937) –
Penelope – oil on canvas – 136 x 91.8cm.
(Christie's) **£101,200 $167,992**

PABLO PICASSO (1881–1973) – The sculptor resting –
signed, inscribed and dated *XXXIII* – gouache, watercolour,
pen and black ink on paper laid down on board –
40.5 x 51cm.
(Christie's) **£275,000 $451,000**

H. WINTHROP PIERCE (b. 1850) – Bundling the wheat
– signed and dated *1884* – oil on canvas – 68.5 x 55.9cm.
(Christie's)   **£870 $1,540**

LUCIEN PISSARRO (1863–1944) – Girl by a trellis –
signed with monogram and dated *1929* – oil on board –
43.2 x 33cm.
(Christie's)   **£4,400 $7,304**

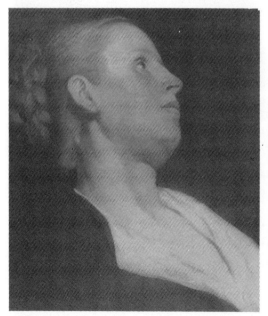

**KARL THEODOR VON PILOTY (German, 1826–
1886)** – Portrait of a woman in profile – signed – oil on
canvas – 41.3 x 35.6cm.
(Butterfield & Butterfield)   **£473 $825**

SIDNEY PIKE – Sheep resting and grazing in a sunlit
orchard – signed and dated *1895* – oil – 8 x 11in.
(G.A. Key)   **£650 $1,151**

OROVIDA PISSARRO (1893–1968) – The stable lantern
– signed and dated *1957* - oil on canvas – 127 x 102cm.
(Christie's)   **£2,035 $3,378**

GIOVANNI BATTISTA PITTONI (1687–1767) – The sacrifice of Polyxena – oil on canvas – 74.5 x 53.9cm.
(Sotheby's) £132,000 $237,600

HERMANN PLATHNER (1831–1902) – The good likeness – signed and dated *1869* – oil on canvas – 62 x 75cm.
(Lempertz) £6,028 $10,248

OGDEN M. PLEISSNER (1905–83) – Netting the salmon – bears inscription on reverse – watercolour, gouache and pencil on paper – unframed – 16.5 x 25.4cm.
(Sotheby's) £2,404 $4,400

THEODOR PIXIS (1831–1907) – Scene from the Gudrun saga – signed and dated *1860* – oil on canvas – 117 x 78cm.
(Lempertz) £4,965 $8,440

OGDEN M. PLEISSNER (1905–83) – La Neige – signed – watercolour on paper – 34.3 x 44.5cm.
(Sotheby's) £1,953 $3,575

ARTHUR POND – Portrait of Sir Frederick Frankland, seated three-quarter length, in a brown coat and breeches – signed with initials and dated *1755* – oil on canvas – 127 x 101.7cm.
(Christie's)   **£1,650 $2,665**

WJATSCHESLAV POBOGENSKIJ (Russian, b. 1943) – Seated nude, back view – signed and dated *1985* – oil on canvas – 150 x 100cm.
(Germann)   **£1,411 $2,244**

SIGMAR POLKE (b. 1941) – Untitled – signed and dated *86* – black ink and acrylic on cardboard mounted on canvas – 75 x 100cm.
(Christie's)   **£23,100 $38,346**

DANIEL HERBERT VAN DER POLL (1877–1963) – Tigers at a waterhole – signed – oil on canvas – 104.7 x 151.1cm.
(Christie's)   **£4,950 $8,118**

PINO PONTI (b. 1905) – Portrait – signed and dated *1941* – oil on board – 16.5 x 12.5cm.
(Finarte)   **£518 $883**

Attributed to BACCIO DELLA PORTA, called Fra Bartolommeo – The Madonna and Child with St. John the Baptist – oil on canvas – unframed – 102 x 78cm.
(Bonhams) **£8,500 $13,515**

GERARD PORTIELJE (Belgian, 1856–1929) – The musician – signed – oil on panel – 21.6 x 15.2cm.
(Butterfield & Butterfield) **£1,198 $2,090**

BERNARD POTHAST (1882–1966) – Awaiting his return – signed – oil on canvas – 31.2 x 25.4cm.
(Christie's) **£3,080 $5,359**

MAURICE B. PRENDERGAST (1859–1924) – Franklin Park, Boston – signed – watercolour on paper – 29.8 x 49.5cm.
(Sotheby's) **£464,444 $836,000**

LEVI WELLS PRENTICE (1851–1935) – Apple harvest – signed with initials – oil on canvas – 38.5 x 48.5cm.
(Christie's) **£15,312 $26,400**

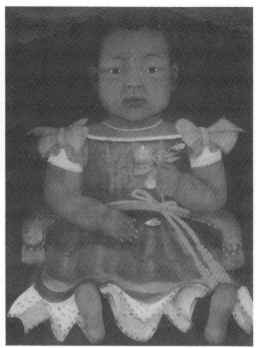

MATTIA PRETI, called Il Cavaliere Calabrese (1613–1699) – Belisarius receiving alms – inscribed on column – oil on canvas – 152.5 x 198.5cm.
(Sotheby's) £440,000 $792,000

VALENTINE CAMERON PRINSEP (1838–1904) – The lady of the Tootni-Nameh; or, The legend of the parrot – signed and indistinctly inscribed – oil on canvas – 91.5 x 116.5cm.
(Christie's) £30,800 $52,360

PRIOR-HAMBLEN SCHOOL (circa 1850) – Portrait of a child – oil on canvas – 20^{1}/4 x 16^{1}/8in.
(Christie's) £22,330 $38,500

Attributed to WILLIAM MATTHEW PRIOR (1806–1873) – Portrait of a young woman – oil on board – 15^{5}/8 x 12^{1}/2in.
(Christie's) £1,276 $2,200

DOD PROCTER (1892–1972) – Girl in a bonnet – oil on canvas – 17 x 12^{1}/2in.
(David Lay) £2,300 $3,657

PIERRE PAUL PRUD'HON (1758–1823) – Portrait of Giovanni Battista Sommariva, bust length – oil on canvas – 65.7 x 54.5cm.
(Christie's) **£15,400 $25,102**

CLIFTON ERNEST PUGH (1924–1990) – The Rape of Europa – signed and dated *59* – oil on masonite – 121.9 x 170.2cm.
(Christie's) **£8,800 $15,488**

JAMES BAKER PYNE (1800–1870) – The lake of Zurich – signed, dated and numbered *1865 no. 659* – oil on canvas – 76.2 x 137.2cm.
(Christie's) **£11,000 $18,700**

JAMES BAKER PYNE (1800–1870) – A Capriccio view of the Port of Genoa from the New Terrace – signed and dated *1861* – oil on canvas – 61 x 91.5cm.
(Christie's) **£7,700 $13,629**

JAMES BAKER PYNE (1800–1870) – Sorting the catch – signed and numbered *No. 1818* – oil on canvas – 30.5 x 46.3cm.
(Christie's) **£990 $1,980**

JAMES BAKER PYNE (1800–1870) – Scarborough, Yorkshire, from the South Sands – signed, inscribed and dated *1857* – oil on paper laid down on canvas – unframed – 38.5 x 56cm.
(Christie's) **£2,200 $3,564**

JAMES BAKER PYNE (1800–1870) – On the Margin of Fair Zurich's Waters – signed, dated and numbered *1865 No. 653* – oil on canvas – 52.7 x 83.2cm.
(Christie's) **£3,080 $5,606**

SIMON QUAGLIO (1795–1878) – The Schrannenplatz,
Munich – signed with initials – pencil and watercolour on
card – 20.2 x 26.3cm.
(Christie's)   **£6,600 $11,550**

R. PYNENBURG (Dutch, 19th–20th century) – Cabin
interior with open door – signed – oil on canvas –
60 x 51cm.
(Butterfield & Butterfield)   **£315 $550**

CAREL MAX GERLACH ANTON QUAEDVLIEG
(1823–1874) – The Meet – signed – oil on panel –
22.8 x 34.3cm.
(Christie's)   **£5,500 $9,570**

AUGUSTE QUERFURT (1696–1761) – Hunting with
falcons – oil on panel – 20.8 x 28cm.
(Christie's)   **£3,127 $5,191**

CORNELIS RAAPHORST (1875–1954) – Chinese lanterns – signed – oil on canvas – 80 x 59.7cm.
(Christie's)   £3,520 $5,773

ARTHUR RACKHAM (1867–1939) – Christmas Night – signed – pencil, pen and black ink and watercolour – 228 x 200mm.
(Christie's)   £3,080 $5,205

FRANZ RADZIWILL (1895–1982) – Meadow landscape at Dangast – signed and dated *1940* – oil on canvas – 70.5 x 94.5cm.
(Lempertz)   £55,363 $88,304

RADZIWILL

FRANZ RADZIWILL (1895–1982) – Still life with jasmin – signed – oil on canvas laid down on wood – 40 x 32.5cm.
(Lempertz) £20,069 $32,010

ARNULF RAINER (b. 1929) – Rainbow – signed and dated *62* – oil, coloured crayon and pencil on canvas – 50.5 x 65cm.
(Christie's) £27,500 $44,550

WILLIAM H. RAINEY (1852–1936) – The game of cards in a Dutch lodging house – signed and dated *1894* – pencil, watercolour and bodycolour – 692 x 558mm.
(Christie's) £1,540 $2,803

THEODORE JACQUES RALLI (1852–1909) – Evening
prayers – signed and dated *90* – oil on canvas –
60.4 x 93.4cm.
(Christie's) £59,400 $96,822

JEAN RANC (1674–1735) – Portrait of a huntsman,
seated, in an extensive landscape - oil on canvas – 147 x
114cm.
(Christie's) £22,334 $37,074

WILLIAM BRUCE ELLIS RANKEN (1881–1941) –
Pygmalion – signed indistinctly – oil on canvas –
110.5 x 85cm.
(Christie's) £4,180 $6,939

RAPHAEL

After RAPHAEL (Italian, 19th century) – The Madonna of the chair – oil on canvas, in an ornate and decorative carved wooden frame – diameter 71cm.
(Sotheby's) £7,150 $12,655

JOSEPH RAPHAEL (1869–1950) – The name-day of Burgomaster Captain N.W. van den Broek of Laren, North Holland – oil on canvas – 204.5 x 226.1cm.
(Butterfield & Butterfield) £23,639 $41,250

ARMAND RASSENFOSSE (Belgian 1862–1934) – Naked dancer (two sided) – signed with monogram – drawing heightened with pastel – 28 x 22cm.
(Hôtel de Ventes Horta) £1,293 $2,250

DE RAYNAL (mid 19th century) – Castel Gandolfo; and Porto di Napoli con il Maschio Angioino – one signed and dated *66*; the other signed and dated *67* – pencil and bodycolour heightened with white on paper – 26.6 x 39cm. – two
(Christie's) £2,200 $3,850

LOUISE RAYNER (1832–1924) – Canterbury Cathedral – signed – watercolour and bodycolour – 280 x 426mm.
(Christie's) £4,620 $7,808

LOUISE RAYNER (1832–1924) – Market day, Chippenham – signed – oil on canvas – 25.4 x 61cm.
(Christie's) £8,800 $15,576

LOUISE RAYNER (1832–1924) – Foss Gate, York – signed – pencil, watercolour and bodycolour – 457 x 292mm.
(Christie's) £4,400 $7,436

LOUISE RAYNER (1832–1924) – Magdalen Bridge, Cambridge – signed – pencil, watercolour and bodycolour – 310 x 228mm.
(Christie's) £2,860 $4,833

MARTIAL RAYSSE (b. 1936) – Variation sur un palmier 2 ordinateur IBM et MR 65 – inscribed with title – gouache, black ink and paper collage – 66 x 50cm.
(Christie's) £2,200 $3,652

NICOLA MARIA RECCO (late 17th–early 18th century) – Still life of fish with a copper vessel upon a sea shore – oil on canvas – 107 x 165.8cm.
(Sotheby's) **£19,800 $35,640**

HENRY REDMORE (1820–1887) – Fishing boats and other vessels on the Scheldt near Rotterdam – signed and dated *1852* – oil on canvas – 31.1 x 46.3cm.
(Christie's) **£7,700 $13,706**

HENRY REDMORE (1820–1887) – Shipping at the entrance of Hull Harbour – signed and dated *1885* – oil on panel – 20.2 x 33cm.
(Christie's) **£6,600 $11,748**

EDWARD W. REDFIELD (1869–1965) – The brook – signed – oil on canvas – 80 x 64.8cm.
(Sotheby's) **£29,027 $52,250**

GRANVILLE REDMOND (1871–1935) – A California sunset – signed – oil on canvas – 46 x 81.3cm.
(Christie's) **£9,570 $16,500**

HENRY REDMORE (1820–1887) – Shipping in the Humber off Burlington Quay, Hull – signed and dated *1873* – oil on canvas – 45.7 x 76.2cm.
(Christie's) **£8,360 $14,888**

PAULA REGO – Untitled composition – acrylic and black ink on paper – 101.6 x 137.2cm.
(Bonhams) £11,000 $19,140

ODILON REDON (1840–1916) – Female profile with laurel wreath – signed – charcoal on paper – 44 x 30.5cm.
(Christie's) £82,500 $133,650

GEORGE PHILIP REINAGLE (English, 1802–1835) – Dutch pinks and merchantmen off a fortified jetty – signed with initials and indistinctly dated – oil on panel – 48.7 x 74.9cm.
(Bonhams) £6,000 $9,900

ODILON REDON (1840–1916) – Head with hood, suspended from a chain – signed – black chalk on paper – 46 x 38cm.
(Christie's) £113,453 $200,812

RAMSEY RICHARD REINAGLE (1775-1862) – Portrait of two boys, seated full length, in green and red velvet suits, with their dog – oil on canvas – 101.6 x 127cm.
(Christie's) £11,550 $18,942

PIERRE-AUGUSTE RENOIR (1841–1919) – The collation – signed with monogram – red chalk on ivory paper – 43 x 32cm.
(Lempertz)   **£259,516 $413,928**

PIERRE AUGUSTE RENOIR (1841–1919) – Countryside near Vence – signed – oil on canvas – 17.5 x 23.5cm.
(Christie's)   **£39,600 $64,152**

Follower of GUIDO RENI – The penitent Magdalen – oil on canvas – 235.6 x 157cm.
(Sotheby's)   **£7,700 $13,860**

SERGE REZVANI (b. 1928) – La Jaline – signed and
dated *1959* – oil and asphalt on canvas – 96.5 x 146cm.
(Christie's) **£2,420 $3,848**

GERMAIN THEODORE RIBOT (1845–1893) –
Geraniums in a jug – signed – oil on panel – 30.5 x 24.3cm.
(Christie's) **£4,620 $7,531**

PIERRE RIBERA – Gipsy – signed and dated *1924* – oil on
canvas – 46 x 35cm.
(Duran) **£474 $851**

OSCAR RICCIARDI (b. 1864) – The Sorrento coast –
signed and inscribed – oil on canvas – 40.6 x 61cm.
(Christie's) **£3,520 $6,125**

PIERRE RIBERA (French, 1867–1932) – Au jardin de
Paris – signed and inscribed – oil on board – 33 x 41cm.
(Sotheby's) **£9,900 $17,523**

WILLIAM TROST RICHARDS (American, 1833–
1905) – Along the coast – signed and dated *1883* – oil on
canvas – 28 x 44in.
(Du Mouchelles) **£8,757 $15,000**

GERHARD RICHTER (b. 1932) – Untitled – signed,
numbered and dated on the reverse *551–8 1984* – oil on
canvas – 65 x 80cm.
(Christie's)   **£27,500 $44,550**

GERHARD RICHTER (b. 1932) – Untitled – signed and
dated *31.1.89* – oil on photograph – 14.8 x 10cm.
(Christie's)   **£1,980 $3,287**

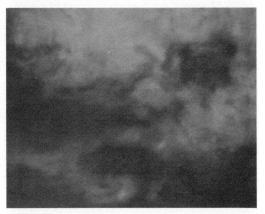

GERHARD RICHTER (b. 1932) – Tourist (with 1 lion) –
signed, numbered and dated on the reverse *370 1975* – oil
on canvas – 200 x 200cm.
(Christie's)   **£159,500 $258,390**

GERHARD RICHTER (b. 1932) – Townscape (M8) –
signed, inscribed with title, numbered and dated *170/8 68* –
oil on canvas – 85 x 90cm.
(Christie's)   **£30,800 $51,128**

GERHARD RICHTER (b. 1932) – Untitled – signed,
numbered and dated on the reverse *675–1 88* – acrylic on
canvas – unframed – 35 x 40cm.
(Christie's)   **£13,200 $21,384**

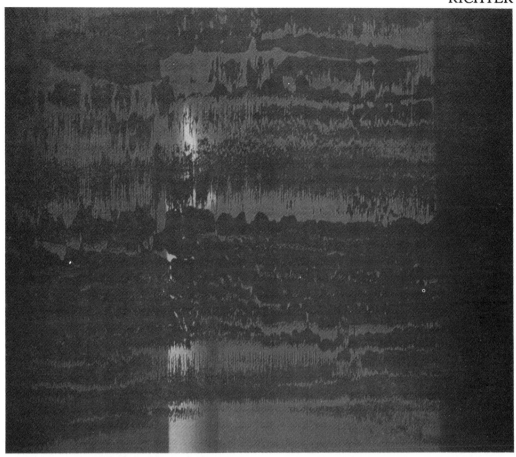

GERHARD RICHTER (b. 1932) – Candle – signed and dated *1989* – oil on photograph – 60 x 62cm.
(Christie's) **£3,850 $6,391**

GERHARD RICHTER (b. 1932) – Small door – signed and dated on the reverse *68* – oil on canvas – unframed – 50 x 50cm.
(Christie's) **£31,900 $56,463**

HERBERT DAVIS RICHTER – The artist's drawing room – signed – 76 x 63.5cm.
(Christie's) **£2,200 $3,498**

LUDWIG RICHTER (1803–1884) – The ox cart – signed and dated *1836* – watercolour on paper – 16 x 23cm.
(Lempertz)   **£8,156 $13,865**

MARTEN RIJCKAERT (1587–1631) – Figures on the banks of a river – oil on panel – 27 x 34.4cm.
(Sotheby's)   **£33,000 $59,400**

AUGUST HEINRICH RIEDEL (1799–1883) – The bathers – signed and dated *1841* – oil on canvas – 98 x 69.8cm.
(Christie's)   **£11,000 $17,930**

PETER RINDISBACHER (1806–1834) – The chase – watercolour on paper – unframed – 19.7 x 29.8cm.
(Christie's)   **£35,090 $60,500**

JEAN-PAUL RIOPELLE (b. 1923) – Arles – signed – oil on canvas – 73 x 99cm.
(Christie's) £42,900 $75,933

DAVID ROBERTS (1796–1864) – Jerusalem (looking south) – signed and dated *1860* – oil on canvas –
122.5 x 183.5cm.
(Christie's) £418,000 $710,600

461

EDWIN THOMAS ROBERTS (1840–1917) – Tea for two – signed – oil on canvas – 63.5 x 50.8cm.
(Christie's) **£6,600** **$7,590**

EDWIN THOMAS ROBERTS (1840–1917) – The fruit seller – signed with monogram and dated *1873* – oil on canvas – 61 x 45.5cm.
(Christie's) **£2,860** **$4,633**

EDWIN THOMAS ROBERTS (British, 1840–1917) – Sweetheart's requited affection – signed – oil on canvas – 18¼ x 14¼in.
(Du Mouchelles) **£3,099** **$5,500**

EDWIN THOMAS ROBERTS (1840–1917) – Her only pair – signed – oil on canvas – 60.9 x 45.2cm.
(Christie's) **£8,250** **$14,603**

EDWIN THOMAS ROBERTS (British, 1840–1917) –
Sweetheart's love at first sight – signed – oil on canvas –
18¼ x 14¼in.
(Du Mouchelles)   £2,536 $4,500

WILLIAM ROBERTS, R.A. (1895–1980) - Pollarding –
signed – pencil, black crayon and watercolour –
55 x 36.5cm.
(Christie's)   £3,520 $5,843

**THOMAS WILLIAM ROBERTS (Australian,
1855–1931)** – The letter – signed and dated *1896* – oil on
canvas laid down on masonite – 67.9 x 50.2cm.
(Butterfield & Butterfield)   £1,576 $2,750

PERCY ROBERTSON (British, 1868–1934) – High
Holborn, London – signed and dated *1903* – watercolour and
gouache on paper – 17.8 x 30.5cm.
(Butterfield & Butterfield)   £1,891 $3,000

JEAN-BAPTISTE ROBIE (1821–1910) – Roses with a blue tit by a stream – signed – oil on panel –
42 x 52cm.
(Christie's)   **£10,780 $17,571**

DOMENICO ROBUSTI, called Tintoretto (1560–1635) – The Lamentation – oil on canvas – 51 x 75cm.
(Sotheby's)   **£93,500 $168,300**

NORMAN ROCKWELL (1894–1978) – Budwine boy –
signed – oil on canvas – 69.9 x 63.5cm.
(Sotheby's) **£15,278 $27,500**

SEVERIN ROESEN (active 1848–1871) – Still life with
fruit and glass of wine – bears signature – oil on canvas –
76 x 63cm – oval
(Glerum) **£20,416 $35,200**

SEVERIN ROESEN (fl. c. 1848–1870) – Vase of flowers
with bird's nest – signed with monogram – oil on canvas –
76.2 x 63.5cm.
(Sotheby's) **£33,611 $60,500**

NORMAN ROCKWELL (1894–1978) – The magician –
signed – oil on canvas – 73.7 x 50.8cm.
(Sotheby's) **£58,056 $104,500**

PHILIP HUTCHINS ROGERS – A view of Millbrook
Lane looking towards Devonport – bears inscription – oil
on canvas – 33.6 x 40.6cm.
(Bonhams) **£2,800 $4,452**

ROHDEN

A. DE ROHDEN (German, 19th century) – Madonna and Child – signed and dated *1878* – oil on panel – unframed – 57 x 37cm.
(Sotheby's) £1,760 $3,115

ROMAN SCHOOL (circa 1640) – The Coronation of the Virgin with Saint John the Baptist, Saint Benedict, Saint Romuald and Saint Andrew – oil on canvas, unstretched – 257.5 x 178cm.
(Sotheby's) £35,200 $63,360

FRANZ ROHDEN (German, 1817–1903) – The Nativity – signed and dated *Roma 1853* – oil on canvas – unframed – 265 x 189cm.
(Sotheby's) £3,520 $6,230

ROMAN SCHOOL (mid 18th century) – Portrait of a gentleman, half-length, seated, wearing the badge of the French military order of St. Louis – oil on canvas – 81 x 64.7cm.
(Sotheby's) £7,150 $12,870

ROMAN SCHOOL (circa 1750) – Allegory of Painting –
oil on canvas – 74 x 97cm.
(Christie's)   **£16,750 $27,805**

ROMAN SCHOOL (circa 1740) – The Sacrifice of Isaac
– oil on canvas – 35.6 x 46.5cm.
(Christie's)   **£7,817 $12,976**

HENRIETTE RONNER-KNIP (1821–1909) – A Bichon
Frizé and a King Charles spaniel with a hen and her chicks
– signed – oil on canvas – 57.8 x 85cm.
(Christie's)   **£4,950 $8,118**

HENRIETTE RONNER-KNIP (1821–1909) – Work, rest
and play – signed and dated *1896* – oil on canvas –
103 x 125.7cm.
(Christie's)   **£93,500 $153,340**

NICOLAAS JOHANNES ROOSENBOOM (Dutch, 1805–80) – Figures in a winter landscape – signed with initials – oil on panel – 20 x 30.5cm.
(Sotheby's)   £2,750 $4,867

MICK ROONEY (b. 1944) – Two women meeting – signed and dated *88* – pastel and gouache – 42 x 33cm.
(Christie's)   £1,375 $2,406

Follower of JACQUES IGNATIUS DE ROORE – An allegorical group with Mars and Juno, Ceres and Venus (?) – oil on canvas – 47 x 55.8cm.
(Christie's)   £1,650 $2,574

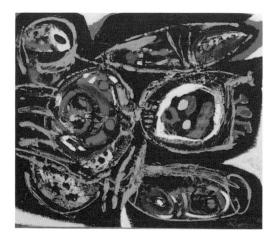

ANTON ROOSKENS (1906–1976) – Symbolen in zwarte Vorm – signed and dated *65* – oil on canvas – 100 x 120cm.
(Christie's) £13,752 $24,341

ALBERTO ROSATI (late 19th century) – Arabs in a street – signed – watercolour heightened with white – 53 x 36cm.
(Christie's) £2,200 $3,828

OTTONE ROSAI (1895–1957) – Four men at a table – signed – oil on canvas – 55.5 x 41.3cm.
(Christie's) £8,800 $14,256

F.H. ROSCOE (19th century) – A tan greyhound bitch in an extensive river landscape – signed and dated *1873* – oil on canvas – 112 x 142cm.
(Christie's) £9,900 $16,236

ROSIER

AMEDEE ROSIER (1821–1891) – Boats on the Lagoon, Venice – signed – oil on canvas – 61.5 x 82.5cm.
(Christie's) £9,680 $16,843

DANTE GABRIEL ROSSETTI (English, 1828–82) – A Christmas carol – signed with monogram and dated *1867* – red and white chalk – 45 x 37.5cm.
(Sotheby's) £33,000 $58,410

JOHANNES ROSIERSE (Dutch, 1818-1901) – The bird's nest – signed - oil on panel – 49 x 63cm.
(Sotheby's) £7,700 $13,629

FEDERICO ROSSANO (1835–1912) – The young harvesters – signed – oil on panel – 19 x 31.8cm.
(Christie's) £6,050 $10,527

ALEXANDER M. ROSSI (fl. 1870–1903) – On the riverbank – signed – oil on card laid down on canvas – 52.1 x 33cm.
(Christie's) £2,640 $4,673

ALEXANDER M. ROSSI (English, fl. 1870–1903) – At the beach – signed and dated *1887* – oil on canvas – 71.2 x 104.2cm.
(Bonhams) £15,000 $23,850

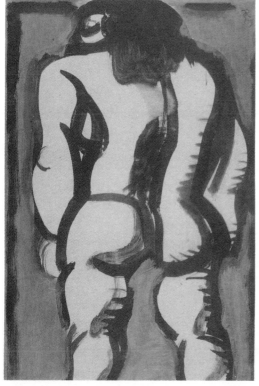

GEORGES ROUAULT (1871–1958) – La Passion – signed – oil on canvas – 10.8 x 25.1cm.
(Christie's) £55,000 $96,800

GEORGES ROUAULT (1871–1958) – Nude, back view – signed with initials and dated *GR 1915* – gouache on paper laid down on card – 39.3 x 25.7cm.
(Christie's) £14,300 $25,168

THEODORE ROUSSEAU (French, 1812–67) – Shepherdess watching her flocks – stamped with the cachet de vente (Lugt 2436) – black chalk – 37 x 51.5cm.
(Sotheby's) £4,400 $7,788

THEODORE ROUSSEAU (1812–1867) – The woodland path – oil on canvas – 79 x 65cm.
(Christie's) **£11,000 $17,930**

CHARLES ROWBOTHAM (1858–1921) – Lake Garda – signed, inscribed and dated *1886* – watercolour heightened with bodycolour – 213 x 505mm.
(Christie's) **£2,420 $3,920**

GEORGE DERVILLE ROWLANDSON (late 19th century) – Over the ditch; and The kill – both signed – oil on canvas – 61 x 91.5cm. – a pair
(Christie's) **£4,400 $7,788**

THOMAS ROWLANDSON (1756–1827) – The comet – signed and dated *1821* – pencil, pen and ink and watercolour – 430 x 270mm.
(Christie's) **£6,600 $10,626**

THOMAS ROWLANDSON (1756–1827) – A sale of English beauties in the East Indies – inscribed as title – pencil, pen and ink and watercolour – 242 x 337mm.
(Christie's) **£12,100 $21,296**

THOMAS ROWLANDSON (1756–1827) – The Breedwell family – pen and ink and watercolour – 98 x 177mm.
(Christie's) **£2,090 $3,678**

FERDINAND ROYBET (French, 1840–1920) – The young prince – signed – oil on cradled woodpanel – 21¹/₂ x 18in.
(Du Mouchelles) £2,043 $3,500

JULES LE ROY (1833–1865) – Tolerance – signed – oil on panel – 40.7 x 32.4cm.
(Christie's) £1,760 $2,886

HERBERT ROYLE (Exh. 1892–1940) – Richmond Castle – signed – oil on canvas – 76 x 102cm.
(Christie's) £3,080 $5,298

JULES LE ROY (1833–1865) – Grandeur déchue – signed on the reverse – oil on canvas – 46.3 x 55.9cm.
(Christie's) £1,430 $2,345

After SIR PETER PAUL RUBENS – Samson taken by the Philistines – oil on canvas – unframed – 101.7 x 174cm.
(Christie's) £3,300 $5,148

JOHN RUSKIN (1819–1900) – The Bridge of Rheinfelden – pencil, pen and brown ink and watercolour, heightened with white, on grey and blue paper – 375 x 552mm.
(Christie's)   **£11,000 $19,360**

S. VAN RUYSDAEL – Landscape near Haarlem – signed with monogram and dated *1653* – oil on canvas – 87 x 83cm.
(Hôtel de Ventes Horta)   **£5,119 $8,754**

JOHN PETER RUSSELL (1858–1930) – Foggy evening at Belle-Ile – signed and dated *10* – watercolour – 25 x 35cm.
(Christie's)   **£3,300 $5,808**

CHAUNCEY FOSTER RYDER (1868–1949) – Deep hollow – signed – oil on canvas tacked over panel – 63.5 x 76.5cm.
(Christie's)   **£5,742 $9,900**

SALOMON VAN RUYSDAEL (1601–1670) – A view along the River Rhine looking upstream towards Arnhem, with cattle watering and vessels under sail – signed and dated *1652* – oil on panel – 62 x 94cm.
(Sotheby's)   **£63,800 $114,840**

THEO VAN RYSSELBERGHE (1862–1926) – Bathers at the seaside – signed with monogram – oil on canvas – 168 x 274cm.
(Christie's)   **£68,200 $110,484**

THEO VAN RYSSELBERGHE (1862-1926) – Southern
landscape – oil on panel – 19 x 24cm.
(Christie's)   **£18,700 $32,912**

THEO VAN RYSSELBERGHE (1862–1926) – View of
Veere, morning mist – signed with monogram and dated *06*
– oil on canvas – 59 x 72cm.
(Christie's)   **£26,400 $46,464**

WALTER DENDY SADLER (1854–1923) – The Connoisseur – signed and dated *84–87* – oil on canvas –
40.8 x 51cm.
(Christie's)   **£1,980 $3,208**

SAILMAKER

Attributed to ISAAC SAILMAKER (circa 1633–1721) –
Two three-deckers and other shipping off Portsmouth – oil
on panel – 28.5 x 39.3cm.
(Christie's) £2,200 $3,916

HENRI SAINTIN (1846–1899) – At the watermill, Spring
– signed and dated *1888* – oil on canvas – 181 x 132cm.
(Christie's) £1,980 $3,445

PAUL SANDBY, R.A. (1725–1809) – Travellers at a well
by the Horns' Inn, near Windsor – signed and dated *1763* –
pencil, black chalk and watercolour – 585 x 416mm.
(Christie's) £14,300 $23,023

Attributed to GIROLAMO DA SANTACROCE I
(Italian, d. 1556) – Sacra conversazione – oil on canvas –
46 x 141cm.
(Butterfield & Butterfield) £7,564 $13,200

PAOLO SALA (1859–1929) – On the Embankment, with Cleopatra's Needle, and Waterloo Bridge beyond,
London – signed – oil on panel – 19.5 x 30.5cm.
(Christie's) £9,350 $16,362

JOHN SINGER SARGENT (1856–1925) – 'Expectancy':
a portrait of Frances Winifred Hill – signed – oil on canvas
– 102.2 x 86.4cm.
(Sotheby's)   **£232,222 $418,000**

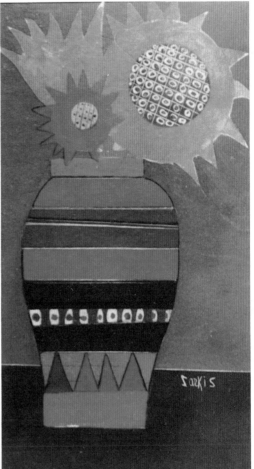

SARKIS SARKISIAN (American, 1909–1977) –
Rasputin – signed – mixed media – 23¹/₂ x 17¹/₄in.
(Du Mouchelles)   **£640 $1,100**

SARKIS SARKISIAN (American, 1909–1977) –
Sunflowers in shaped vase – signed – mixed media on
board – 22¹/₄ x 13³/₄in.
(Du Mouchelles)   **£699 $1,200**

EDGAR SCAUFLAIRE (1893–1960) – Composition with
hat – signed and dated *53* – oil on panel – 50 x 70cm.
(Hôtel de Ventes Horta)   **£2,560 $4,377**

**HENDRIK FRANS SCHAEFFELS (Belgian, 1827–
1904)** – The ballad – signed – oil on canvas – 75 x 100cm.
(Hôtel de Ventes Horta)   **£9,677 $16,450**

**Attributed to BARTOLOMEO SCHEDONI (1578–
1615)** – Charity – oil on canvas – 56.5 x 44cm.
(Sotheby's)   **£4,400 $7,920**

ARY SCHEFFER (1795–1858) – Faust and Margaret in
the garden – signed and dated *1846* – oil on canvas laid
down on panel – unframed – 217.8 x 134.6cm.
(Christie's)   **£126,500 $206,195**

JOSEPH SCHIPPERS (1808–1950) – Lazy kittens – signed – oil on panel – in a painted oval – 37.4 x 47.7cm.
(Christie's) **£2,420 $3,969**

ANDREAS SCHELFHOUT (1787–1870) – Skaters by a booth on a frozen river – signed and dated *1850* – oil on panel – 55 x 74.5cm.
(Christie's) **£71,500 $116,545**

ROBERT SCHEFFER – The Artist's studio – signed – oil on canvas – 81.3 x 63.5cm.
(Christie's) **£3,960 $6,811**

J. ANTON SCHLACHTER (early 19th century) – The Battle of Dresden – signed and dated *1815* – oil on canvas – 94.5 x 137.5cm.
(Christie's) **£12,100 $19,723**

OSKAR SCHLEMMER (1888–1943) – HK 1926 – watercolour and pencil on paper – 55.3 x 40.4cm.
(Christie's) **£143,000 $251,680**

FELIX SCHLESINGER (1833–1910) – Home for tea – signed – oil on panel – 60 x 78.8cm.
(Christie's) **£33,000 $53,790**

FELIX SCHLESINGER (1833–1910) – The departure for America – signed and dated *1859* – oil on canvas – 82.5 x 109.9cm.
(Christie's) **£22,000 $38,500**

HAROLD VON SCHMIDT (1893-1982) – The searchers
– signed and dated *1950* – oil on canvas – 76.2 x 114.3cm.
(Sotheby's)   **£9,167 $16,500**

HANS SCHLIMARSKI (Austrian, b. 1859) – Portrait of
a lady – signed – pastel on cardboard – 63 x 48cm.
(Sotheby's)   **£1,430 $2,531**

HAROLD VON SCHMIDT (1893-1982) – Bunch quitters
– signed and dated *1931* – oil on panel – 61 x 127cm.
(Sotheby's)   **£10,389 $18,700**

HERBERT GUSTAVE SCHMALZ (1857–1935) –
Iphigenia – signed and inscribed – oil on panel –
35.5 x 23.5cm.
(Christie's)   **£1,760 $3,115**

KARL SCHMIDT-ROTTLUFF (1884–1976) – Sea shells
and candlestick – signed – oil on canvas – 65 x 73cm.
(Lempertz)   **£34,602 $55,190**

Follower of JOHANN SCHRANZ (mid 19th century) –
An extensive view of Lisbon on the River Tejo with the
Praça do Terreiro do Paço, The Old Cathedral and the
Castelo de S. Jorge – with inscription – oil on canvas –
91.4 x 152.4cm.
(Christie's)   £24,200 $42,350

JULIAN SCHNABEL (b. 1951) – Fox farm – signed,
numbered and dated *2BB 89* – oil, gesso and marker on
velvet – 244 x 183cm.
(Christie's)   **£115,500 $187,110**

JOSEPH SCHRANZ (b. 1803) – British men-o-war and a
paddle steamer in a squall off Valetta, Malta – signed and
dated *1866* – oil on canvas – 43.7 x 71.1cm.
(Christie's)   **£19,800 $35,244**

JAN CHRISTIANUS SCHOTEL (1787–1838) – A coastal landscape with sailing vessels – signed – oil on
canvas – 64.5 x 86cm.
(Christie's)   **£13,200 $21,516**

LOUIS-MARIE DE SCHRYVER (1862–1942) – Roses in a vase, pears in a porcelain bowl, and fruit on an oak table – signed and dated *1896* – oil on canvas – 90.8 x 81.9cm.
(Christie's) **£12,100 $19,723**

EMIL SCHUMACHER (b. 1912) – Untitled – signed and dated *57* – oil and composition on canvas – 170 x 132cm.
(Christie's) **£88,000 $142,560**

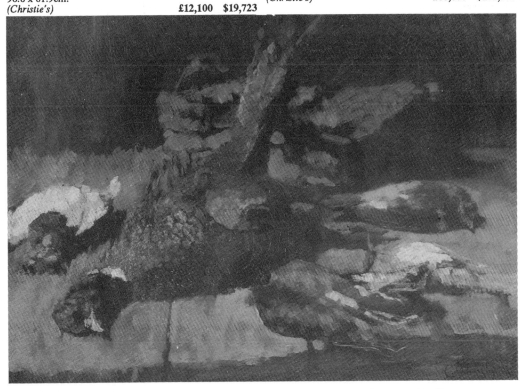

CARL SCHUCH (1846–1903) – A cock pheasant with other dead game on a ledge – signed – oil on canvas – 59 x 79cm.
(Christie's) **£29,700 $48,411**

FRANZ SCHUSTER (1870–1903) – The awakening of Spring – signed – oil on canvas – 77 x 120cm.
(Duran)   **£1,671 $2,999**

CARL SCHWENINGER (1818–1887) – A cosy chat – signed – oil on canvas – 68.5 x 94.6cm.
(Christie's)   **£12,100 $21,175**

WILLIAM SCOTT (1914–1990) – Poem for a jug, blue on white – signed on reverse – oil on canvas – 50.8 x 50.8cm.
(Christie's) **£8,580 $15,015**

EDWARD SEAGO (1910–1974) – The waterfront, Aberdeen–Hong Kong – signed – pencil and watercolour – 33 x 51cm.
(Christie's) **£5,390 $9,460**

WILLIAM SCOTT, R.A. (1914–1990) – Lovers beside a wood – signed and dated *45* – watercolour, bodycolour, pen, brush and black ink – 27.5 x 38cm.
(Christie's) **£5,500 $9,625**

EDWARD SEAGO (1910–1974) – The hayfield, Norfolk – signed – pencil and watercolour – 32.5 x 47.5cm.
(Christie's) **£4,180 $7,190**

CHARLES HENRY SEAFORTH (b. 1801) – Merchantmen off the Indian Coast at dusk – signed and dated *1867* – oil on canvas – 50.2 x 74.8cm.
(Christie's) **£3,520 $6,266**

EDWARD SEAGO (1910–1974) – Norfolk landscape – signed – oil on board – 34 x 50cm.
(Christie's) **£11,000 $18,260**

EDWARD SEAGO (1910–1974) – Summer flowers in a
stoneware jar – signed – oil on canvas – 59.5 x 49.5cm.
(Christie's)   **£8,800 $14,608**

ARTHUR SEGAL (1875–1944) – Sailing boat in harbour
– signed and dated *1912* – oil on canvas – 62.5 x 82cm.
(Christie's)   **£18,700 $32,912**

ADOLF WOLFGANG SEEL (1829–1907) – The orange
seller – signed – oil on board – 66.4 x 48.3cm.
(Christie's)   **£8,800 $14,344**

GOTTARDO SEGANTINI (1882–1974) – Grap da Corn with Piz Corvatsch in the snow – signed and dated *1954* – oil on board – 84 x 122cm.
(Christie's) £15,400 $25,102

ENRIQUE SERRA Y AUQUE (Spanish, 1859–1918) – Ruins by a lake at sunset – signed and inscribed – oil on canvas – 72 x 114cm.
(Sotheby's) £4,400 $7,788

ENRIQUE SERRA Y AUQUE (Spanish, 1859–1918) – A woodland lake at Malmaison – signed and inscribed – oil on canvas – 92 x 67cm.
(Sotheby's) £2,420 $4,283

SERRITELLI (Italian, 19th century) – Figures on a beach near Naples – signed – oil on canvas – 37 x 65cm.
(Sotheby's) £6,050 $10,708

CLEMENT SERVEAU – Reclining nude – signed and
dated *1922* – oval – 132 x 194.3cm.
(Christie's)   **£4,840 $7,696**

WILLIAM EDWARD SETTLE (1821–1897) – A British
frigate and a cutter – signed with monogram and dated
1880 – oil on panel – 18.3 x 26cm.
(Christie's)   **£3,850 $6,853**

DOROTHEA SHARP (1874–1955) – Honeysuckle,
daisies, hollyhocks and fuchsia on a window ledge – oil on
board – 51 x 41cm.
(Christie's)   **£3,300 $5,478**

GINO SEVERINI (1883–1966) – Still life with bottles,
fruit and dessert – signed – oil on canvas – 53.5 x 73cm.
(Finarte)   **£65,737 $112,082**

DOROTHEA SHARP (1874-1955) - In the Luxembourg Gardens – signed – oil on panel – 37 x 44.5cm.
(Christie's) £4,180 $7,190

DOROTHEA SHARP (1874–1955) – Summer flowers –
signed – oil on board – 37 x 43cm.
(Christie's) £5,500 $9,460

DOROTHEA SHARP (1874–1955) – Marcella Smith at
the beach, the Languedoc, South of France – oil on canvas
– 77 x 96.5cm.
(Christie's) £9,900 $16,434

JOSEPH HENRY SHARP (1859–1953) – Aspens,
cottonwoods and spruce, Taos Canyon – signed – oil on
canvas – 64.8 x 76.2cm.
(Butterfield & Butterfield)   £9,455 $16,500

JOSEPH HENRY SHARP (1859–1953) – Autumn in
Taos Canyon – signed – oil on canvas – 55.9 x 68.6cm.
(Butterfield & Butterfield)   £8,825 $15,400

CHARLES GREEN SHAW (1892–1974) – Revolt –
signed – oil on canvas – 127 x 102cm.
(Christie's)   £4,147 $7,150

WILLIAM SHAYER (1787–1879) – An encampment in the New Forest – signed – oil on canvas – 101.6 x 83.8cm.
(Christie's) **£13,200 $23,364**

WILLIAM SHAYER (1787–1879) – The cornfield – signed – oil on canvas – 76.2 x 101.6cm.
(Christie's) **£11,550 $20,444**

WILLIAM SHAYER (1787–1879) – Fishermen bringing in the catch – oil on canvas – 18.4 x 23.5cm.
(Christie's) **£1,650 $2,921**

GEORGE SHEPHERD (1784–1862) – The Gardens at Battlesden House, Bedfordshire – signed and dated *1818* – pencil and watercolour heightened with white – 907 x 540mm.
(Christie's) **£28,600 $46,046**

EVERETT SHINN (1876–1953) – Study of a nude model and study for the Belasco Theatre Proscenium: two works – the first, signed and dated – watercolour and pencil on paper laid down on board (illustrated); the second, watercolour on board - 25.3 x 19cm. and 14.6 x 29.8cm.
(Christie's) **£957 $1,650**

WALTER RICHARD SICKERT (1860–1942) – La Rue du Mortier d'Or, Dieppe – signed and dated *1903* – oil on panel – 19 x 24cm.
(Christie's) **£18,700 $31,042**

491

WALTER RICHARD SICKERT (1860–1942) – Rue
Aguado, Dieppe – signed and dated *1914* – oil on board –
19 x 24cm.
(Christie's)   £5,720 $9,495

AUGUST SIEGEN (late 19th century) – An Arab street
scene – signed – oil on canvas laid down on board –
97.8 x 142.2cm.
(Christie's)   £2,640 $4,595

HENRI LE SIDANER (1862–1939) – The white garden,
Gerberoy – signed – oil on panel – 38 x 58cm.
(Christie's)   £46,200 $81,312

SIENESE SCHOOL (14th century) – The Coronation of
the Virgin with the Infant Christ, Saint Catherine of
Alexandria, and another female saint – oil and tempera,
gold ground, on panel, arched top – painted surface:
22 x 38cm.
(Sotheby's)   £28,600 $51,480

**SAMUEL SIDLEY (1829–1896) and RICHARD
ANSDELL, R.A. (1815–1885)** – Annie and Ernest, the
children of Angus Holden, Esq. – signed and dated *1877* –
oil on canvas – 163 x 122cm.
(Christie's)   £12,100 $19,602

BENJAMIN D. SIGMUND (fl. 1880–1903) – A young
girl with sheep, by a cottage – signed – pencil and
watercolour with touches of white heightening –
254 x 363mm.
(Christie's)   £2,640 $4,277

BENJAMIN D. SIGMUND (fl. 1880–1903) – Feeding time – signed – watercolour heightened with white – 255 x 360mm.
(Christie's) £1,485 $2,406

BENJAMIN D. SIGMUND (fl. 1880–1903) – At George Green, near Windsor – signed – watercolour heightened with white – 255 x 369mm.
(Christie's) £1,980 $3,208

PAUL SIGNAC (1863–1935) – Les Sables d'Olone –
signed, dated and inscribed *Sept. 30* – pencil and
watercolour on paper – 26 x 41.3cm.
(Christie's) £8,800 $15,488

PAUL SIGNAC (1863–1935) – Village on the riverbank –
signed – watercolour and pencil on paper – 26.6 x 38.4cm.
(Christie's) £9,900 $16,038

GIUSEPPE SIGNORINI (1857–1932) – The proposal –
signed and inscribed – watercolour and bodycolour on card
– 45.1 x 59.7cm.
(Christie's) £4,620 $8,039

PAUL SIGNAC (1863–1935) – Harbour view, Paimpol –
signed with initials – watercolour and soft pencil on two
sheets of joined paper – 30.2 x 77.1cm.
(Christie's) £24,200 $42,592

FRANCIS AUGUSTUS SILVA (1835–1886) – Moonrise
– signed and dated 72 – oil on canvas – 35.5 x 61cm.
(Christie's) £20,416 $35,200

TAVIK FRANTISEK SIMON (1877–1942) – Onival Beach – signed and dated *1904* – oil on canvas – 45.7 x 54.6cm.
(Christie's) £5,500 $9,570

MARIA ELENA VIEIRA DA SILVA (b. 1908) – Winter journey – signed and dated *61* – oil on canvas – 162 x 162cm.
(Christie's) £132,000 $213,840

TAVIK FRANTISEK SIMON (1877–1942) – Jardin de Luxembourg, Paris – signed – oil on canvas – 68 x 73cm.
(Christie's) £5,280 $8,606

CHARLES SIMPSON (1885–1938) – Becher's Brook,
The Grand National – signed – oil on canvas – 71 x 102cm.
(Christie's)   **£2,200 $3,784**

JOHN SKEAPING, A.R.A. (1901–1980) – On the gallop.
– signed and dated *69* – oil on canvas – 52 x 75cm.
(Christie's)   **£1,320 $2,270**

JOHN SKEAPING – Coming through the crowd – signed
and dated *'62* – 43 x 37in.
(Bearne's)   **£2,500 $4,425**

ERIC SLOANE (1910–1985) – The slope – signed – oil
on canvasboard – 51 x 61cm.
(Christie's)   **£2,233 $3,850**

JAN SLUIJTERS – 'Apachedans' – signed and dated *1911* – watercolour – 17 x 24cm.
(Glerum) **£5,300 $9,222**

HARALD SLOTT-MØLLER (Danish, 1864–1937) – Morning coffee – signed – oil on canvas – 83 x 67cm.
(Sotheby's) **£14,850 $26,284**

JAN SLUIJTERS (1881–1957) – Wooded landscape with women bathing – signed – pencil, pastel and watercolour on paper – 53.5 x 73cm.
(Christie's) **£5,844 $10,345**

JAN SLUIJTERS (1881–1957) – Moonlight – signed with monogram and dated '10 – oil on canvas – 41 x 33.5cm. *(Christie's)* **£20,628 $36,617**

FRANS SMEERS (Belgian 1873–1960) – On the pier – signed – oil on panel – 55 x 35cm. *(Hôtel de Ventes Horta)* **£3,276 $5,700**

GUSTAVE DE SMET (1877–1943) – River landscape with goat – signed – oil on canvas – 49.5 x 68.5cm. *(Christie's)* **£13,064 $23,124**

FRANK O. SMALL (American, b. 1860) – The welcoming smile – signed – oil on canvas – 22 x 16in. *(Skinner Inc.)* **£1,899 $3,300**

GUSTAVE DE SMET (Belgian, 1877–1943) – Vase of roses – signed – oil on canvas – 40 x 45cm. *(Hôtel de Ventes Horta)* **£11,945 $20,427**

LEON DE SMET (Belgian, 1881–1966) – Woman at her toilet – signed and dated 1930 – oil on canvas – 97 x 67cm.
(Hôtel de Ventes Horta)   £14,505 $24,804

CARLTON ALFRED SMITH (1853–1946) – A girl seated in an interior – signed – pencil and watercolour – 394 x 273mm.
(Christie's)   £3,300 $5,577

CARLTON ALFRED SMITH (1853–1946) – Absent thoughts – signed and dated 1884 – pencil and watercolour – 425 x 325mm.
(Christie's)   £2,860 $4,633

CARLTON ALFRED SMITH (1853–1946) – The jewel box – signed and dated 97 – pencil and watercolour – 489 x 347mm.
(Christie's)   £5,500 $9,295

JOHN BRANDON SMITH (1848–1884) – Fishermen by the falls on the River Conway, North Wales – signed and dated *1881* – oil on canvas – 88.3 x 26.4cm.
(Christie's) **£9,900 $16,038**

GRACE COSSINGTON SMITH (1892–1984) – Still life with leaves – signed and dated *53* – oil on canvas laid down on board – 52.7 x 43.2cm.
(Christie's) **£9,900 $17,424**

HUGHIE LEE SMITH – Reader – signed – oil on canvas – 18 x 24in.
(Du Mouchelles) **£4,367 $7,500**

THOMAS SMYTHE – Work horses by and in a stable with domestic poultry, summer time – signed – oil – 11 x 17in.
(G.A. Key) **£2,800 $4,956**

Attributed to FRANS SNYDERS (1579–1657) and studio – The seller of fruit and vegetables – oil on canvas – 183 x 291cm.
(Christie's)   £61,418 $101,954

Follower of JORIS VAN SON – Still life of a roemer, fruit, together with a lobster, shrimps, oysters and a lemon on pewter dishes arranged on a table – oil on canvas – 39.5 x 57cm.
(Sotheby's)   £12,100 $21,780

PEETER SNYERS (1681–1752) – A still life of flowers in a glass vase, shells, a bird of paradise and a colubrid snake in a glass jar, all on a desk flanked by a maid – signed – oil on copper – 33 x 40.5cm.
(Sotheby's)   £38,500 $69,300

WILLIAM LOUIS SONTAG, JR. – London and Northwestern railroad – oil on canvas – $16^3/4$ x $51^1/2$in.
(Du Mouchelles)   £2,113 $3,750

Studio of FRANCESCO SOLIMENA (Italian, 1657–1747) – Christ and the woman taken in adultery – oil on canvas – 103.5 x 155.5cm.
(Butterfield & Butterfield)   £4,097 $7,150

JOAQUIN SOROLLA Y BASTIDA (1863–1923) – The return from fishing – signed – oil on canvas laid down on board – 47 x 62.5cm.
(Christie's)   £484,000 $788,920

JOAQUIN SOROLLA Y BASTIDA (1863–1923) – The man in the straw hat – with certificate of authenticity – oil on canvas – 55 x 46cm.
(Duran)   **£14,485 $26,000**

GIOVANNI SOTTOCORNOLA (Italian, 1855–1917) – A still life of peaches on foliage – signed and dated *1888* – oil on canvas – 48 x 78cm.
(Sotheby's)   **£11,550 $20,443**

PIERRE SOULAGES (b. 1919) – 19 Mars 60 – signed – oil on canvas – 130 x 130cm.
(Christie's)   **£60,500 $107,085**

EDWARD JOSEPH SOUTHALL – The trippers – signed with monogram and dated *1933* – watercolour – 6¼ x 10in.
(Bearne's)   **£3,600 $6,246**

CHARLES SOUBRE (Belgian, 1821–93) – A violent attack – signed and dated *1847* – oil on canvas – 149 x 109cm.
(Sotheby's)   **£2,200 $3,894**

Attributed to GIOVANNI PAOLO SPADINO (active circa 1687–1703) – Still life of apples, peaches, grapes and a melon – oil on canvas – 24 x 51cm.
(Sotheby's)   **£6,600 $11,880**

SPANISH SCHOOL, after Titian (19th century) –
Venus – oil on canvas – 138 x 220cm.
(Duran)   **£1,681 $2,958**

SPANISH SCHOOL (18th century) – St. Theresa – oil on
canvas – 117 x 93cm.
(Duran)   **£179 $315**

SPANISH SCHOOL (18th century) – St Francis at prayer
– oil on canvas – 142 x 92cm.
(Duran)   **£613 $1,100**

SPANISH SCHOOL (circa 1580–1600) – The
Immaculate Conception – oil on panel – unframed –
115 x 90cm.
(Christie's) **£4,467 $7,415**

SPANISH SCHOOL (20th century) – Guardian angel –
oil on canvas – 215 x 130cm.
(Duran) **£1,253 $2,249**

SPANISH SCHOOL (after Murillo) – The young St.
John – oil on canvas – 119 x 97cm.
(Duran) **£700 $1,246**

SPANISH SCHOOL (late 18th century) – Susannah and
the Elders – oil on canvas – 213 x 150cm.
(Duran) **£2,228 $3,999**

SPANISH SCHOOL (17the century or later) – Virgin and Child – oil on board
(Duran) £532 $936

SPANISH SCHOOL – Adoration of the Magi – oil on canvas – 152 x 109cm.
(Duran) £1,393 $2,500

SPANISH SCHOOL – Still life with dishes and fruit – oil on canvas – 45 x 78cm.
(Duran) £334 $600

SPANISH SCHOOL – Boats – oil on board – 34 x 50cm.
(Duran) £392 $690

CHARLES SPENCELAYH (1865–1958) – Pawning the
clock – signed – oil on board – 15 x 11.5cm.
(Christie's)   **£4,180 $6,772**

CHARLES SPENCELAYH (1865–1958) – A boy seated
on a table, playing a Jew's harp – signed and dated *1899* –
oil on canvas – 66 x 46cm.
(Christie's)   **£26,400 $42,768**

CHARLES SPENCELAYH (1865–1958) – Sweet peas –
signed – oil on canvas – 38 x 30.5cm.
(Christie's)   **£4,180 $7,608**

SIR STANLEY SPENCER, R.A. (1891–1959) – Fernlea,
Cookham – pencil and oil on paper laid over panel –
25.5 x 35.5cm.
(Christie's)   **£14,300 $23,738**

LEON SPILLIAERT (1887–1946) – Boat on the sea –
signed and dated *21* – gouache on card – 50.8 x 83.8cm.
(Christie's) £10,450 $16,929

**JOHANNES FRANCISCUS SPOHLER (Dutch, 1853–
94)** – A Dutch canal scene – signed – oil on canvas –
44 x 35cm.
(Sotheby's) £7,480 $13,240

IGNACE SPIRIDON (fl. 1889–1900) – Feeding time –
signed and dated *1869* – oil on canvas – 76.2 x 99.7cm.
(Christie's) £3,850 $6,699

CORNELIS SPRINGER (1817–1891) – The Rokin,
Amsterdam, towards Langebrugsteeg – signed – oil on
panel – 59.7 x 77.5cm.
(Christie's) £165,000 $288,750

JOSEF MAGNUS STÄCK (1812–1868) – Marina
Grande, Capri – signed and dated *1867* – oil on canvas –
62.2 x 93.3cm.
(Christie's) £6,600 $11,550

**JAN JACOB COENRAAD SPOHLER (Dutch, 1837–
1923)** – The ferry – signed – oil on canvas – 62 x 82.5cm.
(Sotheby's) £13,200 $23,364

STAEL

NICOLAS DE STAEL (1914–1955) – Composition –
signed – oil on canvas – 38 x 46cm.
(Christie's)   **£29,700 $52,272**

HANS STAUDACHER (b. 1923) – Irrtum - signed and
dated *59* – oil, gouache, ink and crayon on board –
90 x 130cm.
(Christie's)   **£7,480 $12,417**

CLARKSON STANFIELD (1793–1867) – Pavia – pencil
and watercolour heightened with white and scratching out –
237 x 362mm.
(Christie's)   **£3,960 $6,970**

PHILIP WILSON STEER, O.M. (1860–1942) – The rape
of the Sabines – signed – oil on canvas – 71.1 x 93.6cm.
(Christie's)   **£7,150 $11,869**

HENRY JOHN SYLVESTER STANNARD (1870–1951)
– A young girl feeding chickens outside a cottage – with
part of a signature – pencil and watercolour with touches of
white heightening – 343 x 489mm.
(Christie's)   **£2,640 $4,805**

THEOPHILE-ALEXANDRE STEINLEN (1859–1923)
– The cat – signed with monogram – gouache and pencil on
brown paper – 51 x 125cm.
(Christie's)   **£8,800 $14,256**

EDWARD BOWRING STEPHENS (1815–1882) –
Portrait of Jane Harris Stephens, the artist's wife, with her
daughter Jane Helen Mary, on a terrace – oil on canvas –
91.5 x 71.1cm.
(Christie's)   **£3,850 $6,237**

JOSEPH STELLA (1880–1946) – Pink flower – signed –
crayon and silverpoint on paper – 55.9 x 38.1cm.
(Christie's)   **£3,190 $5,500**

JOSEPH STELLA (1880–1946) – Telegraph poles –
signed and dated – watercolour on paper – unframed –
16.6 x 22.8cm.
(Christie's)   **£7,656 $13,200**

STEPPE

R. STEPPE (Belgian, 1859–1927) – Moonlight at
Dixmude – signed and dated *1907* – oil on panel –
26.5 x 37cm.
(Hôtel de Ventes Horta)   **£1,210 $2,057**

ALFRED STEVENS (Belgian, 1823–1906) – La
douloureuse certitude – signed – oil on canvas – 80 x 60cm.
(Sotheby's)   **£29,700 $52,569**

ALFRED STEVENS (Belgian, 1823–1906) – Sunday by
the seaside – signed – oil on panel – 47 x 33cm.
(Hôtel de Ventes Horta)   **£1,774 $3,016**

ALLAN STEWART (1865–1951) – William Penn receiving the Charter of Pennsylvania from Charles II –
signed and dated *1913* – oil on canvas – 122 x 183cm.
(Christie's)   **£2,860 $5,062**

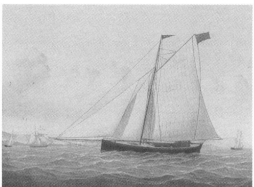

JOHN STEWART (circa 1884) – The yacht Norna in the Clyde – signed and dated *1886* – oil on canvas – 45.8 x 60.9cm.
(Christie's) £1,430 $2,545

MARIE STILLMAN, née Spartali (1844–1927) – Pharmakeutria (Brewing the love philtre) – signed with monogram – watercolour with gum arabic and bodycolour on paper laid down on panel – 52 x 47cm.
(Christie's) £16,500 $28,050

JULIUS LEBLANC STEWART (1855–1919) – Picnic under the trees – signed and dated *96* – oil on canvas – 54 x 100cm.
(Christie's) £47,850 $82,500

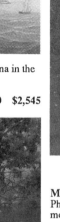

JOSEPH STIELER (German, 1781–1858) – A portrait of King Oskar of Sweden as Crown Prince (1799–1856) – oil on canvas – 73 x 60cm.
(Sotheby's) £7,700 $13,629

MARCUS STONE (1840–1921) – Olivia – signed and dated *1880* – oil on panel – 21.3 x 15.5cm.
(Christie's) £4,180 $7,608

GEORGE HENRY STORY (1835–1923) - Portrait of Abraham Lincoln – signed – oil on canvas – 50.8 x 45.7cm. *(Sotheby's)*   **£12,222 $22,000**

SARAH STONE (fl. 1774–1791) – A little blue heron, Egretta caerulea – signed, dated and numbered *1782/35* – pencil, watercolour and bodycolour – 403 x 292mm. *(Christie's)*   **£1,320 $2,323**

ARTHUR CLAUDE STRACHAN (1865–1935) – Feeding the chickens – signed – watercolour heightened with bodycolour – 290 x 463mm. *(Christie's)*   **£2,090 $3,532**

SARAH STONE (fl. 1774–1791) – A pink flamingo, Plenicopterus ruber – inscribed on mount – pencil and watercolour – 358 x 251mm. *(Christie's)*   **£1,210 $2,130**

SIR ARTHUR ERNEST STREETON (1867–1943) – Banksias against the bay – signed – oil on panel – 20.3 x 66.1cm. *(Christie's)*   **£27,500 $48,400**

SIR ARTHUR ERNEST STREETON (1867–1943) – Kosciusko – signed – 51.4 x 76.8cm.
(Christie's) £29,700 $52,272

HEINRICH STREHBLOW (Austrian, b. 1862) – Ladies embroidering in a workshop – signed and dated
1892 – oil on canvas – unframed – 85 x 125cm.
(Sotheby's) £19,800 $35,046

PHILIP EUSTACE STRETTON (fl. 1884–1919) – Two smooth-haired Fox Terriers by a fishing rod and a creel on a riverbank – signed – oil on board – 46 x 61cm.
(Christie's) £3,410 $5,592

PIERRE-HUBERT SUBLEYRAS (1699–1749) – The Virgin appearing to St. Roch – oil on canvas – 50 x 34cm.
(Christie's) £10,608 $17,609

Circle of PIERRE SUBLEYRAS – Saint Peter baptising the centurion Cornelius – oil on canvas – 71 x 47cm.
(Sotheby's) £6,050 $10,890

HADDON HUBBARD SUNDBLOM (1899–1976) – Sunny afternoon – signed – oil on canvas –
76.2 x 106.7cm.
(Sotheby's)   **£15,278 $27,500**

GUSTAVE SURAND (1860–1937) – Annamese tiger – signed – oil on canvas – 90.1 x 116.8cm.
(Christie's)   **£19,800 $32,472**

SURVAGE

LEOPOLD SURVAGE (1879–1968) – Couple with leaves – signed and dated *35* – gouache on paper – 24.5 x 19cm.
(Christie's) £6,050 $10,648

GRAHAM SUTHERLAND, O.M. (1903–1980) – Study for Pinnacles – signed, inscribed and dated *50* – gouache - 20 x 16cm.
(Christie's) £1,760 $3,080

GRAHAM SUTHERLAND (1903–1980) – Tonnelle de Vine – signed and dated *1947* – pencil and oil on panel – 51 x 97cm.
(Christie's) £66,000 $115,500

GEORGE GARDNER SYMONS (1863–1930) – Winter twilight – signed – oil on canvas – 64 x 76.5cm.
(Christie's) **£10,208 $17,600**

RUDOLPH SVOBODA (Austrian, 1859–1914) – A young lady in Japanese costume – signed and dated *1894* – oil on cardboard – 30 x 18cm.
(Sotheby's) **£2,750 $4,867**

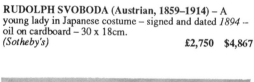

JOHN WARKUP SWIFT (1815–1869) – Approaching harbour; and Fishing boats off a rocky coast – both signed and one dated *1854* – oil on canvas – 45.7 x 62.8cm. – a pair
(Christie's) **£4,620 $8,224**

ARTHUR FITZWILLIAM TAIT (1819–1905) – Trespassers – signed and dated *86* – oil on canvas – 55.9 x 35.9cm.
(Christie's) **£4,466 $7,700**

ARTHUR FITZWILLIAM TAIT – Chickens feeding –
signed and dated *1870* – oil on canvas – 25 x 29½in.
(Du Mouchelles)   **£11,268 $20,000**

ARTHUR F. TAIT (1819–1905) – Spaniel and canvas
back duck – signed and dated *'92* – oil on canvas –
31.1 x 41.3cm.
(Sotheby's)   **£3,757 $6,875**

Follower of FRANZ WERNER VON TAMM – A still
life of melons, grapes and other fruit accompanied by a pair
of doves – oil on canvas – 48.3 x 64.5cm.
(Sotheby's)   **£4,400 $7,920**

DOROTHEA TANNING (b. 1910) – The light in the
hallway – signed – oil on canvas – 74 x 30.4cm. –
asymmetrical
(Christie's)   **£26,400 $42,768**

FREDERICK TAUBES (1900–81) – George Washington Bridge – signed – oil on canvas – 50.8 x 61cm.
(*Sotheby's*)   **£1,082 $1,980**

HUGUES TARAVAL (1729–1785) – The Holy Family – signed – unframed – oil on canvas – 60 x 48.5cm.
(*Christie's*)   **£11,167 $18,537**

FREDERICK TAUBES (1900–1981) – Setting the table – signed – oil on canvas – 88.3 x 127cm.
(*Sotheby's*)   **£2,855 $5,225**

ANTONI TAPIES (b. 1923) – Platter collage – signed on the backing – oil, composition and plate on canvas – 76 x 55cm.
(*Christie's*)   **£55,000 $97,350**

EDWARD TAYLER – A radiant beauty – signed with initials – pencil and watercolour – 12³/₄ x 9in.
(*Christie's*)   **£660 $1,140**

519

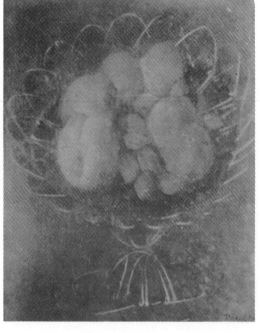

ALFRED HENRY TAYLOR – The Romp – signed and dated 1843 – watercolour heightened with white and gum arabic – 13¹/₂ x 10¹/₂in.
(Christie's) £385 $658

LORETTA TAYLOR – Courting days – signed – watercolour – 22¹/₂ x 30in.
(Du Mouchelles) £174 $300

PAVEL TCHELITCHEW (Russian, 1898–1957) – Still life, fruit – signed – oil on canvas – 28 x 23in.
(Skinner Inc.) £5,065 $8,800

Circle of D'ANTONIO TEMPESTA (1555–1630) – The battle of the Amazons – oil on canvas –
185 x 288.5cm.
(Christie's)   **£22,334 $37,074**

JOHANN MARI TEN KATE (Dutch, 1831–1910) – An artist at rest by his easel – signed – oil on panel –
33.5 x 44cm.
(Sotheby's)   **£12,100 $21,417**

SIEBE JOHANNES TEN CATE – Figures in a street at dusk, Pont Aven – signed – pastel – 40 x 31.8cm.
(Bonhams)   **£700 $1,113**

DOROTHY TENNANT (fl. 1879–1909 d. 1926) – A nude, seated full-length, in a wooded lake landscape – signed and dated *1885* – oil on panel – 19 x 13.6cm.
(Christie's)   **£2,090 $3,699**

HENRY JONES THADDEUS, R.H.A. (1860–1929) – Mediterranean fisherfolk – signed – oil on canvas – 43 x 61cm.
(Christie's)   **£3,080 $4,990**

POLLY THAYER (American, b. 1904) – Tending the garden, Hingham, 1940 – signed – oil on canvas – 20 x 24in.
(Skinner Inc.) £412 $715

FRITS THAULOW (1847–1906) – A river landscape with a moored boat – signed – pastel on paper laid down on canvas – 64.8 x 58.4cm.
(Christie's) £7,480 $13,090

CHARLES JAMES THERIAT – The snake charmers – oil on canvas – 54.4 x 36.8cm.
(Christie's) £1,265 $2,176

CHARLES JAMES THERIAT – Portrait of the Artist –
oil on canvas – 45.7 x 36.8cm. – This lot also includes
official documents relating to the artist
(Christie's)   **£1,320 $2,270**

CHARLES JAMES THERIAT – The goose herder –
signed and dated *95* – oil on canvas – 43.3 x 53.3cm.
(Christie's)   **£2,310 $3,973**

L. THEVENET (Belgian, 1874–1930) – The loveliest of
gardens – signed and dated *1913* – oil on canvas –
60 x 70cm.
(Hôtel de Ventes Horta)   **£5,461 $9,338**

FRED THIELER (b. 1926) – Untitled – signed and dated
64 – gouache and watercolour on irregular torn paper –
95 x 65cm.
(Christie's)   £9,900 $17,523

FRED THIELER (b. 1926) – Flächenrelief Elf – signed
and dated 64 – oil, collage and gouache on canvas –
130 x 92cm.
(Christie's)   £22,000 $35,640

ANTHONY THIEME (1888–1954) – Morning light near Charleston, North Carolina – signed – oil on canvas
– 76 x 91.5cm.
(Christie's)   £9,570 $16,500

THIEME

ANTHONY THIEME (American, 1888–1954) – Custom House Tower, a view of Boston from the harbour – signed – oil on canvas – 27 x 21³/₄in.
(Skinner Inc.) £2,216 $3,850

ANTHONY THIEME (1888–1954) – Seminole Indian village – signed – oil on canvas – 46.2 x 91.4cm.
(Christie's) £3,107 $5,500

ANTHONY THIEME (1888–1954) – Lilac time – signed – oil on canvas – 64.8 x 76.9cm.
(Christie's) £2,486 $4,400

ANTHONY THIEME (1888–1954) – Blossoms, Rockport – signed – oil on canvas – 76.1 x 91.5cm.
(Christie's) £4,350 $7,700

HENRI THOMAS (1878–1972) – Blue dancer – signed – oil on canvas – 100 x 65cm.
(Hôtel de Ventes Horta) £3,870 $6,579

CEPHAS GIOVANNI THOMPSON (1809–1888) –
Portrait of a young man – signed – oil on panel –
71 x 57cm.
(Christie's) **£932 $1,650**

ARCHIBALD THORBURN (1860–1935) – Magpie –
signed – watercolour heightened with white – unframed,
148 x 218mm.
(Christie's) **£3,850 $6,237**

ARCHIBALD THORBURN (1860–1935) – Mergansers,
on Loch Maree – signed and dated *1905* – watercolour
heightened with bodycolour – 380 x 545mm.
(Christie's) **£13,200 $21,384**

HENRY GRINNELL THOMSEN (American, b. 1850) –
Black man eating a watermelon – signed – oil on canvas –
31 x 22in.
(Du Mouchelles) **£2,102 $3,500**

ARCHIBALD THORBURN (1860–1935) – A little crake
– signed – watercolour heightened with white –
228 x 317mm.
(Christie's) **£3,080 $5,205**

THORBURN

ARCHIBALD THORBURN (1860–1935) – A woodcock nesting in autumn leaves – signed and dated *1920* – pencil and watercolour heightened with white –
407 x 508mm.
(Christie's)   **£20,900**   **$33,858**

ARCHIBALD THORBURN (1860–1935) – Blackgame in a pine forest – signed and dated *1925* – watercolour heightened with white – 337 x 547mm.
(Christie's)   **£24,750**   **$40,095**

ARCHIBALD THORBURN (1860–1935) – The Morning of the Twelfth – signed and dated *1910* – watercolour with touches of white heightening – 546 x 763mm.
(Christie's)   **£63,800**   **$103,356**

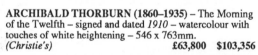

ARCHIBALD THORBURN (1860–1935) – Ptarmigan – signed and dated *1902* – watercolour and bodycolour – 203 x 305mm.
(Christie's)   **£12,100**   **$19,602**

OTTO VON THOREN (1828–1889) – The storm – signed – oil on canvas – 34.2 x 52cm.
(Christie's)   **£1,320**   **$2,297**

Attributed to CHARLES THORNELEY (fl. 1858–1898)
– Fisherfolk unloading their catch at the end of the day; and
Returning home with the catch – with signature and the date
1874 – oil on board – oval – 27.9 x 45.7cm. – a pair
(Christie's)   **£3,850 $6,853**

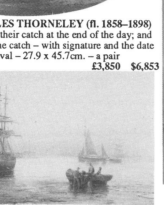

CHARLES THORNELEY (fl. 1858–1898) – Sunrise on
the Essex coast – with signature *James Webb* – oil on canvas
– 25.3 x 40.6cm.
(Christie's)   **£1,045 $1,860**

WILLIAM THORNLEY – Fishermen on a beach below
Mont St Michel – signed – oil on canvas – 61 x 91.5cm.
(Christie's)   **£4,950 $8,811**

GEOFFREY TIBBLE (1909–1952) – The band – signed –
oil on canvas – 63.5 x 76cm.
(Christie's)   **£4,400 $7,304**

GEOFFREY TIBBLE (1909–1952) – Three women –
signed – oil on canvas – 76 x 63.5cm.
(Christie's)   **£3,740 $6,433**

GIOVANNI DOMENICO TIEPOLO – A group of
Oriental magicians and other figures – pen and brown ink –
23.2 x 19.3cm.
(Bonhams)   **£8,000 $12,720**

JOHANN TILL (Austrian, 1827–1894) – Summer –
signed and inscribed – oil on canvas – 68 x 94cm.
(Sotheby's)   £3,850 $6,814

Follower of DOMENICO TINTORETTO – Portrait of a
Venetian senator – oil on canvas – 73.8 x 65.6cm.
(Sotheby's)   £3,850 $6,930

JOE TILSON (b. 1928) – Collage 10/W 1961 – signed –
wood, oil, canvas and mixed media collage – unframed –
122 x 153cm.
(Christie's)   £1,870 $3,272

AURELIO TIRATELLI (1842–1900) – Harvesters in a
cornfield; and Moving to fresh pastures – both signed – oil
on canvas – 16.8 x 36.1cm. – a pair
(Christie's)   £7,150 $12,512

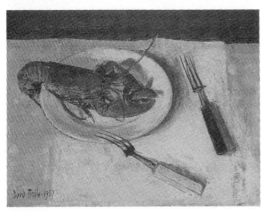

DAVID TINDLE, R.A. (b. 1932) – Still life with lobster –
signed and dated 1957 – oil on board – 30.5 x 40.5cm.
(Christie's)   £1,980 $3,406

Circle of FRANCESCO TIRONI – The Grand Canal,
Venice with San Simeone Piccolo – oil on panel –
54.6 x 94cm.
(Bonhams)   £2,600 $4,134

WILLIAM HOLT YATES TITCOMB (1859–1930) – The church in Cornwall, Rogation Day procession – signed – oil on canvas – 35¹/₂ x 66¹/₂in.
(W.H. Lane & Son) £5,000 $9,213

Manner of TITIAN – The sleeping Magdalen (?) – oil on canvas – 36.5 x 79cm.
(Christie's) £1,100 $1,716

JOHANN HEINRICH TISCHBEIN the Elder (1722–1789) – Portrait of Count Carl von Hessen-Kassel in pilgrim garb, half length – oil on canvas – 73 x 60cm.
(Lempertz) £17,730 $30,141

BEN TOBIAS (1901–1985) – Cornwall – signed and dated *1957* – oil on canvas laid on board – 15¹/₂ x 19¹/₂in.
(W.H. Lane & Son) £700 $1,290

JAMES JACQUES JOSEPH TISSOT (1836-1902) – Type of beauty: portrait of Mrs. Kathleen Newton, in red dress and black bonnet – signed – oil on canvas – 59.5 x 45.7cm.
(Christie's) £176,000 $299,200

BEN TOBIAS (1901–1985) – St Ives harbour – signed and dated *1957* – oil on canvas laid on board – 15¹/₂ x 19¹/₂in.
(W.H. Lane & Son) £650 $1,198

BEN TOBIAS – Rabbis, Frumahs by the sea, 28 – signed,
inscribed and dated *1961* – 40.6 x 50.8cm.
(Christie's)   **£990 $1,574**

BEN TOBIAS – Trouville No. 22 – signed, inscribed and
dated *1948* – 50.8 x 61cm.
(Christie's)   **£1,320 $2,099**

RALPH TODD (Exh. 1880–1928) – Rusty anchors on the
foreshore before Newlyn Pier – signed on label to verso –
watercolour – 13^{1}/2 x 9^{1}/2in.
(W.H. Lane & Son)   **£400 $737**

RALPH TODD (1856–1932) – The letter from abroad –
signed – watercolour – 15 x 11in.
(David Lay) **£1,200 $2,157**

GIOVANNI TOESCHI (late 19th century) – The
introduction – signed and dated *1864* – oil on canvas –
49.5 x 61.6cm.
(Christie's) **£2,640 $4,594**

RALPH TODD (Exh. 1880–1928) – Still life, vase of
daffodils, fruit and pewter jug – signed – watercolour –
10 x 7in.
(W.H. Lane & Son) **£850 $1,373**

EDOUARD TOFANO (Italian, 1838–1920) – Portrait of
a young woman with a bouquet – signed – oil on panel –
10 x 7in.
(Skinner Inc.) **£2,976 $5,170**

GEORGE TOOKER (b. 1920) – Un Ballo in Maschera –
signed – egg tempera on gessoed cardboard –
55.9 x 76.2cm.
(Sotheby's) £42,778 $77,000

JACOB TOORENVLIET – The musician – signed and
dated *1675* – oil on copper – 23.5 x 17.8cm.
(Bonhams) £13,000 $20,670

JAN TOOROP – Self portrait – signed and dated *1921* –
black chalk – 26 x 18cm.
(Glerum) £2,432 $4,232

ROLAND TOPER (b. 1938) – Le Nain IV, L'affaire
Touffard – signed and dated *1976* – pen and black ink and
coloured crayons on paper – 23.5 x 17cm.
(Christie's) £653 $1,156

JAN TOOROP (1858–1928) – Head of an English lady,
Lady H. – signed and dated *1895* – pencil on paper –
41.5 x 32.5cm.
(Christie's) **£17,877 $31,643**

JAN TOOROP (1858–1928) - A portrait of Anna
Smulders reading – signed and dated *1905* – pencil on
paper – 21.5 x 19.5cm.
(Christie's) **£12,033 $21,298**

ROLAND TOPER (b. 1938) – The children and the
panther – signed – pen and black ink and coloured crayons
on paper – 24 x 17cm.
(Christie's) **£687 $1,217**

ADAM WOLFGANG TOPFFER (1766–1847) – A rocky landscape with a lake beyond – signed with monogram and dated *1812* – oil on paper laid down on board – 21 x 29cm.
(Christie's)   **£2,090 $3,637**

FRANK WILLIAM WARWICK TOPHAM (1838–1924) – The morning of the festival, Central Italy – signed and dated *1876* – oil on canvas – 55.3 x 77.5cm.
(Christie's)   **£2,420 $4,283**

SINIBALDO TORDI (1876–1955) – The centre of attention – signed – oil on canvas – 35.6 x 57.8cm.
(Christie's) £1,430 $2,488

GYULA TORNAI (Hungarian, 1861–1928) – In the harem – signed – oil on canvas – 142 x 211cm.
(Sotheby's) £12,100 $21,417

HELEN TORR (1886–1967) – Still life – oil on canvas – 26.4 x 31.3cm.
(Christie's) £1,786 $3,080

HELEN TORR (1886–1967) – Flower rhythm – oil on panel mounted on metal – 29.2 x 21.6cm.
(Sotheby's) £9,778 $17,600

GYULA TORNAI (Hungarian, 1861–1928) – At the shrine – signed and dated *1907* – oil on panel – 85 x 60cm.
(Sotheby's) £2,750 $4,867

HELEN TORR (1886–1967) – Landscape – bears artist's estate stamp – pencil on paper – 12.7 x 17.8cm.
(Christie's) £128 $220

537

JUAN JOSE IZQUIERDO TORRES – Snowy landscape
– signed – oil on board – 19 x 27cm.
(Duran) £134 $236

AUGUSTE TOULMOUCHE (1829–1890) – Awaiting
the visitor – signed and dated *1878* – oil on canvas –
63.5 x 42.5cm.
(Christie's) £9,680 $15,778

GASTON DE LA TOUCHE (French 1854–1913) –
Bateau mouche in Paris – signed – watercolour on paper –
77 x 55cm.
(Hôtel de Ventes Horta) £4,483 $7,800

AUGUSTE TOULMOUCHE (1829–1890) – Good news
– signed and dated *1880* – oil on canvas – 49.5 x 61cm.
(Fraser–Pinneys) £12,531 $21,741

GEORGES DE LA TOUR (1593–1642) – Saint Thomas –
oil on canvas – 65 x 54cm.
(Christie's) **£50,252 $83,418**

FERDINAND TOUSSAINT (1873–1955) – At the opera
– signed – oil on canvas – 99.5 x 80cm.
(Christie's) **£13,200 $23,100**

F. TOUSSAINT (Belgian, 1873–1955) – Still life with
flowers in a vase – signed – oil on canvas – 65 x 81cm.
(Hôtel de Ventes Horta) **£8,065 $13,711**

HENRY SPERNON TOZER (circa 1870–circa 1940) – The game of draughts – signed and dated *1918* – pencil and watercolour – 203 x 279mm.
(Christie's) £880 **$1,487**

HENRY SPERNON TOZER (circa 1870–1940) – The evening news – signed and dated *1925* – watercolour with touches of white heightening – 227 x 330mm.
(Christie's) **£1,210 $1,960**

HENRY SPERNON TOZER (circa 1870–circa 1940) – Reading the news – signed and dated *1913* – pencil and watercolour – 203 x 279mm.
(Christie's) £880 **$1,487**

JULIAN TREVELYAN (1910–1988) – The watermill –
signed and dated *1928* – oil on canvas – 35.5 x 45.8cm.
(Christie's) £990 $1,643

PHOEBE ANNA TRAQUAIR, née Moss (1882–1936) –
The New Creation – signed with monogram and dated *1887*
– oil on canvas (centre painting) and oak panel –
58.5 x 49cm.
(Christie's) £11,000 $18,700

JULIAN TREVELYAN – Gozo – signed and dated *58* –
51 x 61cm.
(Christie's) £2,090 $3,323

JULIAN TREVELYAN (1910–1988) – The Main Line –
signed and dated *44* – oil on panel – 18 x 20cm.
(Christie's) £6,050 $10,587

CARL TRIEBEL (German, 1823–1885) and AUGUST VON RENTZELL (German, 1810–1891) – Genre scene with young shepherd and shepherdess – signed – oil on canvas – unframed – 27¼ x 38¼in.
(Skinner Inc.) £2,374 $4,125

PAUL DESIRE TROUILLEBERT (French, 1829–1900) – A view of Romarantin in the Loire Valley – signed – oil on canvas – 37 x 55cm.
(Sotheby's) £19,800 $35,046

WILLIAM HENRY HAMILTON TROOD (1848–1899) – Too hot – signed and dated *1895* – oil on canvas – 26.7 x 40.7cm.
(Christie's) £1,210 $1,984

JEAN-FRANÇOIS DE TROY (1679–1752) – The battle of the Lapithes and the Centaurs – oil on canvas – 112.5 x 148cm.
(Christie's) £8,934 $14,830

NEWBOLD HOUGH TROTTER (1827–1898) – Cow and calf – signed and dated *1862* – oil on canvas – unframed – 31 x 43.3cm.
(Christie's) £621 $1,100

CONSTANT TROYON (French, 1810–1865) – Herder with cattle – signed – oil on canvas – 21½ x 31in.
(Skinner Inc.) £5,698 $9,900

JAMES WALTER TUCKER (1898–1972) – The homecoming – signed – tempera on canvas – 85 x 117cm.
(Christie's) **£5,280 $8,765**

HENRY SCOTT TUKE, R.A., R.W.S. – A French barque at anchor in Falmouth harbour – signed and dated *1923* – watercolour – 11½ x 17½in.
(Bearne's) **£2,400 $4,164**

HENRY SCOTT TUKE, R.A. (1858–1929) – The Port of St. Tropez – signed and dated *1928* – watercolour – 37 x 26.5cm.
(Christie's) **£2,200 $3,784**

HENRY SCOTT TUKE, R.A. (1858–1929) – The bathers – signed and dated *1922* – watercolour – 28.5 x 44.5cm.
(Christie's) **£6,050 $10,406**

HENRY SCOTT TUKE (1858–1929) – Venice –
initialled, inscribed and dated *1899* – oil on panel –
7 x 10in.
(David Lay)   **£2,500 $4,494**

ANN CHARLOTTE TURNBULL – Portrait of a lady,
seated small full length in a black dress with a lilac wrap –
signed – oil on canvas – 30.5 x 25.4cm.
(Christie's)   **£495 $877**

CHARLES TURNER – Women at market – oil on board –
20 x 30in.
(Du Mouchelles)   **£210 $350**

CHARLES YARDLEY TURNER (1850–1918) – The plainsmen – initialled and dated *1912* – oil on canvas – 68.6 x 144.8cm.
(Butterfield & Butterfield) £567 $990

EDGARD TYTGAT (Belgian, 1879–1957) – Eglise St. Jean – signed and dated *1933* – watercolour – 35 x 50cm.
(Hôtel de Ventes Horta) £3,871 $6,581

GEORGE TURNER (1843–1910) – A ford on the Trent – signed – oil on canvas – 61 x 96.5cm.
(Christie's) £11,000 $17,820

WALTER UFER (1876–1936) – Zuni women carrying water – signed – oil on canvas – 50.8 x 40.6cm.
(Butterfield & Butterfield) £23,639 $41,250

JOSEPH MALLORD WILLIAM TURNER, R.A. (1775–1851) – Figures beneath a colossal arch – pencil, grey wash – 413 x 260mm.
(Christie's) £2,420 $3,896

FRIEDRICH ULRICH (German, 1750?–1808) – Horsemen at a blacksmith's forge – signed – oil on canvas – 43.2 x 53.3cm.
(Butterfield & Butterfield) £1,734 $3,025

FRANZ RICHARD UNTERBERGER (1832–1902) –
Capri – signed – oil on canvas – 52.5 x 70.5cm.
(Christie's) £9,900 $16,137

FRANZ RICHARD UNTERBERGER (1832–1902) – La
Giudecca with San Giorgio Maggiore, Venice – signed – oil
on canvas – 81.3 x 70cm.
(Christie's) £20,900 $36,575

FRANZ RICHARD UNTERBERGER (Belgian, 1832–
1902) – Posilipo, Naples – signed – oil on canvas –
83.2 x 71.1cm.
(Bonhams) £11,500 $18,285

FRANZ RICHARD UNTERBERGER (1832–1902) –
The Grand Canal with Santa Maria della Salute beyond,
Venice – signed – oil on canvas – 84 x 71cm.
(Christie's) £41,800 $73,150

MAURICE UTRILLO (1883–1955) – The Sacré Coeur de
Montmartre – signed and dated *1933* – gouache on paper –
29.5 x 45.5cm.
(Christie's) £33,000 $53,460

FRANZ RICHARD UNTERBERGER (1838–1902) –
Marina Piccola, Capri – signed – oil on canvas –
82 x 66cm.
(Christie's) £12,100 $21,054

MAURICE UTRILLO (1883–1955) – Sannois – signed –
oil on canvas – 24 x 33cm.
(Christie's) £38,500 $67,760

FRANZ RICHARD UNTERBERGER (1838–1902) –
Vietri sul Mare, looking towards Salerno – signed – oil on
canvas – 77 x 127cm.
(Sotheby's) £27,500 $48,675

MAURICE UTRILLO (1883–1955) – The school or
Montmerle (Ain), the Hospital lawn – signed – oil on board
– 66 x 86.5cm.
(Christie's) £38,500 $62,370

MAURICE UTRILLO (1883–1955) – Bourg la Reine –
signed and dated *1935* – oil on canvas – 38 x 55cm.
(Christie's)   **£88,000 $154,880**

MAURICE UTRILLO (1883–1955) – The Café 'Aux Iles
de Neyron' – signed and dated *1923* – gouache on paper
laid down on canvas – 38.2 x 45.8cm.
(Finarte)   **£67,729 $115,478**

MAURICE UTRILLO (1883–1955) – The bouquet –
signed and dated *1927* – pastel and wash on paper –
38 x 32.5cm.
(Christie's)   **£20,900 $33,858**

BERNARD VAILLANT (1632–1698) – Portrait of a boy with a dog – signed and dated *1684* – coloured chalks – 43.8 x 35.7cm.
(Glerum)   £2,041 $3,607

SUZANNE VALADON (1865–1938) – Bare breasted woman (Self portrait) – signed and dated *1917* – oil on canvas – 65 x 50cm.
(Christie's)   £44,000 $71,280

ZSIGMOND VAJDA (Austrian, 1860–1931) – A lady at her toilette – signed – oil on canvas – 139 x 101cm.
(Sotheby's)   £3,080 $5,452

FRANCESCO VALAPERTA (1836–1908) – Portrait of Marguerite de Neufville, seated half length, wearing a cream dress with a blue sash – signed and dated *1881* – oil on canvas – 73.5 x 46.5cm.
(Christie's)   £6,600 $10,758

THEODORE VICTOR CARL VALENKAMPH (1868–1924) – Clipper ship – signed and dated *1904* – oil on canvas – 55.9 x 81.3cm.
(Sotheby's) £1,202 $2,200

FELIX VALLOTTON (1865–1925) – Woman writing in an interior – signed and dated *04* – oil on board – 60.5 x 34.5cm.
(Lempertz) £103,806 $165,571

RICARDO VALERO – Maja smoking – signed – oil on panel – 42 x 26cm.
(Duran) £669 $1,201

LOUIS VALTAT (1869–1952) – The shady terrace – signed with initials – oil on panel – 27.3 x 35.3cm.
(Christie's) £10,450 $16,929

LOUIS VALTAT (1869–1952) – Almond blossoms –
signed – oil on canvas – 81.2 x 65.5cm.
(Christie's) £16,500 $29,040

WILHELM VALTER – A river landscape with cattle on a
bank, a distant church beyond – signed – oil on canvas –
29.2 x 49.6cm.
(Christie's) £2,640 $4,562

JOHN VANDERBANK (1694–1739) – Portrait of John
Sturges, three-quarter length, dressed as an Oriental –
signed – grey and brown wash – unframed – 335 x 257mm.
(Christie's) £1,210 $1,948

CORNELIUS VARLEY – An Irish cart – signed and dated *1848* – pen and black ink and grey wash – unframed – 9¹/₂ x 13¹/₂in.
(Christie's)   **£825**   **$1,462**

JOHN VARLEY (1778–1842) – A fishing boat on the Thames – signed and dated *1831* – pencil and watercolour – 147 x 197mm.
(Christie's)   **£1,650**   **$2,904**

DOROTHY VARIAN (b. 1895) – Still life with plums and melon – signed – oil on canvas – 45.7 x 68.6cm.
(Sotheby's)   **£481**   **$880**

T. VARDON (early 20th century) – Peter, a rough-coated Fox Terrier – signed and dated *1918* – oil on board – 31.7 x 22.8cm.
(Christie's)   **£1,100**   **$1,804**

JOHN VARLEY (1778–1842) – Under the bridge,
Windsor – signed – pencil and watercolour – 267 x 382mm.
(Christie's)   **£2,420 $3,896**

VICTOR VASARELY (b. 1908) – Palota – signed – oil
on canvas – 166 x 126cm.
(Christie's)   **£15,400 $27,258**

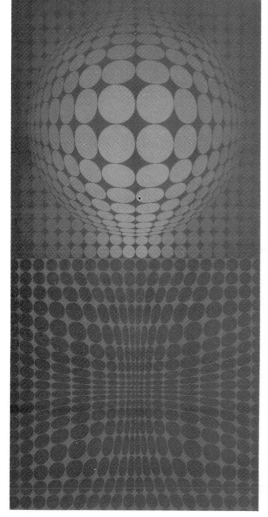

VICTOR VASARELY (b. 1908) – VP–119 - signed –
acrylic on canvas – 260 X 130cm.
(Christie's)   **£16,500 $27,390**

GEZA VASTAGH (1866–1919) – The head of a lion –
signed and dated *1892* – oil on canvas – 101.6 x 83.7cm.
(Christie's)   **£9,020 $15,695**

KEITH VAUGHAN (1912–1977) – Reclining figure –
signed and dated *65* – gouache and coloured crayons –
18 x 15cm.
(Christie's) £528 $876

GEZA VASTAGH (1866–1919) – Portrait of a boy, seated
full length, on a sofa draped with a lion skin – signed and
dated *1895* – oil on canvas – 150.5 x 83.8cm.
(Christie's) £14,300 $24,882

KEITH VAUGHAN (1912–1977) – Foreshore with three
figures – signed and dated *52* – gouache, brush and black
ink – 14 x 17cm.
(Christie's) £2,420 $4,235

KEITH VAUGHAN (1912–1977) – Garden – signed and
dated *1975* – oil on canvas – 102 x 91.5cm.
(Christie's) £9,350 $16,362

ELIHU VEDDER (1836–1923) – The Labyrinth – signed with initial – charcoal and pastel on paper laid down on board – 16 x 22.2cm.
(Christie's) £1,021 $1,760

EDUARD VEITH (Austrian, 1856–1925) – An allegory of Plenty – signed and inscribed – oil on canvas – 140 x 169cm.
(Sotheby's) £2,420 $4,283

BRAM VAN VELDE (1895–1981) – Longinus piercing the side of Christ – oil on canvas – 73 x 54cm.
(Christie's) £1,375 $2,434

AAT VELDHOEN – Kabul in a landscape – signed – oil on canvas – 97.5 x 146cm.
(Glerum) £1,054 $1,805

VENETIAN SCHOOL

VENETIAN SCHOOL (18th century) – Portrait of St. Gregory – oil on canvas – 71.8 x 58.4cm.
(Butterfield & Butterfield) **£630 $1,100**

VENETIAN SCHOOL (circa 1700) – Sleeping Venus with a satyr – oil on canvas – 115 x 168cm.
(Sotheby's) **£66,000 $118,800**

K. VENNEMAN (Flemish, 1802–1875) – Flemish fair – signed – oil on panel – 58 x 73cm.
(Hôtel de Ventes Horta) **£4,113 $6,992**

EUGENE-JOSEPH VERBOECKHOVEN (1798–1881) and HENRY CAMPOTOSTO (d. 1910) – Children with sheep and chickens in a wooded landscape – signed by both artists and dated *1879* – oil on panel – unframed – 66.5 x 87cm.
(Christie's) **£15,950 $27,912**

EUGENE-JOSEPH VERBOECKHOVEN (1798–1881) – A coastal landscape with sheep – signed and dated *1865* – oil on panel – 67.5 x 101.5cm.
(Christie's) **£17,050 $27,792**

EUGENE JOSEPH VERBOECKHOVEN (1798–1881) – A King Charles spaniel seated on a red cushion – signed and dated *1830* – oil on panel – 38.1 x 48.3cm.
(Christie's) **£3,300 $5,412**

JAN HENDRIK VERHEYEN (Dutch, 1778–1846) –
Figures near a church – signed and dated *1810* – oil on
panel – 46 x 59cm.
(Sotheby's) **£4,950 $8,761**

LOUIS VERBOECKHOVEN (Belgian, 1802–89) –
Fishing vessels by the shore – signed and dated *1830* – oil
on canvas – 93 x 128cm.
(Sotheby's) **£11,550 $20,443**

**Circle of JAN HENDRIK VERHEYEN (Dutch, 19th
century)** – A Capriccio scene of a canal – oil on panel –
38 x 45cm.
(Sotheby's) **£2,530 $4,478**

Circle of GASPAR PIETER VERBRUGGEN II – A still
life of tulips, and other flowers in a stone vase on a ledge –
oil on canvas – 91.5 x 67.3cm.
(Bonhams) **£10,000 $15,900**

ARTHUR VEREY (late 19th century) – Mowing clover
– signed – oil on canvas – 76.2 x 127cm.
(Christie's) **£2,200 $3,894**

JAN VERKOLJE (1650–1693) – A lady of quality with a
negro boy, dog and still life in a landscape – signed – oil on
copper – 58 x 49cm.
(Hôtel de Ventes Horta) **£5,461 $9,338**

PAINTINGS PRICE GUIDE

ELIZABETH O'NEILL VERNER (1883–1979) – The flower seller – signed – pastel on linen laid down on board – 22.9 x 22.2cm.
(Sotheby's) £2,855 $5,225

ELIZABETH O'NEILL VERNER (American, b. 1883) – A view of Charleston, St. Michael's Episcopal Church in the distance – signed – pastel on panel – 17¹/₂ x 13³/₈in.
(Skinner Inc.) £2,058 $3,575

ELIZABETH O'NEILL VERNER (American, b. 1883/ 84) – Pipe smoking – signed – pastel on canvasboard – 12³/₄ x 10³/₄in.
(Skinner Inc.) £2,645 $4,675

VERONE (Swiss, 20th century) – In Wonderland – signed – oil on canvas – 61 x 50cm.
(Germann) £1,411 $2,244

M. VERVOORT (Dutch, 18th/19th century) – Two cockerels – signed and dated *1821* – oil on canvas – 78.5 x 89cm.
(Sotheby's) £4,180 $7,399

VERONE (Swiss, 20th century) – Please, don't touch my flowers – signed – oil on canvas – 59 x 60cm.
(Germann) £1,214 $2,162

JULES JACQUES VEYRASSAT (1828–1893) – The harvesters return – signed and dated *1879* – oil on canvas – 61.5 x 101.6cm.
(Christie's) £17,600 $30,800

CHARLES VEZIN (American, 1858–1942) – Manhattan – signed – oil on masonite – 12 x 16in.
(Skinner Inc.) £1,519 $2,640

ALFRED VICKERS (1786–1868) – Windsor Castle from the Brocas Meadows – signed and dated *1854* – oil on canvas – 61.6 x 94.6cm.
(Christie's) **£14,300 $25,311**

ALFRED H. VICKERS – On the River Darent, Kent – signed – oil on canvas – 20.5 x 30.5cm.
(Christie's) **£440 $711**

ALFRED H. VICKERS (British, fl. 1853–1907) – An extensive river landscape – signed – oil on canvas – 40.6 x 81.3cm.
(Butterfield & Butterfield) **£693 $1,210**

VICTORIAN SCHOOL – The cider press – unframed – 26 x 35cm.
(Spencer's) **£750 $1,196**

VICTORIAN ENGLISH SCHOOL – Mother and child seated – oil on panel – 10 x 7¹/₂in.
(G.A. Key) **£240 $383**

EBERHARD VIEGENER (1890–1967) – Still life with cacti and flower pots – signed with monogram and dated *1939* – oil on wood – 24 x 39cm.
(Lempertz) **£5,882 $9,382**

JUAN VILCHES – On the beach – signed – oil on board – 21 x 29cm.
(Duran) **£84 $148**

EUGENIO LUCAS VILLAMIL (1858–1918) –
Courtship – signed – oil on board – 13 x 25cm.
(Duran) **£1,681 $2,958**

EUGENIO LUCAS VILLAMIL (1858–1918) – Sitting in
the meadow – signed – oil on board – 13 x 24cm.
(Duran) **£1,681 $2,958**

JOSE VILLEGAS Y CORDERO (Spanish, 1848–1922)
– Feeding poultry in a backstreet – signed – oil on canvas –
70 x 39cm.
(Sotheby's) **£3,300 $5,841**

JOSE VILLEGAS Y CORDERO (1848–1922) – The letter
– signed – oil on panel – 24 x 18cm.
(Christie's) **£3,960 $6.890**

JOSE VILLEGAS Y CORDERO (Spanish, 1848–1922)
– Papal audience – signed – watercolour on paper –
47 x 64.8cm.
(Butterfield & Butterfield) **£1,261 $2,200**

HARRY AIKEN VINCENT (1864–1931) – Ships in the
harbour – signed – oil on canvas – 71.1 x 91.4cm.
(Butterfield & Butterfield)   £4,413 $7,700

MAURICE DE VLAMINCK (1876–1958) – Beneath the
trees – signed – oil on canvas – 56 x 65cm.
(Christie's)   £55,000 $96,800

HEINRICH VOGELER (1890–1942) – Love – signed –
original etching – 35 x 37.5cm.
(Lempertz)   £1,211 $1,932

ADOLF VOGT – A study of an ox – signed – oil on canvas – 78.8 x 67.3cm.
(Christie's)   **£1,100 $1,892**

MAX VOLKHART (1848–1935) – On the balcony – signed – oil on canvas – 54.5 x 38.1cm.
(Christie's)   **£1,980 $3,445**

JOHANN WILHELM VOLCKER (German, 1812–73) – A still life of flowers on a marble ledge – signed – oil on canvas – 44 x 34cm.
(Sotheby's)   **£6,050 $10,708**

CHARLES VOLKMAR (1841–1914) – Grazing at water's edge – signed – oil on canvas – 119.1 x 89.5cm.
(Christie's)   **£1,595 $2,750**

Follower of FRIEDRICH JOHANN VOLTZ – Cattle watering at a stream – with signature – oil on panel – 16 x 34.3cm.
(Christie's)   **£1,650 $2,838**

Attributed to H. VOORDECKER (19th century Belgian) –The poulterer – oil on canvas – 45.4 x 37cm.
(Hôtel de Ventes Horta)   **£1,552 $2,700**

CORNELIS DE VOS (1585–1651) – Portrait of a lady, said to be Jeanne de Blois – oil on canvas – 118 x 90cm.
(Sotheby's)   **£7,700 $13,860**

Manner of CORNELIS DE VOS – Portrait of a lady, half length in a black dress with a ruff, holding a rose – oil on canvas – unframed – 94 x 71.2cm.
(Christie's)   **£1,100 $1,716**

CORNELIS VREEDENBURGH (Dutch, 1880–1946) –
Putting up the sails/A shore scene – signed – oil on canvas
– 24 x 36in.
(Skinner Inc.) £4,115 $7,150

LOUIS WILLIAM WAIN (1860–1903) – The Silver
Beauty – signed with initials – pencil on buff paper –
8¹/₂ x 12¹/₂in.
(Riddetts) £320 $563

HENDRIK CORNELISZ VROOM (Dutch, 1566–1640)
– Old oak trees in an extensive landscape – dated *1607* – oil
on cradled panel – 73.7 x 57.2cm.
(Butterfield & Butterfield) £2,206 $3,850

EDOUARD VUILLARD (1868–1940) – The dining room
– signed – oil on board laid on cradled panel – 24 x 47cm.
(Christie's) £66,000 $108,240

EDWARD WILKINS WAITE (fl. 1880–1920) – The
brook he loved – signed and dated *1892* – oil on canvas –
54.6 x 43.2cm.
(Christie's) £8,800 $15,576

ROLAND WAKELIN – Still life – signed – oil on board –
35 x 55cm.
(Australian Art Auctions)   **£903 $1,576**

ROLAND SHAKESPEARE WAKELIN (1887–1971) –
Boathouses – signed and dated *1920* – oil on board –
unframed – 26.4 x 31.2cm.
(Christie's)   **£8,800 $15,488**

ERNEST WALBOURN (fl. 1897–1904) – Feeding the
doves – signed – oil on canvas – 50.8 x 76.2cm.
(Christie's)   **£4,950 $9,009**

ROLAND SHAKESPEARE WAKELIN (1887–1971) –
A descriptive sketch in Lincoln's Inn Fields – signed and
dated *1923* – oil on board – unframed – 29.8 x 19.1cm.
(Christie's)   **£3,960 $6,970**

ROLAND SHAKESPEARE WAKELIN (1887–1971) –
Still life – signed and dated *1920* – oil on board – unframed
– 27.9 x 15.9cm.
(Christie's)   **£1,980 $3,485**

ERNEST WALBOURN (fl. 1897–1904) – By the river –
signed – oil on canvas – 50.8 x 76.2cm.
(Christie's)   **£9,350 $17,017**

ERNEST WALBOURN (fl. 1897–1904) – An encounter on
the road – signed – oil on canvas – 61 x 91.5cm.
(Christie's)   £5,500 $9,735

WILLIAM WALCOT – Figures and carriages in front of
the Banqueting House (?) Whitehall – signed – watercolour
and bodycolour – 40 x 53.4cm.
(Bonhams)   £1,900 $3,021

F. WALENN (French, 19th century) – Nudes on a beach
– signed and dated 1914 – oil on canvas – 114.5 x 94.5cm.
(Sotheby's)   £4,400 $7,788

HOWARD WALFORD (circa 1860–1940) – The glory of summer – signed – pencil and watercolour heightened with white – 356 x 273mm.
(Christie's)   £528 $961

DAME ETHEL WALKER (1861–1951) – Female nude study – signed – oil on panel – 35 x 26.5cm.
(Christie's)   £990 $1,643

DAME ETHEL WALKER, A.R.A. (1861–1951) –
Portrait of a lady – oil on canvas – unframed – 76 x 63.5cm.
(Christie's)   £1,375 $2,365

EATON WALKER – The Comedian – signed –
13¹/₂ x 11¹/₂in.
(Bearne's)   £500 $867

JOHN HANSON WALKER (1844–1933) – A shy sitter –
signed – oil on canvas – 60.5 x 90.5cm.
(Christie's) **£8,800 $14,256**

WILLIAM AIKEN WALKER (1839–1921) – Cabin
scene – signed – oil on board – unframed – 15.6 x 31.1cm.
(Sotheby's) **£3,607 $6,600**

WILLIAM AIKEN WALKER (1839–1921) – Cotton
pickers – signed – oil on board – unframed –
15.6 x 31.1cm.
(Sotheby's) **£3,005 $5,500**

WILLIAM AIKEN WALKER (1839–1921) – Wash day
– signed with initials conjoined – oil on board –
23.5 x 30.5cm.
(Christie's) **£6,380 $11,000**

WILLIAM AIKEN WALKER (American, 1839–1921) –
The Sharecroppers' cabin – signed with monogram – oil on
canvas – 6^1/4 x 12^1/4in.
(Skinner Inc.) **£3,112 $5,500**

WILLIAM AITKEN WALKER (American, 1839–1921)
– Black man on a mule near a cotton field – signed – oil on
board – 9^1/2 x 12in.
(Du Mouchelles) **£4,204 $7,000**

WILLIAM WALLS (1860–1942) –A sketchbook of
studies of lions – pencil, one with coloured chalks – twenty
drawings – 242 x 318mm.
(Christie's) **£1,045 $1,766**

WALT DISNEY STUDIOS (American, 20th century) –
'The World is Full of Temptations' from Pinocchio, 1940 –
gouache on celluloid applied to scenic airbrushed
background – 9 x 10³/₄in.
(Skinner Inc.)   **£686 $1,210**

WALT DISNEY STUDIOS (American, 20th century) –
Jiminy Cricket from Pinocchio, 1940 – gouache on
celluloid applied to scenic airbrushed background –
9 x 12in.
(Skinner Inc.)   **£342 $605**

MARTHA WALTER (1875–1976) – French family –
signed - oil on board – 23 x 28cm.
(Christie's)   **£1,531 $2,640**

MARTHA WALTER (1876–1976) – Overhead trestle,
Bass Rocks, Massachusetts – signed – oil on canvas –
102.2 x 81.3cm.
(Sotheby's)   **£24,444 $44,000**

GUSTAVE WAPPERS – Flora – signed with monogram –
oil on canvas – 80 x 64cm.
(Hôtel de Ventes Horta)   **£2,048 $3,502**

CHARLES WARD (fl. 1826–1869) – At the blacksmith's
– signed and dated *1862* – oil on canvas – 63.5 x 88.2cm.
(Christie's) £2,640 $4,673

EDMUND F. WARD (b. 1892) – The swimming hole –
signed – oil on canvas – 45.7 x 61cm.
(Sotheby's) £601 $1,100

EDMUND F. WARD (b. 1892) – The Fusillade – signed –
oil on canvas – 71.1 x 101.6cm.
(Sotheby's) £841 $1,540

ARTHUR WARDLE (1864–1947) – Two Scottish terriers;
and Two Gordon setters – signed – oil on canvas –
55.8 x 35.6cm. – a pair
(Christie's) £6,600 $10,824

ARTHUR WARDLE (British, 1864–1947) – Working a hedgerow, a portrait of two fox terriers – signed – oil on canvas – 16 x 20in.
(Skinner Inc.) £6,014 $10,450

ARTHUR WARDLE – Crossing the burn – signed – oil on canvas – 13⁵/₈ x 17¹/₂in.
(Geering & Colyer) £3,100 $5,131

ANDY WARHOL – Leap frog from 'In the bottom of my garden' – signed – letter-press and watercolour on paper – image size 7³/₄ x 9³/₄in.
(Du Mouchelles) £1,652 $2,750

ANDY WARHOL – Mae West shoe – signed – watercolour on letter-press on paper – image size 3^1/$_2$ x 7^1/$_2$in.
(Du Mouchelles)   £1,502 $2,500

ANDY WARHOL (1930–1986) – In the bottom of my garden 1955 – blotted line print and 3 colour watercolour – 21.5 x 28.1cm.
(Germann)   £717 $1,212

ANDY WARHOL (1930–1986) – Swinging monkey – signed and dated 83 – synthetic polymer silkscreened on canvas – 35.5 x 28cm.
(Christie's)   £5,500 $9,130

EDMUND GEORGE WARREN (1834–1909) –
Harvesting on the South Coast – signed and dated *1869* –
watercolour and bodycolour – 603 x 915mm.
(Christie's) £6,600 $10,692

EDMUND GEORGE WARREN (1834–1909) – Figures on
Eastbourne Beach – signed and indistinctly dated *August 27*
(?) – watercolour heightened with bodycolour –
302 x 483mm
(Christie's) £1,980 $3,208

**ABEL GEORGE WARSHAWSKY (Anglo/American,
1883–1962)** – Still life with poppies and daisies – signed –
oil on masonite – 16 x 13in.
(Skinner Inc.) £285 $495

ABEL GEORGE WARSHAWSKY (1883-1962) –
Woman of Finisterre – signed – oil on canvas –
64.8 x 53.3cm.
(Butterfield & Butterfield) £1,576 $2,750

GEORGES WASHINGTON (1827–1910) – Arab cavalry
fording a stream – signed – oil on canvas – 50.5 x 61cm.
(Christie's) £6,600 $11,484

FRANK WASLEY (English, fl. 1880–1914) – A Roman
Capriccio – signed – oil on canvas – 55.8 x 96.5cm.
(Bonhams) £1,400 $2,226

JOHN WILLIAM WATERHOUSE (1849–1917) – Flora
– inscribed on stretcher – oil on canvas – 102.2 x 68.5cm.
(Christie's) £35,200 $59,840

**JOHN WILLIAM WATERHOUSE (English, 1849–
1917)** – The Loggia – oil on canvas – unframed –
43.2 x 28cm.
(Bonhams) £9,800 $15,582

JOHN WILLIAM WATERHOUSE (1849–1917) –
Miranda, the Tempest – signed and dated *1916* – oil on
canvas – 100.4 x 137.8cm.
(Christie's) £88,000 $149,600

SIR ERNEST ALBERT WATERLOW (1850–1919) – A winter landscape with a flock of sheep by a farm – signed – oil on canvas – 76.2 x 101.6cm.
(Christie's)   **£4,620 $8,408**

FRANKLIN CHENAULT WATKINS (1894–circa 1950) – Temple Bar, looking east – signed – pencil and watercolour with touches of white heightening – 445 x 400mm.
(Christie's)   **£605 $1,022**

HARRY WATROUS (1857–1940) – Kwan-yin – signed – oil on canvas – 50.8 x 45.7cm.
(Sotheby's)   **£1,863 $3,410**

JOHN DAWSON WATSON, R.W.S. (1832–1892) – The model-maker – signed with initials and dated 1867 – pencil, watercolour and bodycolour – 349 x 273mm.
(Christie's) **£660 $1,115**

Circle of JEAN-ANTOINE WATTEAU – The dance – oil on canvas, in a carved and gilt wood frame – 80.5 x 99.6cm.
(Sotheby's) **£18,700 $33,660**

JEAN-ANTOINE WATTEAU (1684–1721) – A man leaning on a pillar – red chalk – 133 x 79mm.
(Christie's) **£10,050 $16,683**

FREDERICK JUDD WAUGH (1861–1940) – The road to nowhere – signed – oil on canvas – 77.5 x 76.2cm.
(Sotheby's) £1,262 $2,310

FREDERICK JUDD WAUGH – Moonlight – signed – oil on canvasboard – 63.5 x 76.3cm.
(Christie's) £2,486 $4,400

JAMES WEBB (1825–1895) – A view of Carthagena, Spain – signed and dated *1881* – oil on canvas – 36 x 61cm.
(Christie's) £3,300 $5,346

JAMES WEBB (1825–1895) – A bit in Holland – signed and dated *83* – oil on panel – 22.8 x 32.4cm.
(Christie's) £5,500 $10,010

JAMES WEBB (1825–1895) – The Castle of Beauvine, Dinant, Belgium – signed and dated *77* – oil on canvas – 60.5 x 91.4cm.
(Christie's) £3,300 $6,006

JAMES WEBB – On the Sussex coast – signed – oil on panel – 6^1/2 x 9^1/2in.
(Michael J. Bowman) £2,200 $3,769

JAMES WEBB (1825–1895) – Heidelberg – signed – oil on canvas – 65.4 x 101.6cm.
(Christie's) £4,180 $7,608

WILLIAM EDWARD WEBB (English, 1862–1903) – Windy day, Peel Harbour – signed – oil on canvas – 61 x 91.4cm.
(Bonhams) £3,600 $5,940

MARIA WEBER (German, fl. circa 1876) – Woman with a parasol – signed, dated and inscribed *1883* – oil on panel – 22 x 11¼in.
(Skinner Inc.) £1,393 $2,420

WESLEY WEBBER (American, 1841–1914) – Fishermen near a tent – signed – oil on canvas – 30 x 25in.
(Du Mouchelles) £1,502 $2,500

SARAH S. STILWELL WEBER (American, 1878–1939) – Lady with leopards – signed – oil on canvas – 40 x 30in.
(Skinner Inc.) £2,956 $5,225

AUGUST WECKESSER (1821–1899) – Maternal love – signed and dated *1886* – arched top – oil on canvas, in a contemporary frame – 96.5 x 68cm.
(Christie's)   **£17,600 $28,688**

HERBERT WILLIAM WEEKES (British, fl. 1864–1904) – Love's call; Guilty – signed – oil on panel – 29.2 x 20.3cm. – a pair
(Butterfield & Butterfield) **£2,206 $3,850**

NILS WEDEL – Refugee – signed – mixed media – 64 x 30cm.
(AB Stockholms Auktionsverk) **£496 $851**

HENRY WEEKES, Jnr. (fl. 1849–1888) – Gundogs with the day's bag – signed and dated *1873(?)* – oil on canvas – 61 x 91.5cm.
(Christie's)   **£2,200 $4,004**

HERBERT WILLIAM WEEKES (1864–1904) – The disputed gate – signed – oil on canvas – 50.8 x 76.2cm.
(Christie's)   **£6,600 $12,012**

EDWIN LORD WEEKS (American, 1849–1903) – Moor at prayer – oil on canvas – unframed – 16½ x 12in.
(Skinner Inc.)   **£622 $1,100**

Circle of JAN WEENIX – A shepherd and shepherdess with goats and dogs in a landscape with drovers and cattle beneath classical ruins beyond – oil on canvas – 78.8 x 142.3cm.
(Christie's) £10,450 $16,302

EDWIN LORD WEEKS (American, 1849–1903) –
Indian gentleman – oil on canvas – 13¹/₂ x 9¹/₂in.
(Skinner Inc.) £529 $935

JOHN REINHARD WEGUELIN (1849–1927) – A pastoral – signed and dated *1905* – pencil and watercolour heightened with white – 372 x 542mm.
(Christie's) £2,090 $3,804

EDWIN LORD WEEKS (American, 1849–1903) – Boy with monkeys – signed and inscribed – oil on canvas – 18¹/₂ x 22¹/₂in.
(Skinner Inc.) £5,912 $10,450

CAREL WEIGHT, R.A. (b. 1908) – A dispute in the shrubbery – signed – oil on board – 16.5 x 21cm.
(Christie's) £1,980 $3,287

WEIGHT

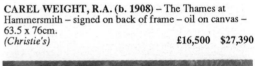

CAREL WEIGHT, R.A. (b. 1908) – The Thames at
Hammersmith – signed on back of frame – oil on canvas –
63.5 x 76cm.
(Christie's) **£16,500 $27,390**

CAREL WEIGHT, R.A. (b. 1908) – Terpiscorah song and
dance; Study for the Parnassian Picnic, Agricultural Hall –
oil on board – 53 x 38cm.
(Christie's) **£2,750 $4,565**

EMILE GEORGES WEISS (French, b. 1861) – The
courtship – signed and dated *90* – oil on panel –
23.5 x 17.1cm.
(Butterfield & Butterfield) **£441 $770**

LUCY ELIZABETH KEMP WELCH (1869–1958) –
Getting in the harvest – signed with initials – oil on board –
58 x 43cm.
(Christie's) £3,850 $6,391

J.S. SANDERSON WELLS, R.I. – Three quarter length
portrait of a cavalier, his left hand resting upon his sword –
signed – oil on board – 24 x 16cm.
(Spencer's) £320 $553

EDGAR E. WEST – Dutch fishing boats in Torbay –
signed – watercolour – 19¹/₂ x 26¹/₂in.
(Bearne's) £560 $972

CORNELIS WESTERBEEK (1844–1903) – A
shepherdess with her flock – signed and dated *99* – oil on
canvas – 61 x 99cm.
(Christie's) £2,860 $4,976

Manner of ROGER VAN DER WEYDEN – The
Deposition – oil on a gold ground on panel – 48.2 x 63.5cm.
(Christie's) £1,100 $1,716

Circle of FRANCIS WHEATLEY – Portrait of a musician, full length, reclining on a sofa, holding a letter – oil on canvas – 130.8 x 194.3cm.
(Bonhams)   **£3,200 $5,088**

WALTER HERBERT WHEELER (1878–1960) – A red Pekingese – signed – oil on board – 22.8 x 25.3cm.
(Christie's)   **£880 $1,443**

JOHN ALFRED WHEELER (British, 1821–1903) – Full cry – signed – oil on canvas – 45.7 x 61cm.
(Butterfield & Butterfield)   **£2,521 $4,400**

Circle of JAMES ABBOTT MCNEILL WHISTLER (American, 1834–1903) – In the Park – oil on panel – bears butterfly motif – 13.6 x 19.6cm.
(Bonhams)   **£1,600 $2,544**

JOHN ARNOLD WHEELER (English, 1821–1877) – A racehorse in a stable – signed – oil on canvas - 50.8 x 61cm.
(Bonhams)   **£1,100 $1,749**

THOMAS WHITCOMBE (English, 1760–1824) – An Indiaman in two positions off Walmer Castle, Kent – oil on canvas – 91.4 x 148cm.
(Bonhams)   **£4,500 $7,425**

ARTHUR WHITE (1865–1953) – The church and fishing craft St. Ives – signed – oil on board – 12 x 9in.
(David Lay)   £360 $647

JOHN BARNARD WHITTAKER (1836–1926) – The cobbler's shop – signed – oil on canvas – 54 x 43.2cm.
(Christie's)   £1,056 $1,870

F. FAULKNER WHITE – Still life of fruit and flower by a claret jug; Still life of roses by a ewer – both signed and dated 1885 – 29¹/₄ x 21¹/₄in. – a pair
(Bearne's)   £780 $1,353

GEORGE WHYATT – A country church at the edge of a village – signed – pencil and watercolour – 10³/₄ x 7in.
(Christie's)   **£198 $340**

JOHN WHORF (1903–1959) – Backyard in spring – signed – watercolour on paper – 58.4 x 36.8cm.
(Sotheby's)   **£601 $1,100**

ROBERT DODD WIDDAS – Picnickers on a hill side overlooking a river estuary – signed and dated *1869* – oil on canvas – unframed – 76.2 x 111.8cm.
(Christie's)   **£1,760 $3,120**

OLAF WIEGHORST (1899–1988) - Watching over the herd – signed – oil on canvas – 50.8 x 77.5cm.
(Butterfield & Butterfield) £5,673 $9,900

GUY WIGGINS (1883–1962) – Wall Street storm – signed – oil on canvasboard – 30.5 x 40.6cm.
(Butterfield & Butterfield) £4,728 $8,250

GUY CARLETON WIGGINS (1883–1962) – Looking down the Avenue from the Plaza, winter – signed – oil on canvasboard – 30.5 x 40.6cm.
(Christie's) £7,656 $13,200

GUY WIGGINS (1883–1962) – New York winter – signed – oil on canvasboard – 40.6 x 30.5cm.
(Butterfield & Butterfield) £3,152 $5,500

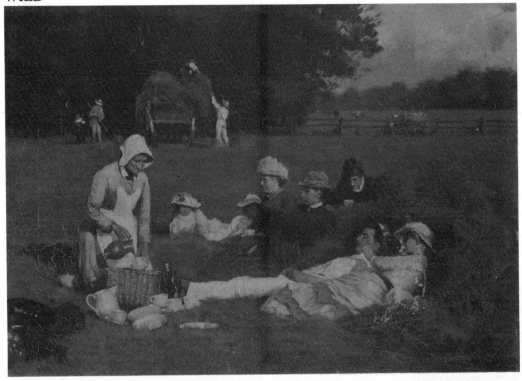

FRANK PERCY WILD (1861–1950) – The picnic – signed and dated *1887* – oil on canvas – 30.5 x 40.8cm.
(Christie's) £17,600 $28,512

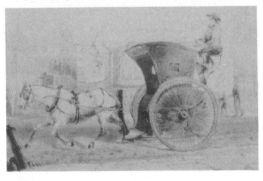

CHARLES WILDAY – The hansom cab - signed and dated *1853* – watercolour – 6 x 9in.
(Christie's) £550 $960

ALFRED WALTER WILLIAMS (1824–1905) – Surrey distance and far away – signed and dated *1882* – oil on canvas – 51 x 76.5cm.
(Christie's) £1,760 $2,851

NORMAN WILKINSON – Coming into port – signed – oil on canvas – 40.7 x 61cm.
(Bonhams) £800 $1,320

EDWARD WILLIAMS (1782–1855) – Countryfolk in wooded landscapes – both signed – oil on panel – 21 x 27cm. – a pair
(Christie's) £4,950 $8,019

HUGH WILLIAM 'Grecian' WILLIAMS (1773–1829) –
Dancing figures overlooking the Bay of Naples – pencil and
watercolour – 515 x 628mm.
(Christie's) £825 $1,452

EDWARD CHARLES WILLIAMS (1807–1881) – The
mill; and Children fishing at a pool – oil on canvas –
21 x 24.8cm. – a pair
(Christie's) £3,850 $7,007

PAUL A. WILLIAMS (American, b. 1934) – Tinka at the
shore – signed – oil on canvas – 8 x 10in.
(Du Mouchelles) £721 $1,200

FREDERICK BALLARD WILLIAMS (1871–1956) –
Seven maidens – oil on canvas – 101.6 x 127cm.
(Butterfield & Butterfield) £1,072 $1,870

GEORGE AUGUSTUS WILLIAMS (1814–1901) – Ice
cart, hazy winter morning – signed with monogram and
dated *1859* – oil on canvas – 61 x 101.6cm.
(Christie's) £6,050 $10,709

TERRICK WILLIAMS (1860–1937) – Coming into
Plymouth Harbour – signed – oil on board – 6 x 9in.
(W.H. Lane & Son) £2,460 $4,533

WILLIAMS

WARREN WILLIAMS – A coastal scene with a gaff-
rigged sailing dinghy in the foreground – signed and dated
(19)18 – 40 x 65cm.
(Spencer's)   **£580 $1,002**

HAROLD WILLIAMSON – The pony ride – signed –
tempera on panel – 45.6 x 43.1cm.
(Christie's)   **£3,960 $6,296**

CAREL WILLINK (1900–1979) – Landscape in Bormis –
signed and dated *1928* – oil on canvas – 97 x 78cm.
(Christie's)   **£27,504 $48,682**

H. WILLIS (mid 19th century) – A Blenheim Cavalier
King Charles spaniel – signed and dated *36* – oil on canvas
– 50.8 x 69.8cm.
(Christie's)   **£6,050 $9,922**

MARIE WILNER (b. 1910) – Bears at the zoo – signed –
oil on canvas – 76.2 x 101.6cm.
(Sotheby's)   **£721 $1,320**   **CHESTER WILSON** – Feeding the rabbits – signed and
dated *1874* – oil on canvas – 60.9 x 50.8cm.
(Christie's)   **£2,090 $3,705**

ANDREW WINTER (American, 1893–1958) – Crow's Nest, a view on Monhegan Island, Maine – signed and dated *42* – oil on canvasboard – 12 x 18in. *(Skinner Inc.)* **£443 $770**

J. CHESTER WILSON – The letter – signed and dated *1873* – 90 x 70cm. *(Spencer's)* **£1,000 $1,775**

J.C. WILSON (mid 19th century) – Artillery practice – signed – oil on canvas – 26.5 x 34cm. *(Christie's)* **£1,320 $2,402**

FRITZ WINTER (1905–1976) – Transformation – signed and dated *53* – oil on canvas – 135.9 x 145.4cm. *(Christie's)* **£44,000 $77,880**

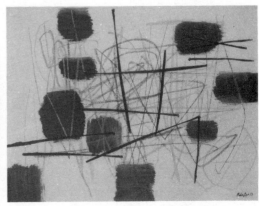

PETER DE WINT (1784–1849) – Figures by a cottage gate – pencil and watercolour – 108 x 152mm. *(Christie's)* **£3,850 $6,776**

FRITZ WINTER (1905–1976) – Lines between red and blue – signed and dated *53* – oil on canvas – 45.5 x 61cm. *(Christie's)* **£23,100 $40,887**

ADRIAN WISZNIEWSKI – The game keeper – signed – gouache – 152.4 x 101.5cm.
(Bonhams)   £5,800 $10,092

FRANZ XAVIER WINTERHALTER (German, 1805–73) – Portrait of a lady – signed, inscribed and dated *1860* – oil on canvas – oval – 130 x 98cm.
(Sotheby's)   £38,500 $68,145

WILLIAM FREDERICK WITHERINGTON (1785–1865) – Dinner time – signed – oil on canvas – 87.6 x 116.9cm.
(Christie's)   £19,800 $33,660

PAINTINGS PRICE GUIDE

WILLIAM FREDERICK WITHERINGTON (1785–1865) – Midsummer; Ye verdant Trees and Underwood, where the poetic Birds rejoice, etc. – signed and dated *1851* – oil on canvas – 69.9 x 90.2cm.
(Christie's)   **£11,000**   **$20,020**

Attributed to WILLIAM FREDERICK WITHERINGTON, R.A. (1785–1865) – Girls gathering corn at harvest – oil on board – 30.5 x 25.5cm.
(Christie's)   **£1,210**   **$1,960**

WALTER WITHERS (1854–1914) – Sheep grazing – signed – 50.8 x 40.6cm.
(Christie's)   **£8,250**   **$14,520**

WALTER WITHERS (1854–1914) – Timber carting – signed and dated *06* – oil on canvas laid down on board – 45.7 x 30.5cm.
(Christie's)   **£6,600   \$11,616**

KARL WITKOWSKI (1860–1910) – Peeling an apple – signed and dated *1900* – oil on canvas – 55.8 x 45.7cm.
(Christie's)   **£2,486   \$4,400**

KARL WITKOWSKI (1860–1910) – Boy with parrot – signed – oil on canvas – 61 x 50.8cm.
(Sotheby's)   **£2,705   \$4,950**

ARTHUR WOELFLE (1873–1936) – Lady in white – signed – oil on canvas – 101.6 x 76.2cm.
(Sotheby's)   **£1,803   \$3,300**

EDWARD WOLFE, R.A. (1897–1982) – Taxco landscape
– signed – oil on canvas – 53 x 77cm.
(Christie's) £3,740 $6,433

EDWARD WOLFE (1897–1982) - Portrait of a young boy
– signed – pastel and watercolour – 51 x 38cm.
(Christie's) £715 $1,187

EDWARD WOLFE (1897–1982) – North African dream –
pencil and pastel – 99 x 70cm.
(Christie's) £1,100 $1,826

EDWARD WOLFE (1897–1982) – Portrait of a soldier –
signed – oil on board – 54.5 x 47cm.
(Christie's) £990 $1,643

EDWARD WOLFE (1897–1982) – Jamieson's farm,
Ardmore, Ireland – signed – pastel – 46 x 61cm.
(Christie's) £880 $1,461

EDWARD WOLFE (1897–1982) – Two Mexican boys –
signed – pastel – 84 x 63.5cm.
(Christie's) £990 $1,643

WOLFE

EDWARD WOLFE, R.A. (1897–1982) – Still life – signed and dated *1920* – oil on canvas – 33 x 46cm.
(Christie's) £1,100 $1,892

JOHANN JAKOB WOLFENSBERGER (1797–1850) – A view of Athens with the Acropolis beyond – signed – pencil and watercolour on paper laid down on canvas – 52 x 75cm.
(Christie's) £3,300 $5,775

ALFRED WOLMARK – Portrait of a girl – on panel – 17^1/$_2$ x 14^1/$_2$in.
(Bearne's) £900 $1,561

GERT HEINRICH WOLLHEIM (1894-1974) – Revue negress – oil on wood – 140 x 96cm.
(Lempertz) £5,190 $8,278

A.V.O. WOOD – Figures gossiping on doorway – signed with monogram – tempera – 27 x 16in.
(G.A Key) £150 $268

ALBERT VICTOR ORMSBY WOOD – New moon –
gouache – 38 x 14in.
(G.A. Key) **£160 $255**

CHRISTOPHER WOOD (1901–1930) – Girl with bread
– oil on canvas-board – 41 x 33cm.
(Christie's) **£4,400 $7,304**
CHRISTOPHER WOOD (1901–1930) – Bringing the
shark ashore – oil on canvas – 19 x 24in.
(W.H. Lane & Son) **£14,000 $22,610**

WOOD

THOMAS WATERMAN WOOD (American, 1823–1903) – Portrait of a woman in a shawl – signed and dated *1858* – oil on canvas – 18 x 14in.
(Skinner Inc.) £3,165 $5,500

DAVID WOODLOCK (1842–1929) – Springtime – signed – pencil and watercolour heightened with white – 425 x 248mm.
(Christie's) £3,300 $5,577

WILLIAM THOMAS WOOD (English, b. 1877) – Souvenir Chinese – signed – oil on canvas –35.6 x 30.5cm.
(Bonhams) £1,300 $2,067

DAVID WOODLOCK (1842–1929) – Old cottage at Sutton Courtney, Berkshire – signed – watercolour with touches of white heightening – 298 x 197mm.
(Christie's) £1,320 $2,402

MABEL WOODWARD (1877–1945) – An afternoon at the beach – signed – oil on canvas laid down on masonite – 39.5 x 49cm.
(Christie's) **£14,036 $24,200**

DAVID WOODLOCK (1842–1929) – A roadside cottage near Sevenoaks, Kent – signed – pencil and watercolour – unframed – 255 x 177mm.
(Christie's) **£825 $1,501**

MABEL WOODWARD (1877–1945) – Polperro and Venice – the first signed, the second signed on reverse – each oil on canvas, the first laid down on board – 25.4 x 33cm. – a pair
(Sotheby's) **£2,855 $5,225**

DAVID WOODLOCK (1842–1929) – Anne Hathaway's cottage – signed – pencil and watercolour heightened with white – 356 x 299mm.
(Christie's) **£1,650 $2,788**

MABEL MAY WOODWARD (American, 1877–1945) – Rockport Pier – signed – oil on masonite – 10 x 12¹/₂in.
(Skinner Inc.) **£1,120 $1,980**

WOODWARD

THOMAS WOODWARD (1801–1852) – An English setter at point – signed with initials and dated *1829* – oil on board – 45.7 x 55.8cm.
(Christie's)   **£880 $1,443**

Follower of PHILIPS WOUWERMAN – Figures in a cave with a horse and dogs – oil on canvas laid down on panel – 36.8 x 48.2cm.
(Bonhams)   **£1,200 $1,908**

THOMAS WORSEY (1829–1875) – Primroses, polyanthus, apple blossom, and a bird's nest on a mossy bank – signed and dated *1856* – oil on canvas – 40.6 x 33cm.
(Christie's)   **£2,860 $5,062**

GEORGE WRIGHT (English, 1860–1942) – Crossing the river – signed – oil on canvas – 28 x 43.2cm.
(Bonhams)   **£3,600 $5,724**

School of PHILIPS WOUWERMAN (Dutch, 1619–1668) – Horsemen bargaining with fishermen on a seashore with a castle beyond – oil on copper – 14.6 x 18.4cm.
(Butterfield & Butterfield)   **£1,261 $2,200**

GILBERT S. WRIGHT – The Charge of the 21st Lancers, Omdurman, 2nd September 1898 – signed – 15½ x 19½in.
(Bearne's)   **£1,500 $2,655**

GILBERT S. WRIGHT (fl. 1900) – Taking the fence –
signed – oil on canvas – 61 x 91.5cm.
(Christie's) **£4,400 $8,008**

MATHIJS WULFRAET – A tavern interior with a
mandolin player and topers seated around a barrel – signed
– oil on panel – 34.6 x 42cm.
(Bonhams) **£4,000 $6,360**

JOHN WRIGHT (circa 1770–circa 1830) - Portrait of
Charles, Earl Grey (1764–1845), three-quarter length,
seated at a desk – signed and dated *1811* – pencil, black
chalk and watercolour – 324 x 242mm.
(Christie's) **£1,320 $2,125**

FRANCIS JOHN WYBURD (English, 1826–93) – The
harem – signed with initials and dated *1873* – oil on canvas
– 71 x 91.5cm.
(Sotheby's) **£20,900 $36,993**

RICHARD HENRY WRIGHT (1857–1930) – The fish
market, Venice – signed – pencil and watercolour –
197 x 260mm.
(Christie's) **£1,210 $2,045**

HAROLD WYLLIE (English, 1880–1973) – H.M.S.
Hornet, with other shipping – signed – oil on canvas –
45 x 81cm.
(Bonhams) **£3,000 $4,950**

BRYAN WYNTER (1915 – ?) – The Old Gas Works, St Ives – signed and dated 1946 – conte with scratching out – 7½ x 9½in.
(W.H. Lane & Son)   **£760 $1,284**

R. YOSHIDA (Japanese, 19th/20th century) – An oriental genre scene – signed – oil on panel – 14¼ x 22¾in.
(Skinner Inc.)   **£760 $1,320**

WILLIAM LIONEL WYLLIE – Florence – signed and inscribed – watercolour – 19.7 x 9.5cm.
(Bonhams)   **£550 $875**

WILLIAM LIONEL WYLLIE (1851–1931) – H.M.S. Shannon and the Second Battle Squadron – signed and dated *1911* – oil on canvas – 68.6 x 109.2cm.
(Christie's)   **£5,500 $9,790**

After DOMENICO ZAMPIERI called Il Domenichino (Italian, 1581–1641) – Santa Cecilia – oil on canvas – 162.6 x 125.7cm.
(Butterfield & Butterfield)   **£4,413 $7,700**

KARL ZERBE (1903–1972) – Marion Square, Charleston – signed and dated *1940* on reverse – encaustic on panel – 73.7 x 81.3cm.
(Butterfield & Butterfield) £315 $550

After DOMENICO ZAMPIERI, called Il Domenichino (Italian, 1581–1641) – Comunione di San Gerolamo – oil on canvas – 119.4 x 74.9cm.
(Butterfield & Butterfield) £3,152 $5,500

Manner of GIUSEPPE ZIAS – Drovers with an ox-cart on a flooded track; and Drovers and cattle in an extensive Italianate landscape – oil on canvas – 30.5 x 41.8cm.
(Christie's) £2,200 $3,432

EUGENIO ZAMPIGHI (Italian, 1859–1944) – Grandpa's pet – signed – oil on canvas – 25.4 x 35.6cm.
(Bonhams) £4,600 $7,314

JOSE RAMON ZARAGOZA (1874–1949) – The lady of the rose – signed and dated *1910* – oil on canvas – 216 x 100cm.
(Duran) £2,100 $3,697

JANUARIUS ZICK (1730–1797) – A peasant family in an interior – signed – oil on canvas – 43 x 57cm.
(Sotheby's) £39,600 $71,280

GUGLIELMO ZOCCHI (Italian, b. 1874) – Seated nude
with mirror and pearl necklace – signed – oil on panel –
15¼ x 11¾in.
(Skinner Inc.) **£1,963 $3,410**

**REINHARD SEBASTIAN ZIMMERMAN (German,
1815–1893)** – Jilted – oil on canvas – 31.8 x 23.5cm.
(Butterfield & Butterfield) **£883 $1,540**

JAN ZOETELIEF-TROMP (1872–1947) – Children
paddling – signed – oil on canvas – 33.5 x 43.8cm.
(Christie's) **£22,000 $35,860**

ANTONIO PIETRO ZUCCHI, A.R.A. (1726–1795) –
Psyche – both with inscription – pen and brown ink, brown
wash – unframed – 270 x 380mm. – a pair
(Christie's) £495 $797

Attributed to JOHANN ZOFFANY, R.A. (1733–1810) –
Study of a black servant carrying a tray – black and white
chalk on blue paper – unframed – 330 x 210mm.
(Christie's) £6,050 $9,740

REINIS ZUSTERS (b. 1918) – Red reflections – signed –
oil on masonite – 45.4 x 60.6cm.
(Christie's) £330 $581

WILLIAM ZORACH (1887–1966) – Cottages near a
woodland path – signed and dated *1937* – watercolour on
paper – 35.5 x 45.7cm.
(Christie's) £932 $1,650

WILLIAM ZORACH (1887–1966) – New England
village – signed and dated *1917* – watercolour and graphite
on paper – 25.4 x 34.3cm.
(Sotheby's) £2,103 $3,850

REINIS ZUSTERS – City meditation – signed – oil on
board – 61 x 76cm.
(Australian Art Auctions) £967 $1,721